Judith White Brockenbrough McGuire

Diary of a Southern Refugee, During the War

Judith White Brockenbrough McGuire
Diary of a Southern Refugee, During the War
ISBN/EAN: 9783337123390
Printed in Europe, USA, Canada, Australia, Japan
Cover: Foto ©ninafisch / pixelio.de

More available books at **www.hansebooks.com**

DIARY

OF A

SOUTHERN REFUGEE,

DURING THE WAR.

BY

A LADY OF VIRGINIA.

"We fare on earth as other men have fared.
Were they successful? Let us not despair.
Was disappointment oft their sole reward?
Yet shall their tale instruct, if it declare
How they have borne the load ourselves are doomed to bear."
BEATTIE'S MINSTREL.

NEW YORK:
E. J. HALE & SON, 16 MURRAY STREET.
1867

TO

MY DEAR LITTLE

GRANDCHILDREN, NEPHEWS, AND NIECES,

This Book

IS MOST AFFECTIONATELY DEDICATED

BY

THE AUTHORESS.

PREFACE.

to keep a true record. Enormous as were the wrongs done us, yet we had no desire to do the slightest wrong to even the bitterest of our enemies. We refused not to do them justice; we were not unwilling to seek for them the mercy of Heaven; to extend to them the hand of Charity; to supply their wants when captured; to attend as far as possible to their sick, and dying, and dead; and asked for nothing from them but that they would leave our borders, never to return. We could not forget the injury done to our country. If what we wrote indicates this, what is it but the voice of nature, which neither fear nor hope could repress? The ruin of the whole South! Where are the colours dark enough for that picture? With her rightful government overturned; her territory seized by lawless hands; her system of domestic labour suddenly broken up; her estates robbed; her fields desolated; her barns destroyed by fire; her temples profaned; her once joyous homes here and there silent as death; her old men and women going with sorrow to the grave, because their gallant sons are not; her fair and fainting daughters mourning for loved ones whom they girded for the fight, and saw again never more; her widows and orphans, whom sorrow may kill, if want does not starve them; her wounded, and scarred, and crippled, and suffering, with no rest for any save in the quiet graves at home, or in the vast cemeteries, where such hosts of her slaughtered children lie. How must we think or speak of all this? Let the coldest heart ever frozen by Northern interest or prejudice answer.

Shall this breach never be healed? Are there no able and patriotic men North and South—no men of God—fitted to achieve this work without further injury or shame to either party? This great revolution cannot be without God—without whom not a sparrow falls to the ground. If there be error or mischief, that is of man. With God "one day is as a thousand years, and a thousand years as one day." He sees the end from the beginning. His great "purposes run along the line of ages," and, worked out as He ordains, produce good, and good only. For ages He has blessed the South with the fairest land, the purest social circle, the noblest race of men, and the happiest people, on earth. Under a mysterious Providence, millions of the coloured race have been saved from the foulest paganism; millions mentally and morally elevated far above those of their native land, and multitudes saved in Christ forever. Is it God's purpose to break up this system? Who can believe that it was His will to do it by war and bloodshed? Or that turning this people loose without preparation, a rapid demoralization, idleness, poverty and vice should doom so many of them to misery, or send them so rapidly to the grave? In this transition state, must the earth remain uncultivated, and its fruits so lessened as to reduce all to comparative poverty, and threaten such numbers with actual starvation? Must a war of races come? Must a spirit of bitter hatred burn on between the sections of our unhappy country? Why not one of peace and forgiveness instead? Why not the healing balm of love? Why not the spirit of Christ, pervading all hearts, and binding up all wounds? God of love, hasten the day! We are verily in need of His gracious assistance. We have cried to Him through many a gloomy day. The days are dark and dreary still. The old South has passed away; her music is all dead; her harp hung where no mortal hand can sweep its chords again, and the very winds of Heaven can bring from it naught save a few wailing notes, sad enough to break every human heart.

"Mourn
Her banished peace, her laurels torn;
Her sons, for valour long renowned,
Lie slaughtered on their native ground.
Her hospitable roofs no more
Invite the stranger to the door;
In smoky ruins sunk they lie,
The monuments of cruelty."

The following pages are, as intimated above, presented to the public more in compliance with the wishes of others than of the writer. She has no experience in matters of this sort, and claims nothing except what may be due to sincerity and truth. Her earnest prayer is, that what is erroneous may be forgiven her, and the whole result be agreeable and useful to her readers.

DIARY

OF A

SOUTHERN REFUGEE.

AT HOME, *May* 4, 1861.—I am too nervous, too wretched to-day to write in my diary, but that the employment will while away a few moments of this trying time. Our friends and neighbors have left us. Every thing is broken up. The Theological Seminary is closed ; the High School dismissed. Scarcely any one is left of the many families which surrounded us. The homes all look desolate ; and yet this beautiful country is looking more peaceful, more lovely than ever, as if to rebuke the tumult of passion and the fanaticism of man. We are left lonely indeed ; our children are all gone— the girls to Clarke, where they may be safer, and farther from the exciting scenes which may too soon surround us; and the boys, the dear, dear boys, to the camp, to be drilled and prepared to meet any emergency. Can it be that our country is to be carried on and on to the horrors of civil war ? I pray, oh how fervently do I pray, that our Heavenly Father may yet avert it. I shut my eyes and hold my breath when the thought of what may come upon us obtrudes itself; and yet I cannot believe it. It will, I know the breach will be healed without the effusion of blood. The taking of Sumter without bloodshed has somewhat soothed my fears, though I am told by those who are wiser than I, that men must fall on both sides by the score, by the hundred, and even by the thousand. But it is not my habit to look on the dark side, so I try hard to employ myself, and hope for the best. To-day our house seems so deserted, that I feel more sad than usual, for on this morning we took leave of our whole household. Mr. —— and myself are now the sole occupants of the house, which usually teems with life. I go from room to room, looking at first one thing and then another, so full of sad associations. The closed piano, the locked bookcase, the nicely-arranged tables, the formally-placed chairs, ottomans and sofas in the parlor! Oh for some one to put them out of order! And then the dinner-table, which has always been so well surrounded, so social, so cheerful, looked so cheerless to-day, as we seated ourselves one at the head, the other at the foot, with one friend,—but one,—at the side. I could scarcely restrain my tears, and but for the presence of that one friend, I believe I should have cried outright. After dinner, I did not mean to do it, but I could not help going into the girls' room, and then into C.'s. I heard my own footsteps so plainly, that I was startled by the absence of all other sounds. There the furniture looked so quiet, the beds so fixed and smooth, the wardrobes and bureaux so tightly locked, and the whole so lifeless! But the writing-desks, work-boxes, and the numberless things so familiar to my eyes! Where were they? I paused, to ask myself what it all meant. Why did we think it necessary to send off all that was so dear to us from our own home? I threw open the shutters, and the answer came at once, so mournfully! I heard distinctly the drums beating in Washington. The evening was so still that I seemed to hear nothing else. As

I looked at the Capitol in the distance, I could scarcely believe my senses. That Capitol of which I had always been so proud! Can it be possible that it is no longer *our* Capitol? And are our countrymen, under its very eaves, making mighty preparation to drain our hearts' blood? And must this Union, which I was taught to revere, be rent asunder? Once I thought such a suggestion sacrilege; but now that it is dismembered, I trust it may never, never be reünited. We must be a separate people—our nationality must be different, to insure lasting peace and good-will. Why cannot we part in peace?

May 10.—Since writing last, I have been busy, very busy, arranging and rëarranging. We are now hoping that Alexandria will not be a landing-place for the enemy, but that the forts will be attacked. In that case, they would certainly be repulsed, and we could stay quietly at home. To view the progress of events from any point will be sad enough, but it would be more bearable at our own home, and surrounded by our family and friends. With the supposition that we may remain, and that the ladies of the family at least may return to us, I am having the grounds put in order, and they are now so beautiful! Lilacs, crocuses, the lily of the valley, and other spring flowers, are in luxuriant bloom, and the roses in full bud. The greenhouse plants have been removed and grouped on the lawn, verbenas in bright bloom have been transplanted from the *pit* to the borders, and the grass seems unusually green after the late rains; the trees are in full leaf; every thing is so fresh and lovely. "All, save the spirit of man, is divine."

War seems inevitable, and while I am trying to employ the passing hour, a cloud still hangs over us and all that surrounds us. For a long time before our society was so completely broken up, the ladies of Alexandria and all the surrounding country were busily employed sewing for our soldiers. Shirts, pants, jackets, and beds, of the heaviest material, have been made by the most delicate fingers. All ages, all conditions, meet now on one common platform. We must all work for our country. Our soldiers must be equipped. Our parlor was the rendezvous for our neighborhood, and our sewing-machine was in requisition for weeks. Scissors and needles were plied by all. The daily scene was most animated. The fires of our enthusiasm and patriotism were burning all the while to a degree which might have been consuming, but that our tongues served as safety-valves. Oh, how we worked and talked, and excited each other! One common sentiment animated us all; no doubts, no fears were felt. We all have such entire reliance in the justice of our cause and the valor of our men, and, above all, on the blessing of Heaven! These meetings have necessarily ceased with us, as so few of any age or degree remain at home; but in Alexandria they are still kept up with great interest. We who are left here are trying to give the soldiers who are quartered in town comfort, by carrying them milk, butter, pies, cakes, etc. I went in yesterday to the barracks, with the carriage well filled with such things, and found many young friends quartered there. All are taking up arms; the first young men in the country are the most zealous. Alexandria is doing her duty nobly; so is Fairfax; and so, I hope, is the whole South. We are very weak in resources, but strong in stout hearts, zeal for the cause, and enthusiastic devotion to our beloved South; and while men are making a free-will offering of their life's blood on the altar of their country, women must not be idle. We must do what we can for the comfort of our brave men. We must sew for them, knit for them, nurse the sick, keep up the faint-hearted, give them a word of encouragement in season and out of season. There is much for us to do, and we must do it. The embattled hosts of the North will have the whole world from which to draw their supplies; but if, as it seems but too probable, our ports are blockaded, we shall indeed be dependent on our own exertions, and great must those exertions be.

The Confederate flag waves from several points in Alexandria: from the Marshall House, the Market-house, and the several barracks. The peaceful, quiet old town looks quite warlike. I feel sometimes, when walking on King's street, meeting men in uniform, passing companies of cavalry, hearing martial music, etc., that I must be in a dream. Oh that it were a dream, and that the last ten years of our country's history were blotted out! Some of our old men are a little nervous, look doubtful, and talk of the impotency of the South. Oh, I feel utter scorn for such remarks. We must not admit weakness. Our soldiers do not think of weakness; they know that their hearts are strong, and their hands well skilled in the use of the rifle. Our country boys have been brought up on horseback, and hunting has ever been their holiday sport. Then why shall they feel weak? Their hearts feel strong when they think of the justice of their cause. In that is *our* hope.

Walked down this evening to see ———. The road looked lonely and deserted. Busy life has departed from our midst. We found Mrs. ——— packing up valuables. I have been doing the same; but after they are packed, where are they to be sent? Silver may be buried, but what is to be done with books, pictures, etc.? We have determined, if we are obliged to go from home, to leave every thing in the care of the servants. They have promised to be faithful, and I believe they will be; but my hope becomes stronger and stronger that we may remain here, or may soon return if we go away. Every thing is so sad around us! We went to the Chapel on Sunday as usual, but it was grievous to see the change—the organ mute, the organist gone; the seats of the students of both institutions empty; but one or two members of each family to represent the absentees; the prayer for the President omitted. When Dr. —— came to it, there was a slight pause, and then he went on to the next prayer—all seemed so strange! Tucker Conrad, one of the few students who is still here, raised the tunes; his voice seemed unusually sweet, because so sad. He was feebly supported by all who were not in tears. There was night service, but it rained, and I was not sorry that I could not go.

May 15.—Busy every moment of time packing up, that our furniture may be safely put away in case of a sudden removal. The parlor furniture has been rolled into the Laboratory, and covered, to keep it from injury; the books are packed up; the pictures put away with care; house linen locked up, and all other things made as secure as possible. We do not hope to remove many things, but to prevent their ruin. We are constantly told that a large army would do great injury if quartered near us; therefore we want to put things out of the reach of the soldiers, for I have no idea that officers would allow them to break locks, or that they would allow our furniture to be interfered with. We have a most unsettled feeling—with carpets up, curtains down, and the rooms without furniture; but a constant excitement, and expectation of we know not what, supplants all other feelings. Nothing but nature is pleasant, and that is so beautiful! The first roses of the season are just appearing, and the peonies are splendid; but the horrors of war, with which we are so seriously threatened, prevent the enjoyment of any thing. I feel so much for the *Southerners* of Maryland; I am afraid they are doomed to persecution, but it does seem so absurd in Maryland and Kentucky to talk of armed neutrality in the present state of the country! Let States, like individuals, be independent—be something or nothing. I believe that the very best people of both States are with us, but are held back by stern necessity. Oh that they could burst the bonds that bind them, and speak and act like freemen! The Lord reigneth; to Him only can we turn, and humbly pray that He may see fit to say to the troubled waves, "Peace, be still!" We sit at our windows, and see the bosom of our own Potomac covered with the sails of vessels employed by the enemies of our peace. I often wish myself far away, that I, at least, might not *see* these things. The newspapers are filled with the boastings of the North, and yet I cannot feel alarmed. My woman's heart does not quail, even though they come, as they so loudly threaten, as an avalanche to overwhelm us. Such is my abiding faith in the justice of our cause, that I have no shadow of doubt of our success.

May 16.—To-day I am alone. Mr. —— has gone to Richmond to the Convention, and so have the Bishop and Dr. S. I have promised to spend my nights with Mrs. J. All is quiet around us. Federal troops quartered in Baltimore. Poor Maryland! The North has its heel upon her, and how it grinds her! I pray that we may have peaceful secession.

17*th.*—Still quiet. Mrs. J., Mrs. B., and myself, sat at the Malvern windows yesterday, *spying* the enemy as they sailed up and down the river. Those going up were heavily laden, carrying provisions, etc., to their troops. I think if all Virginia could see their preparations as we do, her vote would be unanimous for secession.

21st.—Mr. —— has returned. Yesterday evening we rode to the parade-ground in Alexandria; it was a beautiful but sad sight. How many of those young, brave boys may be cut off, or maimed for life! I shudder to think of what a single battle may bring forth. The Federal vessel *Pawnee* now lies before the old town, with its guns pointing towards it. It is aggravating enough to see it; but the inhabitants move on as calmly as though it were a messenger of peace. It is said that an undefended, indefensible town like Alexandria will hardly be attacked. It seems to me strange that they do not go immediately to the Rappahannock, the York, or the James, and land at once in the heart of the State. I tremble lest they should make a direct attack upon Richmond. Should they go at once to City Point, and march thence to the city, I am afraid it could hardly be defended. Our people are busy in their preparations for defence; but time is necessary—every day is precious to us. Our President and military chiefs are doing all that men can do to forward preparations. My ear is constantly pained with the sound of cannon from the Navy-Yard at Washington, and to-day the drum has been beating furiously in our once loved metropolis. Dr. S. says there was a grand dress parade—brothers gleefully preparing to draw their brothers' blood!

Day after to-morrow the vote of Virginia on secession will be taken, and I, who so dearly loved this Union, who from my cradle was taught to revere it, now most earnestly hope that the voice of Virginia may give no uncertain sound; that she may leave it with a shout. I am thankful that she did not take so important a step hastily, but that she set an example of patience and long-suffering, and made an earnest effort to maintain peace; but as all her efforts have been rejected with scorn, and she has been required to give her quota of men to fight and destroy her brethren of the South, I trust that she may now speak decidedly.

FAIRFAX C. H., *May* 25.—The day of suspense is at an end. Alexandria and its environs, including, I greatly fear, our home, is in the hands of the enemy. Yesterday morning, at an early hour, as I was in my pantry, putting up refreshments for the barracks preparatory to a ride to Alexandria, the door was suddenly thrown open by a servant, looking wild with excitement, exclaiming, "Oh, madam, do you know?" "Know what, Henry?" "Alexandria is filled with Yankees." "Are you sure, Henry?" said I, trembling in every limb. "Sure, madam! I saw them myself. Before I got up I heard soldiers rushing by the door; went out, and saw our men going to the cars." "Did they get off?" I asked, afraid to hear the answer. "Oh, yes, the cars went off full of them, and some marched out; and then I went to King Street, and saw such crowds of Yankees coming in! They came down the turnpike, and some came down the river; and presently I heard such noise and confusion, and they said they were fighting, so I came home as fast as I could." I lost no time in seeking Mr. ——, who hurried out to hear the truth of the story. He soon met Dr. ——, who was bearing off one of the editors in his buggy. He more than confirmed Henry's report, and gave an account of the tragedy at the Marshall House. Poor Jackson (the proprietor) had always said that the Confederate flag which floated from the top of his house should never be taken down but over his dead body. It was known that he was a devoted patriot, but his friends had amused themselves at this rash speech. He was suddenly aroused by the noise of men rushing by his room-door, ran to the window, and seeing at once what was going on, he seized his gun, his wife trying in vain to stop him; as he reached the passage he saw Colonel Ellsworth coming from the third story, waving the flag. As he passed Jackson he said, "I have a trophy." Jackson immediately raised his gun, and in an instant Ellsworth fell dead. One of the party immediately killed poor Jackson. The Federals then proceeded down the street, taking possession of public houses, etc. I am mortified to write that a party of our cavalry, thirty-five in number, was captured. It can scarcely be accounted for. It is said that the Federals notified the authorities in Alexandria that they would enter the city at eight, and the captain was so credulous as to believe them. Poor fellow, he is now a prisoner, but it will be a lesson to him and to our troops generally. Jackson leaves a wife and children. I know the country will take care of them. He is the first martyr. I shudder to think how many more there may be.

The question with us was, what was next to be done? Mr. —— had voted for secession, and there were Union people enough around us to communicate every thing of the sort to the Federals; the few neighbours who were left were preparing to be off, and we thought it most prudent to come off too. Pickets were already thrown out beyond Shuter's Hill, and they were threatening to arrest all secessionists. With a heavy heart I packed trunks and boxes, as many as our little carriage would hold; had packing-boxes fixed in my room for the purpose of bringing off valuables of various sorts, when I go down on Monday; locked up every thing; gave the keys to the cook, enjoining upon the servants to take care of the cows, "Old Rock," the garden, the flowers, and last, but not least, J——'s splendid Newfoundland. Poor dog, as we got into the carriage how I did long to take him! When we took leave of the servants they looked sorrowful, and we felt so. I promised them to return to-day, but Mr. —— was so sick this morning that I could not leave him, and have deferred it until day after to-morrow. Mr. —— said, as he looked out upon the green lawn just before we set off, that he thought he had never seen the place so attractive; and as we drove off the bright flowers we had planted seemed in full glory; every flower-bed seemed to glow with the "Giant of Battles" and other brilliant roses. In bitterness of heart I exclaimed, "Why must we leave thee, Paradise!" and for the first time my tears streamed. As we drove by "The Seminary," the few students who remained came out to say "Good-by." One of them had just returned from Alexandria, where he had seen the bodies of Ellsworth and Jackson, and another, of which we had heard through one of our servants who went to town in the morning. When the Federal troops arrived, a man being ordered to take down the secession flag from above the markethouse, and run up the "stars and stripes," got nearly to the flag, missed his foothold, fell, and broke his neck. This remarkable circumstance was told me by two persons who saw the body. Is it ominous? I trust and pray that it may be.

When we got to Bailey's Cross Roads, Mr. —— said to me that we were obliged to leave our home, and as far as we have a *right* to any other, it makes not the slightest difference which road we take—we might as well drive to the right hand as to the left—nothing remains to us but the barren, beaten track. It was a sorrowful thought; but we have kind relations and friends whose doors are open to us, and we hope to get home again before very long. The South did not bring on the war, and I believe that God will provide for the homeless.

About sunset we drove up to the door of this, the house of our relative, the Rev. Mr. B., and were received with the warmest welcome. As we drove through the village we saw the carriage of Commodore F. standing at the hotel door, and were soon followed by the C.'s of our neighbourhood and many others. They told us that the Union men of the town were pointing out the houses of the Secessionists, and that some of them had already been taken by Federal officers. When I think of all this my heart quails within me. Our future is so dark and shadowy, so much may, nay must, happen before we again become quiet, and get back, that I feel sad and dreary. I have no fear for the country—that must and will succeed; but our dear ones!—the representatives of every State, almost every family, from the Potomac to the Gulf of Mexico—how must they suffer, and how must we at home suffer in their behalf!

This little village has two or three companies quartered in it. It seems thoroughly aroused from the quiescent state which it was wont to indulge. Drums are beating, colours flying, and ever and anon we are startled by the sound of a gun. At Fairfax Station there are a good many troops, a South Carolina regiment at Centreville, and quite an army is collecting at Manassas Station. We shall be greatly outnumbered, I know, but numbers cannot make up for the zeal and patriotism of our Southern men fighting for home and liberty.

May 29.—I cannot get over my disappointment; I am not to return home; the wagon was engaged. E. W. had promised to accompany me; all things seemed ready; but yesterday a gentleman came up from the Seminary, reporting that the public roads are picketed far beyond our house, and that he had to cross fields, etc., to avoid an arrest, as he had no pass. I know that there are private roads which we could take, of which the enemy knows nothing; and even if they saw me, they surely would not forbid ingress and egress to a quiet elderly lady like myself. But Mr. —— thinks that I ought not to risk it. The fiat has gone forth, and I am obliged to submit. I hear that the house has been searched for arms, and that J's old rifle has been filched from its corner. It was a wonderfully harmless rifle, having been innocent even of the blood of squirrels and hares for some time past. I wonder if they do suppose that we would leave good fire-arms in their reach when they are so much wanted in the Confederacy, or if it is a mere pretext for satisfying a little innocent curiosity for seeing the interior of Southern homes? Ah, how many Northerners—perhaps the very men who have come to despoil these homes, to kill our husbands, sons and brothers, to destroy our peace—have been partakers of the warm-hearted hospitality so freely offered by our people! The parlours and dining-rooms now so ignominiously searched, how often have they been opened, and the best cheer which the houses could afford set forth for them! I do most earnestly hope that no Northern gentleman, above all, no Christian gentleman, will engage in this wicked war of invasion. It makes my blood boil when I remember that our private rooms, our chambers, our very sanctums, are thrown open to a ruthless soldiery. But let me not do them injustice. I believe that they took nothing but the rifle, and injured nothing but the sewing-machine. Perhaps they knew of the patriotic work of that same machine—how it had stitched up many a shirt and many a jacket for our brave boys, and therefore did it wrong. But this silent agent for our country's weal shall not lie in ruins. When I get it again, it shall be repaired, and shall

"Stitch, stitch, stitch,
Band, and gusset, and seam,"

for the comfort of our men, and it shall work all the more vigorously for the wrongs it has suffered.

I am indulging myself in writing on and on, because I have so little occupation now, and I feel so anxious and restless about those so near and dear to us, who have gone forth to defend us. The loss of property will be as nothing if our boys are spared. I am willing to be poor, but let, oh, let our family circles be unbroken! But I may feel too much anxiety, even on this subject. Our children have gone forth in a just and righteous cause; into God's hands let us consign them; they are doing their duty; to His will let us submit!

29th, Night.—Several of our friends from Alexandria have passed to-day. Many families who attempted to stay at home are escaping as best they may, finding that the liberty of the hoary-headed fathers of patriotic sons is at stake, and others are in peril for opinion's sake. It is too provoking to think of such men as Dr. —— and Dr. —— being obliged to hide themselves in their houses, until their wives, by address and strategy, obtain passes to get them out of town! Now they go with large and helpless families, they know not whither. Many have passed whom I did not know. What is to become of us all?

CHANTILLY, *June* 1.—We came here (the house of our friend Mrs. S.) this morning, after some hours of feverish excitement. About three o'clock in the night we were aroused by a volley of musketry not far from our windows. Every human being in the house sprang up at once. We soon saw by the moonlight a body of cavalry moving up the street, and as they passed below our window (we were in the upper end of the village) we distinctly heard the commander's order, "Halt." They again proceeded a few paces, turned and approached slowly, and as softly as though every horse were shod with velvet. In a few moments there was another volley, the firing rapid, and to my unpractised ear there seemed a discharge of a thousand muskets. Then came the same body of cavalry rushing by in wild disorder. Oaths loud and deep were heard from the commander. They again formed, and rode quite rapidly into the village. Another volley, and another, then such a rushing as I never witnessed. The cavalry strained by, the commander calling out "Halt, halt," with curses and imprecations. On, on they went, nor did they stop. While the balls were flying, I stood riveted to the window, unconscious of danger. When I was forced away, I took refuge in the front yard. Mrs. B. was there before me, and we witnessed the disorderly retreat of eighty-five of the Second United States Cavalry (regulars) before a much smaller body of our raw recruits. They had been sent from Arlington, we suppose, to reconnoitre. They advanced on the village at full speed, into the cross-street by the hotel and court-house, then wheeled to the right, down by the Episcopal church. We could only oppose them with the Warrenton Rifles, as for some reason the cavalry could not be rendered effective. Colonel Ewell, who happened to be there, arranged the Rifles, and I think a few dismounted cavalry, on either side of the street, behind the fence, so as to make it a kind of breastwork, whence they returned the enemy's fire most effectively. Then came the terrible suspense; all was confusion on the street, and it was not yet quite light. One of our gentlemen soon came in with the sad report that Captain Marr of the Warrenton Rifles, a young officer of great promise, was found dead. The gallant Rifles were exulting in their success, until it was whispered that their captain was missing. Had he been captured? Too soon the uncertainty was ended, and their exultant shouts hushed. His body was found in the high grass—dead, quite dead. Two of our men received slight flesh-wounds. The enemy carried off their dead and wounded. We captured four men and three horses. Seven of their horses were left dead on the roadside. They also dropped a number of arms, which were picked up by our men. After having talked the matter over, we were getting quite composed, and thought we had nothing more to fear, when we observed them placing sentinels in Mr. B.'s porch, saying that it was a high point, and another raid was expected. The gentlemen immediately ordered the carriages, and in half an hour Mr. B's family and ourselves were on our way to this place. As we approached the house, after a ride of six miles, the whole family came out to receive us. L. and B. ran across the lawn to meet us, with exclamations of pleasure at seeing us. We were soon seated in the parlour, surrounded by every thing that was delightful—Mrs. S. all kindness, and her daughters making the house pleasant and attractive. It was indeed a haven of rest to us after the noise and tumult of the court-house. They were, of course, in great excitement, having heard wild stories of the fight. We all rejoiced, and returned thanks to God that He had enabled our men to drive off the invaders.

This evening we have been enjoying a walk about these lovely grounds. Nature and art have combined to make it one of the most beautiful spots I ever saw—"So clean, so green, so flowery, so bowery," as Hannah wrote of Hampstead; and we look on it sadly, fearing that the "trail of the serpent may pass over it all." Can it be that other beautiful homes are to be deserted? The ladies of the family are here alone, the sons are where they should be, in the camp; and should the Northern army sweep over it, they cannot remain here. It is pitiful to think of it. They all look so happy together, and then if they go they must be scattered. Colonel Gregg and others of a South Carolina regiment dined here yesterday. They are in fine spirits, and very sanguine.

June 6.—Still at Chantilly. Every thing quiet, nothing particularly exciting ; yet we are so restless. Mrs. C. and myself rode to the camp at Fairfax Court-House a day or two ago to see many friends; but my particular object was to see my nephew, W. B. N., first lieutenant in the Hanover troop. He looks well and cheerful, full of enthusiasm and zeal; but he feels that we have a great work before us, and that we have entered upon a more important revolution than our ancestors did in 1775. How my heart yearned over him, when I thought of his dear wife and children, and his sweet home, and how cheerfully he had left all for the sake of his country. His bright political prospects, his successful career at the bar, which for one so young was so remarkable, his future in every respect so full of hope and promise—all, all laid aside. But it is all right, and when he returns to enjoy his unfettered country, his hardships will be all forgotten, in joy for his country's triumphs. The number in camp there has greatly increased since we came away. We came home, and made havelocks and haversacks for the men. The camp at Harper's Ferry is said to be strong and strengthening.

Mrs. General Lee has been with us for several days. She is on her way to the lower country, and feels that she has left Arlington for an indefinite period. They removed their valuables, silver, etc., but the furniture is left behind. I never saw her more cheerful, and she seems to have no doubt of our success. We are looking to her husband as our leader with implicit confidence; for besides his great military abilities, he is a God-fearing man, and looks for help where alone it is to be found. Letters from Richmond are very cheering. It is one great barracks. Troops are assembling there from every part of the Confederacy, all determined to do their duty. Ladies assemble daily, by hundreds, at the various churches, for the purpose of sewing for the soldiers. They are fitting out company after company. The large stuccoed house at the corner of Clay and Twelfth streets, so long occupied by Dr. John Brockenbrough, has been purchased as a residence for the President. I am glad that it has been thus appropriated. We expect to leave this place in a day or two for Clarke County for the summer, and we part with this dear family with a sad feeling that they may too soon have to leave it too. Mrs. S. has already sent off her plate and paintings to a place of safety. Mrs. C. is here with her mother. She left home when the army approached our neighborhood; she could not stay alone with her little son. Like ourselves, she brought off in her carriage what valuables she could, but necessarily has left much, which she fears may be ruined. Oh, that I had many things that are locked up at home! so many relics—hair of the dead, little golden memorials, etc.—all valueless to others, but very dear to our hearts. Alas, alas! I could not go back for them, and thieves may break through and steal. I trust that the officers will not allow it to be done, and try to rest contented.

THE BRIARS, *June* 12.—We are now in the beautiful Valley of Virginia, having left Chantilly on the 8th. The ride through the Piedmont country was delightful; it looked so peaceful and calm that we almost forgot the din of war we had left behind us. The road through Loudoun and Fauquier was picturesque and beautiful. We passed through the villages of Aldie, Middleburg, and Upperville. At Middleburg we stopped for an hour, and regaled ourselves on strawberries and cream at the house of our excellent brother, the Rev. Mr. K. At Upperville we spent the night. Early next morning we went on through the village of Paris, and then began to ascend the Blue Ridge, wound around on the fine turnpike, paused a moment at the top to "view the landscape o'er," and then descended into the "Valley." The wheat, which is almost ready for the reaper, is rich and luxuriant, foreshadowing an abundant commissariat for our army. After driving some miles over the delightful turnpike, we found ourselves at this door, receiving the warm-hearted welcome of the kindest of relatives and the most pleasant of hosts. Our daughters were here before us, all well, and full of questions about "home." This is all very delightful when we fancy ourselves making a *voluntary* visit to this family, as in days gone by, to return home when the visit is over, hoping soon to see our friends by our own fireside; but when the reality is before us that we were forced from home, and can only return when it pleases our enemy to open the way for us, or when our men have forced them away at the point of the bayonet, then does our future seem shadowy, doubtful, and dreary, and then we feel that our situation is indeed sorrowful. But these feelings must not be indulged; many are already in our situation, and how many more are there who may have to follow our example! Having no houses to provide for, we must be up and doing for our country; idleness does not become us now—there is too much to be done; we must work on, work ever, and let our country's weal be our being's end and aim.

Yesterday we went to Winchester to see my dear S., and found her house full of refugees : my sister Mrs. C., and her daughter Mrs. L., from Berkeley County. Mrs. C.'s sons are in the army; her eldest, having been educated at the Virginia Military Institute, drilled a company of his own county men during the John Brown raid; he has now taken it to the field, and is its commander; and Mr. L. is in the army, with the rank of major. Of course the ladies of the family were active in fitting out the soldiers, and when an encampment was near them, they did every thing in their power to contribute to the comfort of the soldiers; for which sins the Union people around them have thought proper to persecute them, until they were obliged to leave home—Mrs. L. with two sick children. Her house has been searched, furniture broken, and many depredations committed since she left home ; books thrown out of the windows during a rain: nothing escaped their fury.

Winchester is filled with hospitals, and the ladies are devoting their energies to nursing the soldiers. The sick from the camp at Harper's Ferrry are brought there. Our climate seems not to suit the men from the far South. I hope they will soon become acclimated. It rejoices my heart to see how much everybody is willing to do for the poor fellows. The ladies there think no effort, however self-sacrificing, is too great to be made for the soldiers. Nice food for the sick is constantly being prepared by old and young. Those who are very sick are taken to the private houses, and the best chambers in town are occupied by them. The poorest private and the officer of high degree meet with the same treatment. The truth is, the *élite* of the land is in the ranks. I heard a young soldier say, a few nights ago, that his captain was perhaps the plainest man, socially, in the company, but that he was an admirable officer. We heard a good story about a wealthy young private whose captain was his intimate friend, but not being rich, he could not afford to take a servant to camp; it therefore fell to the lot of the privates to clean the captain's shoes. When the turn of the wealthy friend came, he walked up, cap in hand, with an air of due humility, gave the military salute, and said, with great gravity, "Captain, your shoes, if you please, sir." The ludicrousness of the scene was more than either could stand, and they laughed heartily. But the wealthy private cleaned the captain's shoes.

June 15.—Yesterday was set apart by the President as a day of prayer and fasting, and I trust that throughout the Confederacy the blessing of God was invoked upon the army and country. We went to church at Millwood, and heard Bishop Meade. His sermon was full of wisdom and love; he urged us to individual piety in all things, particularly to love and charity to our enemies. He is full of enthusiasm and zeal for our cause. His whole heart is in it, and from the abundance of the heart the mouth speaketh, for he talks most delightfully and encouragingly on the subject. He says that if our ancestors had good reason for taking up arms in 1775, surely we had much better, for the oppression they suffered from the mother-country was not a tithe of the provocation we have received from the Government at Washington.

16th.—Rumours are abundant to-day of a Federal force approaching Strasburg. We are not at all credulous of the flying reports with which our ears are daily pained, and yet they make us restless and uneasy. We thank God and take courage from the little successes we have already had at Pigs Point, Acquia Creek, Fairfax Court-House, and Philippi. These are mere trifles, they say; well, so they are, but they are encouraging to our men, and show that we can hold our own.

A most decided revolution is going on in our social system throughout our old State: economy rules the day. In this neighbourhood, which has been not a little remarkable for indulging in the elegancies of life, they are giving up desserts, rich cake, etc. The wants of the soldiers are supplied with a lavish hand, but personal indulgences are considered unpatriotic. How I do admire their self-denying spirit! I do not believe there is a woman among us who would not give up every thing but the bare necessaries of life for the good of our cause.

16th, Night.—I can scarcely control myself to sit quietly

down and write of the good news brought by the mail of to-day; I mean the victory—on our side almost bloodless victory—at Bethel. It took place on the 10th. Strange that such *brilliant* news was so long delayed! The enemy lost 200 men, and we but one. He, poor fellow, belonged to a North Carolina regiment, and his bereaved mother received his body. She lives in Richmond. It seems to me that Colonel Magruder must have displayed consummate skill in the arrangement of his little squad of men. His " blind battery " succeeded admirably. The enemy had approached in two parties from Fortress Monroe, and, by mistake, fired into each other, causing great slaughter. They then united and rushed into the jaws of death, or, in other words, into the range of the guns of the blind battery. I feel sorry, very sorry, for the individual sufferers among the Yankees, particularly for those who did not come voluntarily; but they have no business here, and the more unsuccessful they are the sooner their government will recall them. I do believe that the hand of God was in this fight, we were so strangely successful. How we all gathered around M. M. as she read the account given in the paper; and how we exulted and talked, and how Mr. P. walked backwards and forwards, rubbing his hands with delight!

The camp at Harper's Ferry is broken up. General Johnston knows why; I am sure that I do not. He is sending out parties of troops to drive off the Yankees, who are marauding about the neighbouring counties, but who are very careful to keep clear of the "Ferry." The Second Regiment, containing some of our dear boys, has been lately very actively engaged in pursuit of these marauders, and we are kept constantly anxious about them.

18*th.*—We go to-day to dine with Bishop Meade. He

wishes us to spend much of our time with him. He says he must have the "refugees," as he calls us, at his house. Dear me, I am not yet prepared to think ourselves *refugees*, for I do hope to get home before long. How often do I think of it, as I left it! Not only blooming in its beauty, but the garden filled with vegetables, the strawberries turning on the vines, the young peach-orchard in full bloom; every thing teeming with comfort and abundance.

But the family is waiting for me; the carriage is at the door, and my sad thoughts must end.

NIGHT.—The day was passed delightfully; the Bishop, his son, and daughter-in-law, all so kind, hospitable and agreeable. It amused me to see with what avidity the old gentleman watches the progress of events, particularly when I remember how much opposed he was to secession only a few months ago. He clung to the Union with a whole-souled love for all that he had been educated to revere, as long as he could do it; but when every proposal for peace made by us was spurned, and when the President's proclamation came out, calling for 75,000 troops, and claiming Virginia's quota to assist in fighting her Southern brethren, he could stand it no longer, and I only hope that the revolution may be as thorough throughout the land as it is in his great mind.

"Mountain View" is beautiful by nature, and the Bishop has been collecting exotic trees and shrubs for many years, and now his collection is perfectly magnificent. This country is so far very peaceful, but we are constantly subjected to the most startling rumours, and the frequent, though distant, booming of cannon is very trying to our nervous and excitable temperaments. Many, so many, of our dear ones are constantly exposed to danger; and though we would not have it otherwise—we could not bear that one of them should hesitate to give his life's-blood to his country—yet it is heart-breaking to think of what may happen.

June 19.—Yesterday evening we heard rumours of the Federal troops having crossed the Potomac, and marching to Martinsburg and Shepherdstown in large force. General Johnston immediately drew up his army at a place called "Carter's," on the Charlestown road, about four miles beyond Winchester. Messrs. B. and R. M. called this morning, and report that the location of the Federals is very uncertain; it is supposed that they have retreated from Martinsburg. Oh, that our Almighty Father, who rules all things, would interpose and give us peace, even now when all seem ready for war! He alone can do it.

June 24.—We have been in Winchester for the last two days, at Dr. S's. General Johnston's army encamped at "The Lick." Some Southern regiments encamped near Winchester. The army at Manassas said to be strongly reinforced. Measles prevailing there, and near Winchester, among the troops. There has been a slight skirmish in Hampshire, on New Creek, and another at Vienna, in Fairfax County. We repulsed the enemy at both places. Captain Kemper, of Alexandria, led our men in the latter fight, and is much extolled for his dexterity and bravery.

July 1.—A rumour of a skirmish, in which the Messrs. Ashby were engaged, and that Richard Ashby was severely wounded. I trust it may not be true.

July 3.—A real fight has occeurred near Williamsport, but on the Virginia side of the Potomac. General Cadwallader crossed the river with, it is said, 14,000 men, to attack our force of 4,000 stationed there under Colonel

Jackson. Colonel J. thought it folly to meet such an army with so small a force, and therefore ordered a retreat ; but quite a body of artillery remained to keep the enemy at bay. They retained with them but one gun, a six-pounder The Rev. Dr. Pendleton, now captain of artillery, commanded this gun, and whenever he ordered its discharge he was heard to say, reverently, "The Lord have mercy upon their souls—fire!" The result was almost miraculous but four of our men were missing, two of whom were killed; twenty were wounded, and have been brought to the Winchester hospitals ; sixty-five prisoners were taken, and are now in Winchester. Many of their men were seen to fall. Our men, who did this deadly firing, retreated in perfect order. I heard this from one who was on the field at the time. It is said that in Dr. Pendleton the soldier and the chaplain are blended most harmoniously. A gentleman who went to the camp to visit his sons, who belong to the "Rockbridge Battery," told me that he arose before daylight, and was walking about the encampment, and when near a dense wood his attention was arrested by the voice of prayer; he found it was the sonorous voice of Dr. P., who was surrounded by his company, invoking for them, and for the country, the blessing of Heaven. What a blessing it is for those young men, away from the influences of home, and exposed to the baneful associations of the camp, to have such a guide! It has almost reconciled me to the clergy going upon the field as soldiers. The Bishop of Louisiana has been to Mountain View, to consult Bishop Meade on the subject of his taking the field. I do not know what advice was given. These reverend gentlemen, who were educated at West Point, are perfectly conscientious, and think it their duty to give their military knowledge to their country, and their presence may do much for the spiritual good of the army.

Brave Richard Ashby is dead; how I grieve for his family and for his country, for we cannot afford to lose such men!

July 4.—This day General Scott promised himself and his Northern friends to dine in Richmond. Poor old renegade, I trust he has eaten his last dinner in Richmond, the place of his marriage, the birthplace of his children, the home of his early friendships, and so near the place of his nativity and early years.

How can he wish to enter Richmond but as a friend? But it is enough for us to know that he is disappointed in his amiable and *patriotic* wish to-day. So may it be.

I have seen W. H., who has just returned from Fairfax. Last week he scouted near our house, and gives no very encouraging report for us. Our hills are being fortified, and Alexandria and the neighbourhood have become one vast barracks. The large trees are being felled, and even houses are falling by order of the invader! Our prospect of getting home becomes more and more dim; my heart sinks within me, and hope is almost gone. What shall we do, if the war continues until next winter, without a certain resting-place? Our friends are kind and hospitable, open-hearted and generous to a wonderful degree. In this house we are made to feel not only welcome, but that our society gives them heartfelt pleasure. Other friends, too, are most kind in giving invitations "for the war"—" as long as we find it agreeable to stay," etc.; but while this is very gratifying and delightful, yet we must get some place, however small and humble, to call home. Our friends here amuse themselves at my fears; but should the war continue, I do not think that they have any guarantee that they will not be surrounded by an *unfriendly host.* They think that they will not leave their homes under any circumstances; perhaps not, because they are surrounded by so much property that they must protect; but the situation will be very trying. Whenever I express a feeling of despondency, Mr. —— meets it with the calm reply, that the "Lord will provide," so that I am really ashamed to give place to fear. The situation of the people of Hampton is far worse than ours—their homes reduced to ashes; their church in ruins! That venerable colonial church, in which for generations they have been baptized, received the Holy Communion, been married, and around which their dead now lie. Their very graves desecrated; their tomb-stones torn down and broken; the slabs, sacred to the memory of their fathers, children, husbands, wives, which have been watched and decorated perhaps for years, now converted into dining-tables for the Yankee soldiery. How can human hearts bear such things and live? We have not yet been subjected to any thing of the kind, and I humbly trust that so dire a calamity may be averted.

July 5.—Yesterday M. P. and myself spent several hours riding about to visit our friends. The news of the day was, that General Patterson, with a large force, had crossed the river and taken possession of Martinsburg, and that General Johnston had sent Colonel Stuart, with his cavalry, to reconnoitre and cut off his supplies, and to prevent a retreat. All these things make us anxious, particularly as the booming of cannon is not unfrequent; but my faith in the justice of our cause is strong.

6*th.*—No army news to be relied on. We spent our time as usual. Knitting for the soldiers is our chief employment. Several suits of clothes for them are in progress in the house.

Sunday, 9th.—About to go to church. I trust that this Sabbath may be instrumental of much spiritual good, and that the hearts of the people may be busy in prayer, both for friends and enemies. Oh, that the Spirit of God may be with the soldiers, to direct them in keeping this holy day! We are in the Lord's hands—He alone can help us.

July 18.—During the last ten days we have been visiting among our friends, near Berryville, and in Winchester. The wheat harvest is giving the most abundant yield, and the fields are thick with corn. Berryville is a little village surrounded by the most beautiful country and delightful society. Patriotism burns brightly there, and every one is busy for the country in his or her own way. It is cheering to be among such people; the ladies work, and the gentlemen— the old ones—no young man is at home—give them every facility. But Winchester, what shall I say for Winchester that will do it justice? It is now a hospital. The soldiers from the far South have never had measles, and most unfortunately it has broken out among them, and many of them have died of it, notwithstanding the attention of surgeons and nurses. No one can imagine the degree of self-sacrificing attention the ladies pay them; they attend to their comfort in every respect; their nourishment is prepared at private houses; every lady seems to remember that her son, brother, or husband may be placed in the same situation among strangers, and to be determined to do unto others as she would have others to do unto her.

War still rages. Winchester is fortified, and General Johnston has been reinforced. He now awaits General Patterson, who seems slowly approaching.

While in Winchester, I heard of the death of one who has been for many years as a sister to me—Mrs. L. A. P., of S. H., Hanover County. My heart is sorely stricken by it, particularly when I think of her only child, and the many who seemed dependent on her for happiness. She died on Saturday last. With perfect resignation to the will of God, she yielded up her redeemed spirit, without a doubt of its acceptance. *In cœlo quies.* There is none for us here.

We have been dreadfully shocked by the defeat at Rich Mountain and the death of General Garnett! It is the first repulse we have had, and we should not complain, as we were overpowered by superior numbers; but we have so much to dread from superior numbers—they are like the sand upon the sea-shore for multitude. Our men say that one Southern man is equal to three Yankees. Poor fellows! I wish that their strength may be equal to their valour. It is hard to give up such a man as General Garnett. He was son of the late Hon. Robert S. Garnett, of Essex County; educated at West Point; accomplished and gallant. His military knowledge and energy will be sadly missed. It was an unfortunate stroke, the whole affair; but we must hope on, and allow nothing to depress us.

I have just returned from a small hospital which has recently been established in a meeting-house near us. The convalescent are sent down to recruit for service, and to recover their strength in the country, and also to relieve the Winchester hospitals. The ladies of the neighbourhood are doing all they can to make them comfortable. They are full of enthusiasm, and seem to be very cheerful, except when they speak of home. They are hundreds of miles from wife, children, and friends. Will they ever see them again? I have been particularly interested in one who is just recovering from typhoid fever. I said to him as I sat fanning him: "Are you married?" His eyes filled with tears as he replied, "Not now; I have been, and my little children, away in Alabama, are always in my mind. At first I thought I could not leave the little motherless things, but then our boys were all coming, and mother said, 'Go, Jack, the country must have men, and you must bear your part, and I will take care of the children;' and then I went and 'listed, and when I went back home for my things, and saw my children, I 'most died like. 'Mother,' says I, 'I am going, and father must take my corn, my hogs, and every thing else he likes, and keep my children; but if I never get back, I know it will be a mighty burden in your old age; but I know you will do your best.' 'Jack,' says she, 'I will do a mother's part by them; but you must not talk that way. Why should you get killed more than another? You will get back, and then we shall be so happy. God will take care of you, I know He will.'" He then took a wallet from under his pillow, and took two locks of hair: "This is Peter's, he is three years old; and this is Mary's, she is a little more than one, and named after her mother, and was just stepping about when I left home." At that recollection, tears poured down his bronzed cheeks, and I could not restrain my own. I looked at the warm-hearted soldier, and felt that he was not the less brave for shedding tears at the recollection of his dead wife, his motherless children, and his brave old mother. I find that the best way to nurse them, when they are not too sick to bear it, is to talk to them of home. They then cease to feel to you as a stranger, and finding that you take interest in their "short and simple annals," their natural reserve gives way, and they at once feel themselves among friends.

July 19.—This day is perhaps the most anxious of my life. It is believed that a battle is going on at or near Manassas. Our large household is in a state of feverish anxiety; but we cannot talk of it. Some sit still, and are more quiet than usual; others are trying to employ themselves. N. is reading aloud, trying to interest herself and others; but we are all alike anxious, which is betrayed by the restless eye and sad countenance. Yesterday evening we were startled by the sound of myriads of horses, wheels, and men on the turnpike. We soon found the whole of General Johnston's army was passing by, on its way to join Beauregard, below the mountain. A note from J. M. G., written with a pencil at the Longwood gate, was soon brought in, to say that they would halt at Millwood. The carriages were soon ready, and as many of the family as could go went to Millwood to meet them. I gave up my seat to another, for I felt too sad to meet with those dear boys marching on to such danger. Mr. —— and the girls went. They saw my nephews, R. C. W. and B. B., and others who were very dear to us. They report them all as in fine spirits. The people all along the road, and in the village of Millwood, went out to meet them with refreshments. While halting at Millwood, General Johnston announced to them that General Beauregard had been successful in a fight the day before, near Manassas, and that another fight was hourly pending. The troops became wild with excitement. It is said that General Patterson has gone to join McDowell. I trust that General Johnston may get there in time. They were passing here from about four in the afternoon until a late hour in the night. After midnight the heavy army wagons were lumbering by, and we ever and anon heard the tap of the drum. We did not retire until all was still, and then none of us slept.

July 20.—R. P. arrived to-night from Norfolk. He passed Manassas yesterday, and saw J. very busy with the wounded. The fight of the 18th quite severe; the enemy were very decidedly repulsed; but another battle is imminent. We were shocked by the death of Major C. Harrison. J. wrote to his father. He fears to-morrow may be a bloody Sabbath. Oh, that Providence would now interpose and prevent further bloodshed! Oh, that strength may be given to our men. Let not the enemy overcome them. Oh, God of Nations! have mercy on the South!

The fight on Thursday lasted several hours; our loss was fifteen killed, about forty wounded; in all about eighty to eighty-five missing. It is believed that at least 900 of the enemy were left on the field; 150 of their slightly wounded have been sent to Richmond as prisoners. Their severely wounded are in the hands of our surgeons at Manassas.

Sunday, 21.—We were at church this morning and heard Bishop Meade, on the subject of "Praise." He and his whole congregation greatly excited. Perhaps there was no one present who had not some near relative at Manassas, and the impression was universal that they were then fighting. This suspense is fearful; but we must possess our souls in patience.

Monday.—We can hear nothing from Manassas at all reliable. Men are passing through the neighbourhood giving contradictory reports. They are evidently deserters. They only concur in one statement—that there was a battle yesterday.

Tuesday.—The victory is ours! The enemy was routed. The Lord be praised for this great mercy.

Evening.—Mr. —— and myself have just returned from a neighbouring house where we heard the dread particulars of the battle. We saw a gentleman just from the battle field, who brought off his wounded son. It is said to have been one of the most remarkable victories on record, when we consider the disparity in numbers, equipments, etc. Our loss, when compared with that of the enemy, was small, very small; but such men as have fallen! How can I record the death of our young friends, the Conrads of Martinsburg, the only sons of their father, and such sons! Never can we cease to regret Tucker Conrad, the bright, joyous youth of the "High School," and the devoted divinity student of our Theological Seminary! Noble in mind and spirit, with the most genial temper and kindest manners I have ever known. Mr. —— saw him on Thursday evening on his way to the battle-field, and remarked afterwards on his enthusiasm and zeal in the cause. Holmes, his brother, was not one of us, as Tucker was, but he was in no respect inferior to him—loved and admired by all. They were near the same age, and there was not fifteen minutes between their deaths. Lovely and pleasant in their lives, in their deaths they were not divided. But my thoughts constantly revert to that desolated home—to the parents and sister who perhaps are now listening and waiting for letters from the battle-field. Before this night is over, loving friends will bear their dead sons home. An express has gone from Winchester to tell them all. They might with truth exclaim, with one of old, whose son was thus slain, "I would not give my dead son for any living son in Christendom." But that devoted father, and fond mother, have better and higher sources of comfort than any which earthly praise can give! Their sons were Christians, and their ransomed spirits were wafted from the clash and storm of the battle-field to those peaceful joys, " of which it has not entered into the heart of man to conceive." I have not heard which was there to welcome his brother to his home in the skies; but both were there to receive the spirit of another, who was to them as a brother. I allude to Mr. Peyton Harrison, a gifted young lawyer of the same village. He was lieutenant of their company, and their mother's nephew, and fell a few moments after the last brother. He left a young wife and little children to grieve, to faint, and almost to die, for the loss of a husband and father, so devoted, so accomplished, so brave. Like his young cousins, he was a Christian; and is now with them rejoicing in his rest. Martinsburg has lost one other of her brave sons ; and yet another is fearfully wounded. I thank God, those of my own household and family, as far as I can hear, have escaped, except that one has a slight wound.

We certainly routed the enemy, and already wonderful stories are told of the pursuit. We shall hear all from time to time. It is enough for us now to know that their great expectations are disappointed, and that we have gloriously gained our point. Oh, that they would now consent to leave our soil, and return to their own homes! If I know my own heart, I do not desire vengeance upon them, but only that they would leave us in peace, to be forever and forever a separate people. It is true that we have slaughtered them, and whipped them, and driven them from our land, but they are people of such indomitable perseverance, that I am afraid that they will come again, perhaps in greater force. The final result I do not fear; but I do dread the butchery of our you men.

"MOUNTAIN VIEW," *July* 29.—Mr. —— and mys came over here on Friday, to spend a few days with t Bishop and his family. He delivered a delightful addre yesterday in the church, on the thankfulness and praise d to Almighty God, for (considering the circumstances) o unprecedented victory at Manassas. Our President a Congress requested that thanks should be returned in all our churches. All rejoice for the country, though there a many bleeding hearts in our land. Among our acquain ances, Mr. Charles Powell, of Winchester, Col. Edmu Fontaine, of Hanover, and Mr. W. N. Page, of Lexin ton, each lost a son; and our friend, Mr. Clay Ward, Alexandria, also fell. The gallant Generals Bee and Ba tow were not of our State, but of our cause, and we a mourn their loss. Each mail adds to the list of casualtie The enemy admit their terrible disaster, and are busy i quiring into *causes*.

This house has been a kind of hospital for the last mont Several sick soldiers are here now, men of whom they kno nothing except that they are soldiers of the Confederac They have had measles, and are now recruiting for servic One who left here two weeks ago, after having been car fully nursed, was killed at Manassas. The family seem lament him as an old friend, though they never saw hi until he came here from the Winchester hospital. Two so of this house were in the fight; and the Bishop had sever other grandchildren engaged, one of whom, R. M., lost h right arm. His grandfather has been to Winchester to s him, and is much gratified by the fortitude with which l bears his suffering. He says, "R. is a brave boy, and h done his duty to his country, and I will try to do my duty to him, and make up the loss of his arm to him, as far as possible." It is delightful to be with Bishop Meade. There is so much genuine hospitality and kindness in his manner of entertaining, which we perhaps appreciate more highly now than we ever did before. His simple, self-denying habits are more conspicuous at home than anywhere else. We sit a great deal in his study, where he loves to entertain his friends. Nothing can be more simple than its furniture and arrangements, but he gives you so cordial a welcome to it, and is so agreeable, that you forget that the chair on which you sit is not cushioned. He delights in walking over the grounds with his friends, and as you stop to admire a beautiful tree or shrub, he will give you the history of it. Many of them he brought with him from Europe; but whether native or foreign, each has its association. *This* he brought in his trunk when a mere scion, from the tide-water section of Virginia; that from the "Eastern Shore;" another from the Alleghany mountains; another still, from the Cattskill mountains. Here is the oak of old England; there the cedar of Lebanon; there the willow from St. Helena, raised from a slip which had absolutely waved over the grave of Napoleon. Here is another, and prettier willow, native of our own Virginia soil. Then he points out his eight varieties of Arbor Vitæ, and the splendid yews, hemlocks, spruces, and firs of every kind, which have attained an immense size. Our own forest trees are by no means forgotten, and we find oaks, poplars, elms, etc., without number. He tells me that he has more than a hundred varieties of trees in his yard. His flowers, too, are objects of great interest to him, particularly the old-fashioned damask rose. But his grape-vines are now his pets. He understands the cultivation of them perfectly, and I never saw them so luxuriant. It has been somewhat the fashion to call him stern, but I wish that those who call him so could see him among his children, grandchildren, and servants. Here he is indeed a patriarch. *All* are affectionately respectful, but none of them seem at all afraid of him. The grandchildren are never so happy as when in "grandpapa's room;" and the little coloured children frequently come to the porch, where he spends a great deal of his time, to inquire after "old master's health," and to receive bread and butter or fruit from his hands.

July 30th.—I have just been conversing with some young soldiers, who joined in the dangers and glories of the battle-field. They corroborate what I had before heard of the presence of Northern females. I would not mention it before in my diary, because I did not wish to record any thing which I did not *know* to be true. But when I receive the account from eye-witnesses whose veracity cannot be doubted, I can only say, that I feel mortified that such was the case. They came, not as Florence Nightingales to alleviate human suffering, but to witness and exult over it. With the full assurance of the success of their army they meant to pass over the mutilated limbs and mangled corpses of ours, and to go on their way rejoicing to scenes of festivity in the halls of the vanquished, and to revel over the blood of the slain, the groans of the dying, the wails of the widow and the fatherless. But "Linden saw another sight," and these very delicate, gentle, *womanly* ladies, where were they? Flying back to Washington, in confusion and terror, pell-mell, in the wildest excitement. And where were their brave and honourable escorts? Flying, too; not as protectors to their fair friends, but with self-preservation alone in view. All went helter-skelter—coaches, cabriolets, barouches, buggies, flying over the roads, as though all Fairfax were mad.

> "Ah, Fear! ah, frantic Fear!
> I see—I see thee near.
> I know thy hurried step, thy haggard eye!
> Like thee, I start; like thee, disordered fly!

Each bush to their disordered imaginations contained a savage Confederate. Cannon seemed thundering in the summer breeze, and in each spark of the lightning-bug, glinted and gleamed the sword and Bowie-knife of the blood-thirsty Southerner. Among the captured articles were ladies' dresses, jewels, and other gew-gaws, on their way to Richmond to the grand ball promised to them on their safe arrival. There were also fine wines, West India fruits, and almost everything else rich, or sweet, or intoxicating, brought by the gay party, for a right royal pic-nic on the field of blood. The wines and brandies came in well for our wounded that night, and we thank God for the superfluities of the wicked.

July 30.—News from home. Mr. McD., of the Theological Seminary, an Irish student, who was allowed to remain there in peace, being a subject of Great Britain, has just arrived at this house as a candidate for ordination. He says that our house has been taken for a hospital, except two or three rooms which are used as headquarters by an officer. Bishop Johns' house is used as headquarters; and the whole neighbourhood is one great barracks. The families who remained, Mrs. B., the Misses H., and others, have been sent to Alexandria, and their houses taken. Mr. J's and Mr. C's sweet residences have been taken down to the ground to give place to fortifications, which have been thrown up in every direction. Vaucluse, too, the seat of such elegant hospitality, the refined and dearly-loved home of the F. family, has been levelled to the earth, fortifications thrown up across the lawn, the fine old trees felled, and the whole grounds, once so embowered and shut out from public gaze, now laid bare and open—Vaucluse no more! There seems no probability of our getting home, and if we cannot go, what then? What will become of our furniture, and all our comforts, books, pictures, etc.! But these things are too sad to dwell on.

Mr. McD. gives an amusing account of the return of the Northern troops on the night of the 21st, and during the whole of the 22d. Such a wild, alarmed, dispirited set he had never an idea of. He had seen them pass by thousands and thousands, first on one road and then on the other, well armed, well mounted, in every respect splendidly equipped, only a few days before. As a Southern sympathizer, he had trembled for us, and prayed for us, that we might not be entirely destroyed. He and one or two others of similar sentiments had prayed and talked together of our danger. Then what was their surprise to see the hasty, disordered return!

August 1.—This whole neighbourhood is busy to-day, loading a wagon with comforts for the hospital at Fairfax Court-House. They send it down once a week, under the care of a gentleman, who, being too old for the service, does this for the sick and wounded. The hospitals at Centreville and the Court-House are filled with those who are too severely wounded to be taken to Richmond, Charlottesville, and the larger hospitals. They are supplied, to a very great degree, by private contributions. It is beautiful to see the self-denying efforts of these patriotic people.

Everybody sends contributious on the appointed day to Millwood, where the wagon is filled to overflowing with garments, brandy, wine, nice bread, biscuit, sponge cake, butter, fresh vegetables, fruit, etc. Being thoroughly packed, it goes off for a journey of fifty miles.

THE BRIARS, *August* 10.—Nothing new from the army. All seems quiet; no startling rumours within the past week. The family somewhat scattered : M. P. has gone to the "Hot Springs," J. to Capon Springs, both in quest of health; E. P. and E. M. are at "Long Branch" (Mr. H. N's) on a visit to a young friend.

J. P. has just called, having resigned his commission in the United States Navy, and received one in the Confederate ; he is on his way to Richmond for orders. He tells me that my dear W. B. P. has come in from Kentucky, with the first Kentucky Regiment, which is stationed near Centreville. It is right he should come; and I am glad he has, though it is another source of painful anxiety to me.

12*th*.—Still nothing from the army. We go on here quietly and happily—as happily as the state of the country will allow. The household peaceful and pleasant. The ladies, all of us, collect in one room generally, and work, while one reads some pleasant book. We are mercifully dealt with, and I hope we are grateful for such blessings.

The Northern papers tell us that General Patterson has withdrawn from the Northern army. The reason thereof is not mentioned ; but we shrewdly suspect that the powers at Washington are not entirely satisfied that he was so completely foiled by General Johnston. General Johnston was fighting the battle of Manassas before General P. knew that he had left the Valley. The rumour that he had gone to join McDowell was unfounded. For many days there was no intercourse between the section occupied by the Federal army and that occupied by ours; pickets were placed on every road, to prevent any one from passing towards General P. Gentlemen who had come to Winchester and Berryville on business for a few hours, were not allowed to return home for days. So how could the poor man know what was going on? We only fear that his place may be supplied by one more vigilant. General Scott, too, has been *almost* superseded by General McClellan, who seems just now to be the idol of the North. The Philadelphia papers give a glowing description of his reception in that city. It was his luck, for it seems to me, with his disciplined and large command, it required no skill to overcome and kill the gallant General Garnett at Rich Mountain. For this he is feted and caressed, *lionized* and *heroized* to the greatest degree. I only hope that, like McDowell and Patterson, he may disappoint their expectations.

August 20.—We are rejoicing over a victory at Springfield, Missouri—General Lyon killed and his troops routed. Our loss represented large. I have only seen the Northern account.

No news from home, and nothing good from that quarter anticipated. We are among dear, kind friends, and have the home feeling which only such genuine and generous hospitality can give; but it sometimes overpowers me, when I allow myself to think of our uncertain future.

NORWOOD, NEAR BERRYVILLE, *August* 26.—On a visit of a few days to our relative, Dr. M. The people of this neighbourhood occupied as they are in the one I left. All hearts and hands seem open to our army. Four heavily laden wagons have left Berryville within a few days, for the hospitals below. We are all anxious about Western Virginia, of which we can hear so little. General Lee and General Floyd are there, and if they can only have men and ammunition enough we have nothing to fear.

The army in Fairfax seems quiet. Colonel Stuart, with his cavalry, has driven the enemy back, and taken possession of " Chestnut Hill " as head-quarters. There they are overlooking Washington, Georgetown, and our neighbourhood, all bristling with cannon, to prevent their nearer approach. Some of those young men can almost point from the hills on which they are encamped, to chimneys of their own firesides, the portals of their own homes. The woods are cleared away for miles; even the yard trees are gone, leaving the houses in bold relief, with nothing to shade, nothing to obscure them. I do pity those who were obliged to stay in Southern homes, with Southern hearts, surrounded by bitter and suspicious enemies. My old friend Mrs. D. is sometimes in their lines, sometimes in ours. When our men are near her, they are fed from her table, and receive all manner of kindness from her hands. Some of my nephews have been invited to her table, and treated as her relations. When they entered her house she advanced towards them with outstretched hands. "You don't know me, but I knew your mother, father, and all your relations; and besides, I am connected with you, and you must come to my house while near me, as to that of an old friend." Nothing could be more grateful to a soldier far away from home and friends. But these were her bright moments. She has had many trials while in the enemy's lines. Her husband and grown son are in the Confederate service; she has sent her two young daughters to her friends in the lower country, and has remained as the protector of her property, with her two sons of eight and ten, as her companions. On one occasion her servant was driving the cows from her yard to be milked; from very loneliness she called to the servant to remain and milk them where they were; the very tinkling of the cow-bell was pleasant to her. It was scarcely done when a posse of soldiers came with their bayonets gleaming in the moonlight, and demanded, "Why did you have a bell rung in your yard this evening?" "Do you mean, why did the cow-bell ring? Because the cow shook her head while she was being milked." "But you don't have the cows milked in the yard every evening. It was a signal to the rebels—you know it was—and your house shall be burnt for it." She then had to plead her innocence to save her house, which they pretended not to believe until the servants were called up to prove her statements. They then, with threats and curses, went off. Another night she carried a candle from room to room to seek some missing article. In a short time several soldiers were seen running to her house with lighted torches, yelling "Burn it, burn it to the ground!" She ran to the yard to know the cause; instantly this lonely woman was surrounded by a lawless, shouting soldiery, each with a burning torch, revealing, by its lurid and fitful light, a countenance almost demoniac. They seemed perfectly lawless, and without a leader, for each screamed out, "We are ordered to burn your house." "Why?" said she. "Because you have signal-lights at your windows for the d——d rebels." She immediately suspected that no such order had been given, and summoning firmness of voice and manner to her aid, she ordered them off, saying that she should send for an officer. They did go, uttering imprecations on her defenceless head. But a still more trying scene occurred a short time ago. Our soldiers were surrounding her house, when Colonel Stuart sent off a raiding party. During that night the Yankees advanced, and our men retired. The Yankees at once heard that the raiders were out; but in what direction was the question. They came up to her house, and knowing the mother too well to attempt to extort any thing from her, ordered the little boys to tell them in what direction Colonel Stuart had gone. The boys told them that they could tell nothing. Threats followed; finally handcuffs and irons for the ankles were brought. Still those little heroes stood, the one as pale as ashes, the other with his teeth clenched over his under lip, until the blood was ready to gush out, but not one word could be extorted, until, with a feeling of hopelessness in their efforts, they went off, calling them cursed little rebels, etc. The mother saw all this, and stood it unflinchingly—poor thing! It is harrowing to think of her sufferings. Yet, if she comes away, her house will be sacked, and perhaps burnt.

We are sometimes alarmed by reports that the enemy is advancing upon Winchester; but are enabled to possess our souls in patience, and hope that all may be well. I see that they are encroaching upon the Northern Neck. I trust they may be repulsed from that fair land.

"The Briars," *Sept.* 6.—We returned home, as we are wont to call this sweet place, yesterday, and are just now taken up with family matters of deep interest. The army in Virginia seems quiet; but our arms had a severe reverse on Thursday. Fort Hatteras was bombarded and taken by Federal vessels. They also secured many prisoners.

General Floyd, in Western Virginia, had a severe skirmish with the enemy, about a week ago, and drove them off with considerable loss. Our loss was small.

Sept. 12*th.*—Yesterday was the wedding of our dear ——.

The marriage of a child is always melancholy when it involves separation, but particularly so under such circumstances. But surely never were refugees so blessed with friends. Our plan was to have the ceremony in the church, and then to proceed to Winchester, where the bridal party would take the stage for Strasburg, and thence by the cars to Richmond; but we were overruled by Mr. P., who invited his and our friends for the evening, and a beautiful entertainment was prepared for them. We all exercised our taste in arranging the table, which, with its ices, jellies, and the usual etceteras of an elegant bridal supper, made us forget that we were in a blockaded country. A pyramid of the most luscious grapes, from Bishop Meade's garden, graced the centre of the table. The bridesmaids were *three*, and groomsman *one*, and he, poor fellow, had to go off in the storm of last night, because his furlough lasted but forty-eight hours, and his station is Culpepper Court-House. The groom had a furlough of but three days, to come from and return to Richmond. The Bishop and Mrs. J. arrived in the morning. The party consisted of *ladies*, and gentlemen too old for the service. Bishop J. performed the ceremony. Bishop Meade professed to be too old for such occasions, and declined coming. We feel very lonely this morning, and turn to the newspapers more than we have done for some time.

I saw a young soldier the other day, who told me he could see the *top* of our house distinctly from "Munson's Hill." Oh, that I could know what is going on within those walls, all encompassed by armies as it is. With my mind's eye I look into first one room and then another, with all the associations of the past; the old family Bible, the family pictures, the library, containing the collection of forty years, and so many things which seemed a part of ourselves. What will become of them? Who are now using or abusing them?

Sept. 16*th.*—Just returned from Annfield, where we have spent a charming day, with most delightful society. The papers brought us news of success in the West, General Floyd having overcome Rosecranz on Gauley River. This gave us great satisfaction, as we are peculiarly anxious about that part of Virginia. We passed the time in talking over the feats of our heroes, as well as in enjoying the *elegancies* by which we were surrounded.

Sept. 18*th.*—I have been greatly interested in a letter, which has been sent me, written by my nephew, Lt. W. B. N., to his wife, the day after the battle of Manassas. I copy it here because I want his little relations, for whom I am writing this diary, to have a graphic description of the fight, and to know what their family and friends suffered for the great cause.

"CENTREVILLE, *July* 22, 1861.

"MY DEAR ———.:—For the last four days we have never been longer than two hours in any one place, have slept upon the ground in good weather and bad, eaten nothing but crackers and fried bacon, and rest little at any time; for all of which privations and a thousand others we have been more than compensated (thanks to the just God who governs the councils of history and decrees the destiny of nations) in the glorious results of yesterday. On the morning of the 17th, we had received reliable information that the enemy was advancing, over 50,000 strong, and were not surprised, at five o'clock in the morning, to hear the fire of our pickets, who were slowly retiring before the advancing foe. The order was given to pack. In ten minutes baggage was packed, tents struck, and the wagons driven to the rear; and the whole command forward to line of battle. In a few minutes the glittering bayonets of the enemy lined the neighbouring hills. From the heavy signal-guns being fired at intervals along our line—commencing at Germantown and stretching along to Fairfax Court-House—it was evident that the enemy was endeavouring to surround our little band; but our "Little Trump," as the men call Beauregard, was not to be taken by any such game. Every preparation was made to deceive the enemy, by inducing him to believe that we meditated a vigorous resistance. Meantime our column defiled through a densely wooded road, and was far on the way to Centreville when the enemy discovered his mistake. He followed on very cautiously. To our troop, with Kemper's Battery, was assigned the post of honour, and charged with the duty of covering the retreat. We were the last to leave the village, and as we went out at one end of the street, his column appeared at the other. We halted at this place about four o'clock in the afternoon, and again made show of battle—slept until twelve o'clock at the heads of our horses. We silently left the place, the enemy's pickets being within hailing distance of our own. At daybreak we were across Bull Run, having marched very slowly to keep pace with the infantry. We found beds of leaves in the woods, wrapped ourselves in our blankets, and slept for an hour or two, until we were aroused by the roar of the enemy's guns as he opened his batteries upon our lines. For two mortal hours shot and shell flew thick along our whole line. This day's work was evidently intended only to draw the fire of our artillery, and show where our batteries were. In consequence of which our gunners were ordered not to fire a single shot, unless within point-blank range. After thus opening the ball, two dense masses of infantry were sent to defile to the right and left, to make two separate attacks. It was indeed a beautiful sight as they came down in perfect order, and with the stealthy step of veterans. They came nearer and yet nearer, and yet no shot from our guns. Our men began to mutter, and say that we were preparing for another retreat. But in a few moments the appointed time arrived. A single shot from the Washington Artillery gave the signal of death, and for half an hour there was nothing but a continuous sheet of flame along the right of our lines. The enemy fell back, rallied, and charged again, with a like result. Again they rested, and rushed forward, but old Virginia was true to herself, and the gallant Seventeenth and Eighteenth Regiments charged them with the bayonet, and drove them back in utter confusion. The cavalry were held in reserve, and although within range of the artillery, and constantly experiencing the sensation which men may be supposed to indulge, who know there is a hidden danger hovering in the air, without knowing where it is to light, took no part in the action. Our time came yesterday, however. Our troop was for four hours in the hottest of the fight, and every man in it won the applause and approbation of the whole camp. The action commenced at eight o'clock on the sweet Sabbath morning. The enemy commenced with quite a heavy cannonade upon our right, which proved to be a mere feint, to distract our attention, as his main attack was directed to our left wing. At ten o'clock the enemy had crossed the river on our left, and then the fighting commenced in earnest. From the hill on which we stood, we could see, from the smoke and dust, though at the distance of several miles, how the fight was waging on our left. Some thought the enemy was retreating; others that our men had fallen back. It was an hour of painful interest. At eleven o'clock an aid-de-camp rode up in a gallop, and said our men were retiring—the cavalry was ordered to the left. We were temporarily attached to Radford's regiment—ours was the first company, and mine was the first platoon. On we dashed in a gallop, and as we passed within range of a battery of rifled cannon a ball was fired at us which passed between Wickham and myself, knocking up a cloud of dust. Without wavering in their ranks, the men and horses dashed forward at a gallop. As we reached the scene of action the sight was discouraging in the extreme. The enemy had at first the advantage of every attacking party. He had concentrated his forces for an attack upon one point. The First Louisiana Regiment and the Fourth Alabama, attacked in flank and centre by 30,000 men, were literally cut to pieces. They refused to surrender, but retired slowly, disputing every inch of ground. As we rode up we could meet parts of companies which had been utterly overwhelmed—the men wounded, their arms broken, while some of them were carrying off their dead in blankets. Every thing looked like retreat. We were ordered up to within five hundred yards of the enemy's artillery, behind a hill which afforded some protection against their destructive fire. For one hour the fire raged with incessant fury. A ball passed over the hill and through our ranks, grazing one of our men. A shell exploded just under Radford's horse, and every minute shot and shell were continually whistling by us. I can give you no conception of that awful hour. Not a man shrank from his post. Two of our men were taken exceedingly sick, one fainting from the heat and excitement. Such calmness and composure I never witnessed. To make the matter worse, despondency, if not despair, was fast writing itself upon every face. The fire was evidently approaching us. Our friends were retiring, and the whispered rumour passed from lip to lip that our artillery ammunition was running low. In a moment, however, a cloud of dust in our rear showed the approach of our wagons, coming up at a dashing rate, with a fresh supply. Our reinforcements now commenced pouring in. Georgia, South Carolina, Alabama, Mississippi, and Tennessee swept by in their glittering array with the calm light of battle on their faces, and their bayonets gleaming in the quiet Sabbath sunshine. No man faltered, no man lagged behind. Neither the groans of the dying nor the shrieks of the wounded, as they passed by in crowded ambulances, seemed to produce any impression except to fix the determination upon the countenances of all, to win or to die upon the field. The tide now seemed to ebb, just enough to keep us from despair. The firing did not advance, although the explosion of their shells was terrific in the extreme. A gleam of hope, too, gradually broke in upon us, when Kemper's Battery, which had been posted in our centre, galloped up and opened a destructive fire upon our extreme left. The advance was evidently checked, when a loud cheer in the front told us that something unusual had happened. What was it? Was it the triumph of our enemies over our poor stricken friends; or was it some advantage gained by courage in defence of right? The suspense was awful. Men stood straight in their stirrups and stretched their eyes as if they could pierce the rugged bosom of the barren hill which raised its scarred front between them. An aid passed up. His message is written on his face, and before he speaks a word a wild shout breaks from the throats of thousands. When he speaks, another, another and another round of cheers told the story to our hitherto sinking hearts. The Fourth Virginia Regiment had taken Sprague's Rhode Island Battery of six pieces, at the point of the bayonet. Scarcely had the echo of our cheers died away when again the noise of shouting broke upon the air. What was it? Had the enemy rallied and retaken the guns? Fear struggled with hope. But no: the gallant Twenty-seventh, envious of the glorious achievement of the Fourth, at a single dash had charged a regiment of regulars, swept them from the field, and taken every gun in Sherman's Battery. [*See note at end of Book.*] The firing of musketry and the rattling of bayonets was now terrible beyond description. For one hour there was an incessant cracking of rifles, without a single moment's pause. The enemy were evidently retiring, and unless reinforced from the left and centre, the day was ours.

"To prevent this, our field telegraph had already given the signal for movement upon our own right, and a heavy fire of musketry and artillery told us that Bonham's Brigade, to which we had been attached in the morning, had crossed the run and were pouring it into the enemy's centre. The South Carolina boys dashed up the hill in face of a murderous fire, bayoneted their gunners, and took quiet possession of their central battery. It was three o'clock, and the day was ours. The Washington Artillery galloped up the hill on which we were posted, and opened a perfect Vesuvius of shot and shell upon the receding foe. Colonel Lay then rode up and told us that the time for us to act had arrived. Our whole body of cavalry, 2,700 strong, now rushed like the wind to the front. It was indeed a brilliant spectacle, as, with slackened rein and sabres drawn, the whole command dashed past. The whole line resounded with continued cheering. The force was divided into different detachments. Colonel Radford, with six companies, was ordered to cross a short distance below the enemy's extreme right, and intercept his column. Our company was in front, and I was riding in front of my platoon, when, after crossing the swamp, we came suddenly on a detachment of the enemy concealed in the bushes, with their pieces levelled. The Colonel ordered the charge, and our boys rushed on. Poor E. F. was at my side when we rode over two of them, and they grounded their arms to E. W., who was just in our rear. We galloped on in pursuit of the rest, who retreated across a field, towards the road on which the enemy was retreating. Fontaine was just behind me. Saunders, a fine young fellow, just twenty-four years of age, and splendidly mounted, dashed by us. The enemy had concealed themselves behind a fence ; we rode up, and I demanded their surrender ; they made no reply. I ordered Saunders to fire; before he levelled his carbine the whole squad poured in a volley. Saunders fell dead at my feet, and Edmund Fontaine reeled in his saddle, exclaiming, "Save me, boys ; I am killed!" He was caught in the arms of his cousin, who was just in my rear. Three of my platoon fired, and the two who had shot Fontaine and Saunders fell dead in their tracks. We were now in full view of the enemy's columns, passing in rapid and disorderly retreat along the road, with two pieces of artillery, a large number of baggage-wagons, and some officers' carriages. Colonel Radford, who is a soldier of experience, knew the strength of the enemy and ordered a halt, commanding the men to form. But such a thing was utterly impossible. The men seemed perfectly delirious with excitement, and with a wild shout of, "The guns, the guns!" our whole company rushed pell-mell upon the battery, which proved to be another detachment of the Rhode Island Artillery. Such a scene of wild excitement I never witnessed. My platoon had been detached from the company, and the company from the regiment. There were two caissons and two guns; the guns behind the caissons. My platoon, which was furthest down the road, rushed upon the men who guarded them. One fellow was standing on the caisson, whipping the horses to make them run; they had become so much alarmed that they stood perfectly still, and trembled. I made a blow at him with my sabre, knocked him off the caisson, and he was shot twice before he reached the ground. Meantime W. (who behaved admirably), with the main body, crossed the road higher up, and when the main body of the regiment came up, our company, with some of the Alexandria cavalry, had killed and wounded every man at the guns, and driven the infantry supports in rapid retreat. When we left we expected to be supported by infantry and artillery, and you may imagine our astonishment when, with not quite 300 men, we found that we had nearly cut into the enemy's column, and upon looking one hundred yards down the road, we found them preparing to open on us with two guns supported by six regiments of infantry. The Colonel at once ordered a retreat, so we shot the horses to the caissons, so as to block up the road, and retreated, not, however, before they had poured in upon us four rounds of grape and canister at one hundred and fifty yards' distance. How we escaped a perfect massacre I cannot say. Had they not been so close to us the slaughter would have been terrible. Four of our men were killed. Captain Radford, brother of the Colonel, was literally blown to pieces.

I escaped without a scratch, (as did all the rest of the officers,) excepting quite a severe bruise caused by my horse having pressed my leg against the wheel to the gun-carriage. We brought off several prisoners, a great many pistols, and several horses. Just ahead of the guns was a very handsome open carriage. As soon as they saw us, such a rush! It is suspected, or rather hoped, that Wilson, of Massachusetts, (who was, it is known, on the field,) was in it. One of our men, Linkey by name, took it into his head that General Scott was in it, pursued and overtook it, but at the distance of thirty steps fired his musketine, with eighteen buck-shot, right into the back window.

"As we returned, a melancholy mistake occurred. Bowles, our second lieutenant, who was carrying poor Fontaine to the hospital, with one or two others, met a detachment of four of the Appomattox cavalry, who hailed him. It is said that, instead of giving the signal agreed upon in our camp, by raising the hand to the top of the head, he took them for the enemy, and answered "Federal troops." They fired and he fell dead. Our company received, upon its return, the congratulations of every officer on General Bonham's staff, to whom Colonel R. had spoken of the conduct of our men. To-day it has been raining incessantly. Our column pushed on this morning to this place. Our company was assigned the advance-guard, and this morning at ten o'clock, I had the honor of occupying the *city of Centreville*. The citizens tell us that about twelve o'clock last night the cry passed through the camp that the Virginia horsemen were upon them, when they left in wild confusion. Our triumph has been complete. In two days our noble army has driven them back to Alexandria, captured forty-two guns, many colors, and how many prisoners I will not venture to say. After we reached this place, we were ordered to explore the surrounding country in quest of fugitives. We took eighteen prisoners, and got back just at night, very wet. You never saw such a collection of property as was left in their flight. Hundreds of muskets, gun-carriages, wagon horses; thousands of knapsacks, oil-cloths and blankets, hogsheads of sugar, barrels of pork, beans, etc.; in short, every thing you can conceive. We found to-day over five hundred splendid army overcoats.

"The men are amusing themselves to-night reading letters, of which there were thousands left on the field. Some of them were directed to Mr. So-and-So, expected at Manassas Junction. Some asked for a piece of the floor of the house in which Ellsworth was killed, with blood on it; while others confidently express the belief that Beauregard's scalp was to be carried to Washington. When I tell you that we supped to-night on Yankee crackers, Yankee coffee, and a nice beef-tongue, actually left on the hearth of one of the officers' quarters, in a kettle, ready to be set on the fire—that this is written with a Yankee pencil, given me by one of the men, and on Yankee paper, taken from their wagons, and that I am sitting on a Yankee camp-stool, and writing by a Yankee candle, you can form some idea of the utter rout. I have a pincushion for L., picked up on the field, a needle-case for K., and a sword taken from a Vermont volunteer, for W. Our troops occupy Fairfax Court-House to-day. I will try and see you soon. Good-night. God bless and protect you. I feel that he has protected me in the last few days, in answer to the prayers of a pious wife. I hope that I feel grateful for my preservation."

"MOUNTAIN VIEW," *September* 22.—Came down here

with Mr. ——, a few days ago. Spent this day not quite so profitably as I desired. The ride to the "old chapel," where we had service, is so long, that we spent a great deal of time upon the road. Bishop Meade delivered a most interesting address. He mentioned with great feeling the death of Mr. John A. Washington, of Mount Vernon, who fell at "Cheat Mountain" a few days ago, while, with some other officers, he was observing the movements of Rosecranz. It is heart-rending to hear of the number of valuable lives which are lost in this cruel war.

25th.—The last two days spent with pleasant friends—one day with Miss M. M., and the other with my old acquaintance, Mrs. Dr. F., of the "White Post." These ladies, like all others, are busy for the soldiers. To-day I received a copy of "Headley Vicars," abridged for the camp, by my friend J. J. Mr. M. will take it to-morrow to the camp, when he goes with the wagon. To-day we have been helping the Bishop to pack a barrel of grapes, and another with tomatoes and other fresh vegetables; and yet another Mrs. M. has packed with bread, biscuit, and a variety of things for the sick.

"THE BRIARS," *October 2d.*—We returned yesterday, everybody anxious and apprehensive. Battles seem to be imminent, both in Western Virginia and on the Potomac. Constant skirmishing reported in both places.

General Price, it is said, has taken Lexington, Missouri, with a large number of prisoners. Our army in Fairfax has fallen back from "Munson's Hill" to the Court-House; thus leaving our dear homes more deeply buried in the shades of Yankeeism than ever. There are many refugees in this neighbourhood, like ourselves, wandering and waiting. Mrs. General Lee has been staying at Anufield, and at Media, sick, and without a home. All Virginia has open doors for the family of General Lee; but in her state of health, how dreadful it is to have no certain abiding place. She is very cheerful, and showed me the other day a picture of "Arlington," in a number of *Harpers' Magazine*, which had mistaken its way and strayed to Dixie. She thought the representation good, as it certainly is of what Arlington was; but it is said that those fine trees are living trees no more—all felled to make room for the everlasting fortifications. She clings to the hope of getting back to it; but I begin to feel that we may all hang our harps upon the willows; and though we do not sit by the waters of a strange land, but among our whole-souled friends in our own Virginia, yet our "vine and fig-tree" is wanting. Home and its surroundings must ever be our chief joy, and while shut out from it and its many objects of interest, there will be a feeling of desolation. The number of refugees increases fearfully as our army falls back; for though many persons, still surrounded by all the comforts of home, ask why they do not stay, and protect their property, my only answer is, "How can they?" In many instances defenceless women and children are left without the means of subsistence; their crops destroyed; their business suspended; their servants gone; their horses and other stock taken off; their houses liable at any hour of the day or night to be entered and desecrated by a lawless soldiery. How can they remain without even the present means of support, and nothing in prospect? The enemy will dole them out rations, it is said, if they will take the oath! But who so base as to do that? Can a Southern woman sell her birthright for a mess of pottage? Would she not be unworthy of the husband, the son, the brother who is now offering himself a willing sacrifice on the altar of his country? And our old men, the hoary-headed fathers of heroic sons, can they bear the insults, the taunts of an invading army? Can they see the spot of earth which they have perhaps inherited from their fathers covered with the tents of the enemy; their houses used as head-quarters by officers, while they and their families are forced into the poorest accommodations; ancestral trees laid low, to make room for fortifications, thrown across their grounds, from which cannon will point to the very heart of their loved South? How can the venerable gentlemen of the land stay at home and bear such things? No—let them come out, and in some way help the Confederacy. Our new government will want officers, and the old men had better fill them, and leave the young ones free to swell the army. But I will no longer indulge in this strain; it makes me sad, and it is my duty to give at least the meed of cheerfulness to our kind friends; in truth, we have a right cheerful household. It would be amusing to an observer to see us on mail days. The papers are read aloud, from "Terms" to "finis," by N., who, being a good reader, and having the powers of endurance to a great degree, goes on untiringly, notwithstanding the *running* commentaries kept up throughout from many voices.

October 5.—M. P. and myself drove to Millwood yesterday, and heard various rumours of victories in Western Virginia, and in Missouri; but we are afraid to believe them. At home we go on as usual.

October 8.—At church yesterday; the services interesting; the Communion administered. Rev. Dr. A. delivered an address, perhaps a little too political for the occasion.

The news from Western Virginia not confirmed. Another rumour of a fight on Cheat Mountain, in which General Jackson, with some regiments of Georgians, repulsed the Federal General Reynolds.

11*th.*—Every thing apparently quiet, and we, in the absence of bad news, are surrounded by a most peaceful and pleasant atmosphere. Our communication with the outer world cut off by the freshet in the Shenandoah, so that we had no mail yesterday. Mr. —— has gone to Richmond on business. He wrote from Culpeper Court-House, at which place he stopped to see J., a most pleasing account of the hospitals, and the care taken of the sick.

12*th.*—M. P. and myself drove to Millwood for the mail, and then made an agreeable visit to Mr. and Mrs. J. We found several letters from family and friends; one from my sister, Mrs. C., who with her whole family (except her sons,) married daughters and single, are about to rent the Presbyterian Parsonage, in Hanover, and keep house. As they are all refugees, and have the means, it is a most pleasant idea. The Rev. Mr. H., who was the occupant of the house, has gone to the army as captain of a company which he raised for the purpose.

The papers mentioned the capture of a vessel called "The Fanny," on the coast of North Carolina, laden with blankets, greatcoats, arms and ammunition. A most valuable prize.

October 16.—We had a pleasant evening. While N. read the papers we were knitting for the soldiers. An account is given of some small successes. Our men, near Pensacola, have broken up the camp of "Billy Wilson's Zouaves," of which we have heard so much; and Captain Hollins of the navy has broken the blockade at New

Orleans, sunk the "*Vincennes,*" and captured a sloop, without the least damage to himself and men. Rosecranz has retreated before our men at Big Sewell Mountain. For these things we desire to be truly grateful, without rejoicing in the misfortunes of our enemies, except as they tend to the welfare of our invaded and abused country.

Sunday Night.—To-day went to church, and heard an admirable sermon from Mr. J. As we returned, we called at the post-office, and received a newspaper from Dr. Drane, of Tennessee, in which is recorded the death of his son James. He belonged to the army in Western Virginia, and died there of typhoid fever. He was one of the late pupils of the E. H. S., a most amiable, gentlemanly youth; and it seems but as yesterday that I saw him, light-hearted and buoyant, among his young companions. He is constantly before my mind's eye. His parents and young sister—how my heart bleeds for them! Our poor boys! What may not each battle bring forth? Scarcely a battalion of the army, in any part of the Confederacy, where they are not.

Thursday, 24th.—An account reached us to-day of a severe fight last Monday (21st), at Leesburg—a Manassas fight in a small way. The Federals, under General Stone, came in large force to the river; they crossed in the morning 8,000 or 10,000 strong, under command of Colonel Baker, late Senator from Oregon. They came with all the pomp and circumstance of glorious war, and rushed on as if to certain victory over our small force. "But when the sun set, where were they?" They were flying back to Maryland, that her hills might hide and her rocks shelter them. They crowded into their boats, on their rafts; multitudes plunged into the water and swam over; any thing, any way, that would bear them from "old Virginia's shore." Our men were in hot pursuit, firing upon them incessantly, until the blue waters of the Potomac ran red with blood. It was a "famous victory," as old Caspar would say, and I am thankful enough for it; for if they come to kill us, we must kill or drive them back. But it is dreadful to think of the dead and the dying, the widows and the orphans. Mr. William Randolph, who brought us this account, says there were between five and six hundred prisoners, a number of wounded, and 400 killed and drowned—among them Colonel Baker killed. They had no business here on such an errand; but who, with a human heart, does not feel a pang at the thought that each one had somebody to grieve for him—somebody who will look long for the return of each one of the four hundred! The account goes on to state with exultation, that we lost but twenty-seven *killed*. There are but twenty-seven bereaved households in the length and breadth of this Confederacy from this one fight—a great disparity, and very few considering the violence of the fight; but it is difficult to think with composure of the lacerated hearts in those twenty-seven homes!

Tuesday, 29th.—A little reverse to record this morning. It is said that Colonel McDonald's cavalry made an unfortunate retreat from Romney the other day, as the enemy approached. It may have been wise, as the enemy outnumbered us greatly.

Mr. —— and myself have just returned from a delightful walk to Pagebrook. We were talking of our future, about which he will not allow me to despond. The Lord will provide, he says, and begins at once to count up our mercies. We constantly hear that our children and near relatives are well—none of them have been wounded, all mercifully spared; so that we would be ungrateful indeed to encourage or allow a feeling of despondency.

Wednesday.—Captain and Mrs. W. N. dined with us to-day. It was gratifying to see him look so well, after the intense suffering through which he has passed. He was borne from the field of Manassas, with what seemed to be a mortal wound; a ball had passed through his body. But, thanks to a merciful Providence, good nursing and surgery have saved his valuable life. We are now planning to go to the lower country, but when and where we do not know.

November 3d.—To-day we were at church, and heard a good sermon from the Rev. Mr. Walker, of Alexandria—a refugee in pursuit of an abiding-place.

An immense Federal fleet left Hampton Roads a few days ago, for what point destined we do not know. Oh, that it may find its resting-place in the bottom of the ocean! The terrific storm yesterday gave us comfort. The mighty rushing of the winds was music to our ears. We thought of the Spanish Armada, thanked God and took courage. Was this wicked? I think not. They must lose their lives, or we must lose ours; and if it will please the Almighty Ruler of the wind and waves to use them in our defence, we shall be most grateful.

6th.—Mr. —— gone to the prayer-meeting at Millwood, accompanied by Mr. ——; both will cast their votes for Mr. Davis to be President of these Confederate States for the next six years. We yesterday dined at "Mountain View," with the Rev. Mr. Walker and family. He has been called to South Carolina to be professor in the Episcopal Theological Seminary of that State. He will go, as there is no hope of his getting back to Alexandria during the war.

Nothing from the "Fleet."

November 9.—Our hearts cheered by news from the fleet. A part of it stranded—one vessel on the coast of North Carolina, from which seventy prisoners have been taken; others on the coast of South Carolina. Unfortunately, a part is safe, and is attacking Tybee Island. The fortifications there are said to be strong and well manned.

10*th*.—Returning from church to-day, we were overtaken by W. B. C., on horseback. We were surprised and delighted. He soon explained his "position." Jackson's Brigade has been ordered to take charge of the Valley, and is coming to-day to Strasburg, and thence to Winchester. He rode across on R's horse. He dined with us, and told us a great deal about the army, particularly about our own boys. We are greatly relieved to have that noble brigade in our midst; we have felt, for a long time, the want of protection.

Monday Night.—To-day M. P. and myself went to Winchester, and thence to the camp. We took Mr. P. N's children to see their father. There we saw W. B., J. M. G., and many other young friends, and were much pleased at their cheerfulness. They look sunburnt and soldierly. I returned to Winchester to see my dear S. S. R. C. was sitting with her, looking well and happy. Camp-life agrees with him. These poor boys expect to be ordered to Romney; but wherever they go, they hope, by God's help, to repel the invaders.

15*th*.—This was fast-day—a national fast proclaimed by our President. I trust that every church in the Confederacy was well filled with heart-worshippers. The Rev. Mr. Jones preached for us at Millwood. This whole household was there—indeed, the whole neighbourhood turned out.

We have been anxiously awaiting the result of an anticipated fight between Price and Fremont; but Fremont was superseded while almost in the act of making the attack. We await further developments.

WINCHESTER, *December* 9.—Mr. —— and myself have been here for three weeks, with Dr. S. and our dear niece. Jackson's Brigade still near, which gives these warm-hearted people a good opportunity of working for them, and supplying their wants. We see a great deal of our nephews, and never sit at the table without a large addition to the family circle. This is always prepared for, morning, noon, and night, as it is a matter of course that soldiers will be brought in just at the right time, and so cordially received that they feel that they have a perfect right to come again when it is convenient to them.

A regiment or two have been sent to protect the Chesapeake and Ohio Canal near Honeywood. Affairs in the army are very quiet. I hope that the calm does not portend a storm; I pray that it may be averted.

"THE BRIARS," *December* 18.—Sadly negligent of my diary lately. Nothing new has occurred. We pleasantly pursue the even tenor of our way, but are now preparing to go to my brother's, in Hanover, next week. We have been to "Mountain View" for a couple of days, on a farewell visit to the family. The Bishop has sent his study-carpet to the camp, along with every thing he could possibly spare, for the soldiers' comfort. He looks cheerfully upon our prospects, and is now listening to "Motley's Dutch Republic" with "infinite zest." It is read to him by his daughter-in-law, on these long winter nights. His manner of life is certainly most amiable, as well as pleasant to himself and instructive to others.

Newspapers have just come, giving an account of a fight at Cheat Mountain, on the 13th of December, in which we were successful. Rumours also of a fight on the Chesapeake and Ohio Canal; and another rumour that England has demanded the restoration of "Mason and Slidell," and in case of non-compliance with the demand, that Lord Lyons should demand his passports. How ardently I do wish that England would break up the blockade!

1862.

WESTWOOD, HANOVER COUNTY, *January* 20, 1862.—I pass over the sad leave-taking of our kind friends in Clarke and Winchester. It was very sad, because we knew not when and under what circumstances we might meet again. We left Winchester, in the stage, for Strasburg at ten o'clock at night, on the 24th of December. The weather was bitter cold, and we congratulated ourselves that the stage was not crowded. Mr. —— and the girls were on the back seat, a Methodist clergyman, a soldier, and myself on the middle, and two soldiers and our maid Betsey on the front seat. We went off by starlight, with every prospect of a pleasant drive of eighteen miles. As we were leaving the suburbs of the town, the driver drew up before a small house, from which issued two women with a baby, two baskets, several bundles, and a box. The passengers began to shout out, "Go on, driver; what do you mean? there's no room for another; go on." The driver made no answer, but the women came to the stage-door, and began to put in their bundles; the gentlemen protested that they could not get in—there was no room. The woman with the baby said she *would* get in; she was "agwine to Strasburg to spend Christmas with her relations, whar she was born and raised, and whar she had not been for ten year, and nobody had a better right to the stage than she had, and she was agwine, and Kitty Grim was agwine too—she's my sister-law; and so is baby, 'cause baby never did see her relations in Strasburg in her life. So, Uncle Ben!" she exclaimed to the driver, "take my bag, basket, and box by you, and me and Kitty and baby, and the bundles and the little basket, will go inside." All this was said amidst violent protestations from the men within: "You can't get in; driver, go on." But suiting the action to the word, she opened the door, calling, "Come, Kitty," got on the step, and thrust her head in, saying: "If these gentlemen is gentlemen, and has got any politeness, they will git out and set with Uncle Ben, and let ladies come inside." A pause ensued. At last a subdued tone from the soldier on the middle seat was heard to say: "Madam, if you will get off the step, I will get out." "Very well, sir; and why didn't you do that at first? And now," said she, looking at a man on the front seat, "there's another seat by Uncle Ben; sposen you git out and let Kitty Grim have your seat; she's bound to go." The poor man quietly got out, without saying a word, but the very expression of his back, as he got out of the stage, was subdued. "Now, Kitty, git in, and bring the little basket and them two bundles; they won't pester the lady much." The door was closed, and then, the scene being over, the passengers shouted with laughter.

Our heroine remained perfectly passive until we got to the picket-post, a mile from town. The driver stopped; a soldier came up for passports. She was thunder-struck. "Passes! Passes for white folks! I never heard of such a thing. *I* ain't got no pass; nuther is Kitty Grim." I suggested to her to keep quiet, as the best policy. Just at that time a Tennessee soldier had to confess that he had forgotten to get a passport. "You can't go on," said the official; and the soldier got out. Presently the woman's turn came. "Madam, your passport, if you please." "I ain't got none; nuther is Kitty Grim (that's my sister-in-law); we ain't agwine to git out nuther, 'cause we's gwine to Strasburg to spend Christmas with my relations, and I ain't been thar for ten year, and I never heard of white folks having passes." "But, madam," began the official——"You needn't to 'but, madam,' me, 'cause I ain't agwine to git out, and I'd like to see the man what would put me out. This is a free country, and I'se agwine to Strasburg this night; so you might as well take your lantern out of my face." "But, madam, my orders," began the picket. "Don't tell me nothing 'bout orders; I don't care nothing 'bout orders; and you needn't think, 'cause the Tennessee man got out, that I'se agwine to git out—'cause I ain't. Ain't I got three sons in the army, great sight bigger than you is? and they fit at Manassas, and they ain't no cowards, nuther is their mother; and I ain't agwine to git out of this stage this night, but I'm gwine to Strasburg, whar I was born and raised."

The poor man looked non-plussed, but yet another effort; he began, "My dear madam." "I ain't none of your dear madam; I'se just a free white woman, and so is Kitty Grim, and we ain't no niggers to git passes, and I'se gwine 'long this pike to Strasburg. Now I'se done talking." With this she settled herself on the seat, and leant back with a most determined air; and the discomfited man shut the door amid peals of laughter from within and from without. In a few minutes we were quiet again, and all began to settle themselves for sleep, when the silence was broken by our heroin' "Kitty, is you sick?" "No," said Kitty J's "W care. We im- wonder. Gentlemen, can't one of you ta and give her yourn? she gits monstrous sick when she is a-riding with her back to the horses." There was a death-like silence, and my curiosity was aroused to know how she would manage that point. After a few moments she began again. "Kitty, is you sick?" "No," says Kitty, "not yit." "Well, I do wish one of you gentlemen would give Kitty his seat." Still no reply. All was becoming quiet again, when she raised her voice: "Kitty Grim, *is* you sick?" "Yes," said Kitty, "just a little." "I knowed it; I knowed she was sick; and when Kitty Grim gits sick, she most *in gineral flings up!*" The effect was electric. "My dear madam," exclaimed both gentlemen at once, "take my seat; by all means take my seat." The Methodist clergyman being nearest, gave up his seat and took hers. The change was soon effected amidst the most uproarious laughter, all feeling that they were fairly outgeneralled the third time. From that time until we reached Strasburg, at two o'clock, she kept up a stream of talk, addressed to the baby, never interrupted except once, when the quiet-looking soldier on the front seat ventured to say, "Madam, do you never sleep?" "Never when I'm a-travelling," was the curt reply; and she talked on to the baby: "Look at all them mules—what a sight of fodder they must eat! The Yankees come down to fight us, 'cause we'se got niggers and they ain't got none. I wish there warn't no niggers. I hate Yankees, and I hate niggers too," etc., until we got to Strasburg. She then called out to "Uncle Ben" not to carry her to the depot—she was "agwine to her uncle's." "Whar's that?" cried Uncle Ben. "I don't know, but monstrous nigh a tailor's." One of the passengers suggested that time might be left by the cars, and had better go on to forgotten to get a... objected, and we had become a singularly non-resisting company, and allowed her to take—what we knew she would have—her own way.

In the mean time the cars arrived, crowded with soldiers. It was very dark and cold; the confusion and noise were excessive—shouting, hallooing, hurrahing. We passed through the dense crowd, and into the cars, with some difficulty. Mr. —— returned to look for the baggage. At last all seemed ready, and off we went ; but what was our horror to find that Mr. —— was not in the cars ! All the stories that we had ever heard of persons being thrown from the train as they attempted to get on, arose to our imagination. The darkness and crowd were great. Might he not have been thrown from the platform ? We became more and more uneasy. The conductor came by; I questioned him, thinking he might be in another car. He replied, "No, madam, there is no such gentleman on the train." At this moment the Methodist minister, who had been in the stage, introduced himself as the Rev. Mr. Jones; he knew Mr. —— ; he offered me his purse and his protection. I can never forget his kindness. He thought Mr. —— had not attempted to get on the train; there was so much baggage from the stage that there was some difficulty in arranging it ; he would telegraph from Manassas when we stopped to change cars, and the answer would meet us at Culpeper Court-House. All this was a great relief to us. At Manassas he attended to our baggage; one piece was wanting—a box, which Mr. J. had seen in Mr. ——'s hands, just before the train set off; he seemed convinced that Mr. —— was detained by an ineffectual effort to get that box on the car. At Culpeper Court-House we found J. waiting for us at the depot. Our kind and Rev. friend did not give up his supervision of us until he saw us under J's care. We immediately applied at the office for our expected telegram; but it was not there. As it was Christmas-day, the office was closed at a very early hour, which seemed to me a strange arrangement, considering the state of the country. J. felt no uneasiness about his father, but was greatly disappointed, as he had expected to pass that day with him. I had heard in Winchester that my nephew, W. B. Phelps, had been wounded in the unfortunate fight at Dranesville, and felt great uneasiness about him; but J. had seen persons directly from Centreville, who reported him slightly wounded. This relieved my mind, but it was most unfortunate; for, had I known the truth, I should have gone on the return train to Manassas, and thence to Centreville, for the purpose of nursing him. We spent Christmas-day at the hotel, and dined with a number of soldiers. In the afternoon we were very much gratified to meet with the family of our neighbour, Captain J. The Captain is stationed here, and the ladies have made themselves very comfortable. We took tea with them, and talked over our mutual troubles: our lost homes—our scattered families and friends.

The next morning the train came at the usual hour, bringing Mr. ——. Some difficulty in putting a small box of books on the car had caused a slight detention, and as he was almost in the act of stepping on board, the train moved off, and there he was, left in the dead of a winter's night, without shelter, (for, strange to say, there is no station-house at Strasburg,) without light, and with no one to whom he could apply for assistance. He walked back to the village, and there, to use his own expression, he "verily thought he should have to spend the freezing night in the street." At a number of houses he knocked loud and long, but not a door was opened to him. At last a young man in an office, after giving scrutinizing glances through the window, opened his door and gave him a chair by his fire, assigning as a reason for the difficulty in getting accommodations, that the number of disorderly soldiers passing through the village made it dangerous to open the houses during the night. At daybreak he got on a freight train, hoping to find at Manassas the means of getting to Culpeper Court-House that night. In this he was disappointed, and had a most unpleasant trip on the train, which did not reach Manassas until sunset. There he found no place to sleep, and nothing to eat, until a colonel, whose name he unfortunately had forgotten, invited him to his quarters in the country. He accepted the invitation most gladly, and as it was very dark, he took a servant as a guide, who proved to know no more about the way than he did; so that both blundered and stumbled along a muddy lane, over fences, through a corn-field, over the stalks and corn-beds, until, by what seemed a mere accident, they came upon the longed-for house and found rest for the night. Next morning we joined him on the train, delighted to see him safe and sound, feeling that "all's well that ends well;" we proceeded pleasantly on our journey. J. accompanied us as far as Gordonsville, that he might have two hours with his father. That evening we reached this place after dark, and found a house full of friends and relatives—the house at S. H. also full—so that it was a real family gathering, as in days of yore; and to add to our pleasure, our dear W. B. N. was at home on furlough. Here we see nothing of war, except the uniform of the furloughed soldiers and the retrenchment in the style of living. Desserts and wine are abolished; all superfluities must go to the soldiers. In some respects we are beginning to feel the blockade; groceries are becoming scarce and high in price, but the ladies are becoming wonderfully ingenious—coffee is so judiciously blended with parched corn, wheat or rye, that you scarcely detect the adulteration. The dressy Southern girls are giving up their handsome bonnets, wrappings, and silk dresses; they are perfectly willing to give up what once they considered absolutely necessary to their wardrobes. They say they do not enjoy such things now; they are, however, bright and cheerful; they sing patriotic songs to their furloughed friends, and listen with undying interest to anecdotes of the battle-field, with tears for the fallen, sympathy for the wounded, and the most enthusiastic admiration for deeds of daring, or for the patient endurance of the soldier. It is delightful to see the unanimity of feeling, the oneness of heart, which pervades Virginia at this time; and we believe it is so throughout the South.

We were, however, soon saddened by a letter from Centreville, from a comrade of our dear Willie Phelps to my brother, saying that the wound was more severe than it was at first supposed. He immediately set out for Centreville, but none of us dreamed of real danger. The reports came from him less and less favourable; I wanted to go to him, but the letters were discouraging to me—"There was no room for me; ladies would be in the way in so small a hospital;" and some strange hallucination and blindness to danger led us to abandon the idea of going to him. We knew that he had lost his arm, but did not dream of danger to his life. His mother, at her home in Covington, Kentucky, saw his name among the wounded, and notwithstanding the cold and ice, set off alone—came through Pittsburg and to Baltimore without difficulty, thence to Washington; but there no passport could be obtained to come to Virginia. Her son was but twenty miles off, certainly wounded; she knew no more. She applied in person to the proper authorities: "Is your son in the rebel camp?" was asked. "Then no passport can be given you to visit him." She remembered that General McClellan (who had been a friend in the old army of her son-in-law, General McIntosh) was in the city. She drove to his house. Mrs. McClellan expressed great sympathy for her, and for "your son, the interesting young man I met with in Cincinnati," but regretted that General McClellan was too ill to be spoken to on any subject; he was under the influence of anodynes, etc, etc. She then drove to the house of Mr. Chase, who had been for many years at the bar with her husband, and on most friendly terms. The servant replied pompously that Mr. Chase never saw company at that hour. She then sent for Miss C. The daughter very politely regretted that her father could not be seen until the next day at ten. She could do nothing but return to the hotel for another night of suspense. Next morning, in passing through the parlours, she encountered a lady from her own State, who greeted her pleasantly; she was preparing to entertain her friends—it was New Year's day. "Won't you be with us, Mrs. P.? You may meet some old friends." An apology for declining the invitation was given, by a simple statement of her object in coming to Washington. "Where is your son?" "In the Southern army." "Oh," she exclaimed, "not in the rebel camp! Not a rebel!" and she curled her loyal lip in scorn. "Yes," was the quiet reply, "he is what you call a rebel; but it is the honoured name which Washington bore;" and with a spirit not soothed by her countrywoman, she passed on to the street, got into a carriage, and proceeded to the house of Mr. Chase. It was ten o'clock—surely there could be no obstacle now. He soon entered—she introduced herself and her subject. Mr. C. was polite, but professed to be able to do nothing for her: "I am not the proper person to whom such an application should be made." "I know that; but to whom shall I apply?" He said, "He did not know how to advise her; the case was a difficult one; your son is in the rebel camp; I think that you cannot get a passport." She then, in a state of despair, exclaimed, "Oh, Mr. Chase, he is the son of your old acquaintance, Mr. ——!" He was at once touched. "Are you his widow?" "Yes." "But how came your son to join the rebels?" "Because his father and myself were both Virginians; he was educated in Virginia, and his whole heart is in the Southern cause." He immediately wrote a note to Mr. Seward, which he advised her to deliver in person; it would probably produce the desired effect. To Mr. Seward's she drove. The servant invited her in, but supposed that the Secretary could not attend to business, as it was New Year's day. The note was sent up; an *attaché* soon came down to say that the Secretary could not be seen, but that a passport would be given her, to go at least as far as Fortress Monroe—no passport could be given to go immediately to Centreville. She was thankful for this permission; but it seemed too hard that she should be obliged to go around hundreds of miles, when the object could be accomplished by going twenty.

She took the evening train to Baltimore, thence, next morning, to Fortress Monroe; she reached it in safety that evening. The boat was visited by a provost-marshal as soon as it touched the wharf, who, after examining passports, took hers, and some others, to General Wool. An answer from this high officer was long delayed, but at last it was brought. She could not land, but must return in the boat to Baltimore; it would leave for Baltimore next morning. She poured out her griefs to the officer, who, sympathizing with her story, said he would again apply to General Wool. He soon returned to say that she might land, and her case would be examined into next morning. Next day she was requested to walk into General Wool's office. He asked why she wanted to go to Virginia. The story was soon told. Then the stereotyped question: "Is your son in the rebel army?" with the usual answer. "Then," he replied, "you cannot go." Despair took possession of her soul. She forgot her own situation, and, with the eloquence of a mother, almost frantic with anxiety, she pleaded her cause. Even the obdurate heart of General Wool was moved. He asked her what she knew of the army at Washington. She replied, that she knew nothing; she had only seen the soldiers who passed her on the street. "What have you seen of our army here?" "Nothing, for I have been too unhappy to think of it, and only left my room when summoned by you." "Then," said he, "you may take the first boat to Norfolk." The hour for the departure of the boat came, her trunk was duly searched, and she came off to the dearly-loved Confederacy. She reached Norfolk too late for the cars, and had to wait until next day. On reaching Richmond, she heard that her son had been brought to this place, and was doing well. The next evening she arrived here in a carriage, and was shocked and disappointed to find that she had been misinformed. Heavy tidings reached us that night: he was not improving, as we had hoped, but decidedly worse. At two o'clock in the morning I accompanied her to the depot, eight miles off, and we went on to Manassas; reached the junction after night, and were met by our brother and W. B. N. They knew that we would be in the cars, and came to meet us. As they approached us, I saw, by the dim light of the car-lamp, that their countenances were sad. My heart sunk within me. What could it be? Why had they both left him? She had not seen them, and said to me, "Come, we must get an ambulance and go to Centreville to-night." But in another moment the whole was told. Her child had died that morning, just ten hours before. Who can describe that night of horrors? We spent it in a small house near the depot. Friends and near kindred were full of sympathy, and the people in whose house we were, were kind and considerate. The captain of his company, a noble young friend from her own home, Covington, came to see her, and to condole with her; but her first-born was not—the darling of her heart had passed away! At daylight we were in the cars again, on our melancholy return. On the third day his dear remains were brought to us, and the mother saw her heroic son, in his plain soldier's coffin, but beautiful in death, committed to God's own earth, having fallen in a glorious cause, in the faith of the Gospel, and with a bright hope of a blessed immortality. The young Kentucky friend who accompanied his remains told her his last words, which were a wonderful consolation to her: "Tell my mother that I die in the faith of Christ; her early instructions have been greatly blessed to me; and my last word is, Mother." This was said in extreme weakness. He soon slept, and never awoke in this world. One young soldier said to me that night, at Manassas: "He was one of the bravest men I ever saw, and met death like a soldier." Another said: "He died like a Christian." Scarcely had we buried him,

when news was brought us that her younger, now her only
son, was desperately ill on the steamer "Jamestown," on
James River—he belongs to our navy. She hurried to
Richmond, and thence down the river to the steamer, but
found him better. He was soon well enough to accompany
her to this place. She had left her home suddenly, and
must return to it; so, after a few days with her boy, who
is now decidedly convalescent, she has left him in our care,
and has set off on her weary way home. She will probably
meet with no difficulties on her return, from officials, as she
has passports through our lines; but she has a lonely,
dreary way before her, and a sorrowful story for her young
daughter at home. God be with her!

RICHMOND, *February 5.*—For two weeks my diary has
been a closed book. After another week at W., we went
to the Presbyterian Parsonage, to join the refugee family
who had gathered within its walls. They had made themselves comfortable, and it had quite a *home-like* appearance.
After remaining there a day or two, Mr. —— received a
letter, announcing his appointment to a clerkship in the Post-
Office Department. The pleasure and gratitude with which
it is received is only commensurate with the necessity which
made him apply for it. It seems a strange state of things
which induces a man, who has ministered and served the
altar for thirty-six years, to accept joyfully a situation purely
secular, for the sole purpose of making his living; but no
chaplaincy could be obtained except on the field, which
would neither suit his health, his age, nor his circumstances.
His salary will pay his board and mine in Richmond, and
the girls will stay in the country until they or I can obtain
writing from Government—note-signing from Mr. Memminger, or something else. We are spending a few days with

our niece, Mrs. H. A. C., until we can find board. Mr. —— has entered upon the duties of his office, which he finds confining, but not very arduous. To-morrow I shall go in pursuit of quarters.

The city is overrun with members of Congress, Government officers, office-seekers, and strangers generally. Main Street is as crowded as Broadway, New York; it is said that every boarding-house is full.

February 6.—Spent this day in walking from one boarding-house to another, and have returned fatigued and hopeless. I do not believe there is a vacant spot in the city. A friend, who considers herself *nicely* fixed, is in an uncarpeted room, and so poorly furnished, that, besides her trunk, she has only her wash-stand drawer in which to deposit her goods and chattels; and yet she amuses herself at it, and seems never to regret her handsomely furnished chamber in Alexandria.

7*th*.—Walking all day, with no better success. "No vacant room" is the universal answer. I returned at dinner-time, wearied in mind and body. I have been cheered by suggestions that perhaps Mrs. ——, with a large family and small income, may take boarders; or Mrs. ——, with a large house and small family, may do the same.

8*th*.—I have called on the two ladies mentioned above. The lady with the small income has filled her rooms, and wishes she had more to fill. She of the large house and small family had "never dreamed of taking boarders," was "surprised that such a thing had been suggested," looked cold and lofty, and meant me to *feel* that she was far too rich for that. I bowed myself out, feeling not a little scornful of such airs, particularly as I remembered the time when she was not quite so grand I went on my way speculating on the turning of the wheel of fortune, until I reached the house of an old acquaintance, and rang her bell, hoping that she might take in wanderers. This I did not venture to suggest, but told her my story in pitiful tones. She was all sympathy, and would be glad to take us in, but for the reserve of a bachelor brother to whom the house belonged. She appreciated the situation, and advised me to call on Mrs. —— on —— Street. Nothing daunted by past experience, I bent my steps to —— Street, and soon explained my object to Mrs. ——. She had had vacant rooms until two days ago, but a relative had taken both. Though she spoke positively, she looked doubtful, and I thought I saw indecision in the expression of her mouth. I ventured to expostulate: "Perhaps the lady might be induced to give up one room." She hesitated, and gave me an inquiring look. I told her my history. "An Episcopal minister," she exclaimed; "I'm an Episcopalian, and would be delighted to have a minister in the house. Do you think he would have prayers for us sometimes?" "Oh, certainly, it would gratify him very much." "Well, the lady is not at home to-day, but when she comes I will try to persuade her to do it. Call on Monday." I thanked her, and was walking out, when she called me back, saying, "You will not expect a constant fire in the parlour, will you?" "Oh, no; I can take my visitors to my own room." "Well, I may be out on Monday morning; come in the evening." I returned very much pleased, and received the congratulations of my friends, who are taking much interest in our welfare.

We are suffering great uneasiness about the country. The enemy is attacking Roanoke Island furiously. General Wise is there, and will do all that can be done; but fears are entertained that it has not been properly fortified.

Sunday Night.—Painful rumours have been afloat all day. Fort Henry, on Tennessee River, has been attacked. We went to St. James's this morning, and St. Paul's to-night. When we returned we found Mr. N. and Brother J. awaiting us. They are very anxious and apprehensive about Roanoke Island.

Monday Night.—Still greater uneasiness about Roanoke Island. It is so important to us—is said to be the key to Norfolk; indeed, to all Eastern North Carolina, and Southeastern Virginia. We dread to-morrow's papers.

The lady on —— Street has disappointed me. She met me with a radiant smile when I went to see her this evening, saying, "She agrees; she must, however, remove the wardrobe and bureau, as she wants them herself; but there's a closet in the room, which will answer for a wardrobe, and I reckon that a table with a glass on it will do for a bureau." "Oh, yes; only give me a good bed, some chairs and a washstand, and I can get along very well. Can I see the room?" "Yes; it is a back-room in the third story, but I reckon you won't mind that." My heart did sink a little at that communication, when I remembered Mr. ——'s long walks from Bank Street; but there was no alternative, and I followed her up the steps. Great was my relief to find a large airy room, neatly carpeted, and pleasant in all respects. "This will do," said I; "take the wardrobe and bureau out, and put a table in, and I shall be very well satisfied." "I have a small table," she replied, "but no glass; you will have to buy that." "Very well, I will do that. But you have not yet told me your terms." "Will you keep a fire?" "Oh, certainly, in my room." "Then my charge

FEBRUARY, 1862.   91

is ———." I stood aghast! "My dear madam," said I, "that is twenty dollars more than the usual price, and three dollars less than our whole salary per month." "Well, I can't take a cent less; other people take less because they want to fill their rooms, but I was only going to take you for accommodation; and I can fill my rooms at any time." Now the lines of her face were not undecided. I turned, and as I walked up the already lighted streets of my native city, feeling forlorn and houseless,

> "In happy homes I saw the light
> Of household fires gleam warm and bright;"

and hope that I was not envious. My friends were very sympathetic when I returned, not, however, without a certain twinkle of the eye denoting merriment, as it exactly coincided with a most provoking prophecy made by Mr. C. as I set out; and I joined in a hearty laugh at my own expense, which was a real relief to my feelings.

No good news from Roanoke Island. Fort Henry has fallen; that loss is treated lightly, but the enemy have turned their attention to Fort Donelson, on Cumberland River, which, if taken, would give them free access into the heart of Tennessee.

Tuesday.—Roanoke Island has fallen—no particulars heard.

12th.—The loss of Roanoke Island is a terrible blow. The loss of life not very great. The "Richmond Blues" were captured, and their Captain, the gifted and brave O. Jennings Wise, is among the fallen. My whole heart overflows towards his family; for, though impetuous in public, he was gentle and affectionate at home, and they always seemed to look upon him with peculiar tenderness. He is a severe loss to the country. Captain Coles, of Albemarle, has also fallen. He was said to be an interesting young man, and a gallant soldier. The Lord have mercy upon our stricken country!

13*th*.—Donelson is holding out bravely. I shudder to think of the loss of life.

Notwithstanding the rain this morning, I renewed my pursuit after lodgings. With over-shoes, cloak and umbrella, I defied the storm, and went over to Grace Street, to an old friend who sometimes takes boarders. Her house was full, but with much interest she entered into my feelings, and advised me to go to Mr. L., who, his large school having declined, was filling his rooms with boarders. His wife was the daughter of a friend, and might find a nook for us. I thought of the "Hare and many friends," and bent my steps through the storm to the desired haven. To my surprise, Mrs. L. said we could get a room; it is small, but comfortable, the terms suit our limited means, and we will go as soon as they let us know that they are ready for us.

We have just been drawn to the window by sad strains of martial music. The bodies of Captains Wise and Coles were brought by the cars, under special escort. The military met them, and in the dark, cold night, it was melancholy to see the procession by lamplight, as it passed slowly down the street. Captain Wise has been carried to the Capitol, and Captain Coles to the Central Depot, thence to be carried to-morrow to the family burying-ground at Enniscorthy, in Albemarle County. Thus are the bright, glorious young men of the Confederacy passing away. Can their places be supplied in the army? In the hearts and homes of families there must ever be a bleeding blank.

Sunday, 16th.—This morning we left home early, to be present at the funeral of Captain Wise, but we could not even approach the door of St. James's Church, where it took place. The church was filled at an early hour, and the street around the door was densely crowded. The procession approached as I stood there, presenting a most melancholy *cortège*. The military, together with civil officers of every grade, were there, and every countenance was marked with sorrow. As they bore his coffin into the church, with sword, cap, and cloak resting upon it, I turned away in sickness of heart, and thought of his father and family, and of his bleeding country, which could not spare him. We went to St. Paul's, and heard an excellent sermon from the Rev. Mr. Quintard, a chaplain in the army. He wore the gown over the Confederate gray—it was strange to see the bright military buttons gleam beneath the canonicals. Every thing is strange now!

Tuesday Morning.—The wires are cut somewhere between this and Tennessee. We hear nothing farther West than Lynchburg; rumours are afloat that Donelson has fallen. We are too unhappy about it to think of any thing else.

Evening.—It is all true. Our brave men have yielded to overpowering numbers. The struggle for three days was fearful. The dread particulars are not known. Wild stories are told of the numbers captured. God in his mercy help us!

Wednesday, 19th.—We are now in our own comfortable little room on Grace Street, and have quite a home-like feeling. Our children in the city are delighted to have us so near them, and the girls have come on a visit to their cousin, Mrs. C., and will be present at the inauguration on the 22d.

February 22.—To-day I had hoped to see our President inaugurated, but the rain falls in torrents, and I cannot go. So many persons are disappointed, but we are comforted by knowing that the inauguration will take place, and that the reins of our government will continue to be in strong hands. His term of six years must be eventful, and to him, and all others, so full of anxiety! What may we not experience during those six years? Oh, that all hearts may this day be raised to Almighty God for his guidance! Has there been a day since the Fourth of July, 1776, so full of interest, so fraught with danger, so encompassed by anxiety, so sorrowful, and yet so hopeful, as this 22d of February, 1862? Our wrongs then were great, and our enemy powerful, but neither can the one nor the other compare with all that we have endured from the oppression, and must meet in the gigantic efforts of the Federal Government. Our people are depressed by our recent disasters, but our soldiers are encouraged by the bravery and endurance of the troops at Donelson. It fell, but not until human nature yielded from exhaustion. The Greeks were overcome at Thermopylæ, but were the Persians encouraged by their success? Did they still cherish contempt for their weak foe? And will the conquerors of Donelson meet our little army again with the same self-confidence? Has not our Spartan band inspired them with great *respect* for their valour, to say nothing of awe?

Our neighbour in the next room had two sons in that dreadful fight. Do they survive? Poor old lady! she can hear nothing from them; the telegraphic wires in Tennessee are cut, and mail communication very uncertain. It is so sad to see the mother and sister quietly pursuing their avocations, not knowing, the former says, whether she is not the second time widowed; for on those sons depend not only her comfort, but her means of subsistence, and that fair young girl, always accustomed to perfect ease, is now, with her old mother, boarding—confined to one room, using her taste and ingenuity, making and altering bonnets for her many acquaintances, that her mother may be supplied with the little luxuries to which she has always been accustomed, and which, her child says, "mother must have." "Our property," she says, "is not available, and, of course, 'the boys' had to give up their business to go into the army."

23*d*.—Notwithstanding the violence of the rain yesterday, the Capitol Square, the streets around it, and the adjacent houses, were crowded. The President stood at the base of that noble equestrian statue of Washington, and took the oath which was taken by the "Father of his Country" more than seventy years ago—just after the "great rebellion," in the success of which we all, from Massachusetts to Georgia, so heartily gloried. No wonder that he spoke as if he were inspired. Was it not enough to inspire him to have the drawn sword of Washington, unsheathed in defence of his invaded country, immediately over his head, while the other hand of his great prototype points encouragingly to the South? Had he not the life-like representations of Jefferson, George Mason, and, above all, of Patrick Henry, by his side? The latter with his scroll in his outstretched hand, his countenance beaming, his lips almost parted, and seeming on the point of bursting into one blaze of eloquence in defence of his native South. How could Southern tongues remain quiet, or Southern hearts but burn within us, when we beheld our heroes, living and dead, surrounding and holding up the hands of our great chief? By him stood his cabinet, composed of the talent and the patriotism of the land; then was heard the voice of our beloved Assistant Bishop, in tones of fervid eloquence, beseeching the blessings of Heaven on our great undertaking. I would that every young man, from the Potomac to the Rio Grande, could have witnessed the scene.

Last night was the first levee. The rooms were crowded. The President looked weary and grave, but was all suavity and cordiality, and Mrs. Davis won all hearts by her usual unpretending kindness. I feel proud to have those dear old rooms, arousing as they do so many associations of my childhood and youth, filled with the great, the noble, the *fair* of our land, every heart beating in unison, with one great object in view, and no wish beyond its accomplishment, as far as this world is concerned. But to-day is Saturday, and I must go to the hospital to take care of our sick—particularly to nurse our little soldier-boy. Poor child, he is very ill!

27th.—Nothing new or important in our army. We were relieved to hear that the number who surrendered at Donelson was not so great as at first reported; the true number is 7,000, which is *too* many for us to lose! I trust they may be kindly treated. I know that we have friends at the North, but will they dare to be friendly openly? Oh, I hope they may have mercy on our prisoners! We have had some hope of recognition by France and England, but they still look on with folded arms.

March 3.—Last Friday was the third day appointed by our President as a day of fasting and prayer within nine months. The churches were filled to overflowing, with, I trust, heart-worshippers, and I believe that God, in his great mercy, will direct our Government and our army.

4th.—In *statu quo* as far as our armies are concerned.

The *Nashville*, a Confederate steamer, that has been watched by eight Federal war vessels, came into port the other day, at Beaufort, North Carolina, after many hair-breadth escapes, bringing a rich burden.

Ash-Wednesday, March 5.—This morning Dr. Wilmer gave us a delightful sermon at St. Paul's. He will be consecrated to-morrow Bishop of Alabama. To-night Bishop Elliott of Georgia preached for us, on the power of thought for good or evil. I do admire him so much in every respect.

6th.—To-day we saw Bishop Wilmer consecrated—Bishop Meade presiding, Bishops Johns and Elliott assisting. The services were very imposing, but the congregation was grieved by the appearance of Bishop Meade; he is so feeble! As he came down the aisle, when the consecration services were about to commence, every eye was fixed on him; it seemed almost impossible for him to reach the chancel, and while performing the services he had to be supported by the other Bishops. Oh, how it made my heart ache! and the immense crowd was deeply saddened by it.

7th.—Just returned from the hospital. Several severe cases of typhoid fever require constant attention. Our little Alabamian seems better, but so weak! I left them for a few moments to go to see Bishop Meade; he sent for me to his room. I was glad to see him looking better, and quite cheerful. Bishops Wilmer and Elliott came in, and my visit was very pleasant. I returned to my post by the bedside of the soldiers. Some of them are very fond of hearing the Bible read; and I am yet to see the first soldier who has not received with apparent interest any proposition of being read to from the Bible. To-day, while reading, an elderly man of strong, intelligent face sat on the side of the bed, listening with interest. I read of the wars of the Israelites and Philistines. He presently said, "I know why you read that chapter; it is to encourage us, because the Yankee armies are so much bigger than ours; do you believe that God will help us because we are weak?" "No," said I, "but I believe that if we pray in faith, as the Israelites did, that God will hear us." "Yes," he replied, "but the Philistines didn't pray, and the Yankees do; and though I can't bear the Yankees, I believe some of them are Christians, and pray as hard as we do; ["Monstrous few on 'em," grunted out a man lying near him;] and if we pray for one thing, and they pray for another, I don't know what to think of our prayers *clashing*." "Well, but what do you think of the justice of our cause? don't you believe that God will hear us for the justice of our cause?" "Our cause," he exclaimed, "yes, it is just; God knows it is just. I never thought of looking at it that way before, and I was *mighty* uneasy about the Yankee prayers. I am *mightily obleeged* to you for telling me." "Where are you from?" I asked. "From Georgia." "Are you not over forty-five?" "Oh, yes, I am turned of fifty, but you see I am monstrous strong and well; nobody can beat me with a rifle, and my four boys were a-coming. My wife is dead, and my girls are married; and so I rented out my land, and came too; the country hasn't got men enough, and we mustn't stand back on account of age, if we are hearty." And truly he has the determined countenance, and bone and sinew, which make a dangerous foe on the battle-field. I wish we had 50,000 such men. He reminds me of having met with a very plain-looking woman in a store the other day. She was buying Confederate gray cloth, at what seemed a high price. I asked her why she did not apply to the quartermaster, and get it cheaper. "Well," she replied, "I *knows* all about that, for my three sons is in the army; they gets their clothes *thar;* but you see this is for my old man, and I don't think it would be fair to get his clothes from *thar*, because he ain't never done nothing for the country as yet—he's just *gwine* in the army." "Is he not very old to go into the army?" "Well, he's fifty-four years old, but he's well and hearty like, and ought to do something for his country. So he says to me, says he, 'The country wants men; I wonder if I could stand marching; I've a great mind to try.' Says I, 'Old man, I don't think you could, you would break down; but I tell you what you can do—you can drive a wagon in the place of a young man that's driving, and the young man can fight.' Says he, 'So I will—and he's agwine just as soon as I gits these clothes ready, and that won't be long.'" "But won't you be very uneasy about him?" said I. "Yes, indeed; but you know he ought to go—them wretches must be drove away." "Did you want your sons to go?" "Want 'em to go!" she exclaimed; "yes; if they hadn't agone, they shouldn't a-staid whar I was. But they wanted to go, *my* sons did." Two days ago, I met her again in a baker's shop; she was filling her basket with cakes and pies. "Well," said I, "has your husband gone?" "No, but he's agwine to-morrow, and I'm getting something for him now." "Don't you feel sorry as the time approaches for him to go?" "Oh, yes, I shall miss him mightily; but I ain't never cried about it; I never shed a tear for the old man, nor for the boys neither, and I ain't agwine to. Them Yankees must not come a-nigh to Richmond; if they does, I will fight them myself. The women must fight, for they *shan't* cross Mayo's

Bridge; they *shan't* git to Richmond." I said to her, "You are a patriot." "Yes, honey—ain't you? Ain't everybody?" I was sorry to leave this heroine in homespun, but she was too busy buying cakes, etc., for the "old man," to be interrupted any longer.

8*th.*—The family of Captain ——, of the navy, just arrived. They have been "*refugeeing*" in Warrenton; but now that there is danger of our army falling back from the Potomac to the Rappahannock, they must leave Warrenton, and are on their way to Danville. Their sweet home is utterly destroyed; the house burned, etc. Like ourselves, they feel as though their future was very dark.

March 11*th.*—Yesterday we heard good news from the mouth of James River. The ship "Virginia," formerly the Merrimac, having been completely incased with iron, steamed out into Hampton Roads, ran into the Federal vessel Cumberland, and then destroyed the Congress, and ran the Minnesota ashore. Others were damaged. We have heard nothing further; but this is glory enough for one day, for which we will thank God and take courage.

13*th.*—Our hearts are overwhelmed to-day with our private grief. Our connection, Gen. James McIntosh, has fallen in battle. It was at Pea Ridge, Arkansas, on the 7th, while making a dashing cavalry charge. He had made one in which he was entirely successful, but seeing the enemy reforming, he exclaimed, "We must charge again. My men, who will follow me?" He then dashed off, followed by his whole brigade. The charge succeeded, but the leader fell, shot through the heart. The soldiers returned, bearing his body! My dear J. and her little Bessie are in Louisiana. I groan in heart when I think of her. Oh that I were near her, or that she could come to us!

These are the things which are so unbearable in this war. That noble young man, educated at West Point, was Captain in the army, and resigned when his native Georgia seceded. He soon rose to the rank of Brigadier, but has fallen amid the flush of victory, honoured, admired and beloved by men and officers. He has been buried at Fort Smith. The Lord have mercy upon his wife and child! I am thankful that he had no mother to add to the heart-broken mothers of this land. The gallant Texas Ranger, General Ben McCulloch, fell on the same day; he will be sadly missed by the country. In my selfishness I had almost forgotten him, though he doubtless has many to weep in heart-sickness for their loved and lost.

Bishop Meade is desperately ill to-day—his life despaired of.

March 14*th*.—Our beloved Bishop Meade is dead! His spirit returned to the God who gave, redeemed, and sanctified it, this morning about seven o'clock. The Church in Virginia mourns in sackcloth for her great earthly head. We knew that he must die, but this morning, when we had assembled for early prayers, it was announced to us from the pulpit, a thrill of anguish pervaded the congregation, which was evident from the death-like stillness. A hymn was read, but who could then sing? A subdued effort was at last made, and the services proceeded. Like bereaved children we mingled our prayers and tears, and on receiving the benediction, we went silently out, as in the pressure of some great public calamity, and some bitter, heartfelt sorrow. Thus, just one week after the solemn public services in which he had been engaged, it pleased Almighty God to remove him from his work on earth to his rest in heaven. During his last illness, though often suffering intensely, he never forgot his interest in public affairs. The blessed Bible was first read to him, each morning, and then the news of the day. He had an eye for every thing; every movement of Government, every march of the troops, the aspect of Europe, and the Northern States, every thing civil and military, and all that belonged to God's Church upon earth—dying as he had lived, true to Virginia, true to the South, true to the Church, and true to the Lord his God.

Saturday Night.—Spent to-day at the hospital. Heard of the shelling of Newbern, N. C., and of its fall. My heart sickens at every acquisition of the Federals. No further news from Arkansas. Yesterday evening I went to see the body of our dear Bishop ; cut a piece of his hair; kissed his forehead, and took my last look at that revered face.

Monday Night.—This morning I was at the funeral, at St. Paul's Church; the service was read by the Rev. J. P. McGuire and Rev. C. J. Gibson. Bishop Johns made a most solemn address. The procession, long and sad, then wended its way to Hollywood Cemetery.

15th.—Our army has fallen back to the Rappahannock, thus giving up the splendid Valley and Piedmont country to the enemy. This, I suppose, is right, but it almost breaks our hearts to think of it. Winchester was occupied last Wednesday! Lord, how long shall our enemies prosper? Give us grace to bear our trials.

24th.—Our people continue to make every effort to repel the foe, who, like the locusts of Egypt, overrun our land, carrying the bitterest enmity and desolation wherever they go. Troops are passing through Richmond on their way to Goldsborough, N. C., where it is said that Burnside is expected to meet them. Everybody is busy in supplying their wants as they pass through. On Sunday, just as the girls of one of the large seminaries were about to seat themselves at table, the principal of the school came in: "Young ladies," said he, "several extra trains have arrived, unexpectedly, filled with troops. The committee appointed to attend them are totally unprepared. What can we do to help our hungry soldiers?" "Give them our dinner," cried every young voice at once. In five minutes baskets were filled and the table cleared. When the girls reached the cars, the street was thronged with ladies, gentlemen, children, servants, bearing waiters, dishes, trays, baskets filled with meats, bread, vegetables, etc. Every table in Richmond seemed to have sent its dinner to Broad Street, and our dear, dusty, hungry gray coats dined to their hearts' content, filled their haversacks, shouted "Richmond forever!" and went on their way rejoicing.

March 27.—This has been a day of uneasiness to us all. General Jackson has had a fight at Kernstown, near Winchester. No particulars, except that the enemy were repulsed, and our loss heavy. Many that are so dear to us are in that "Stonewall Brigade;" and another day of suspense must pass before we can hear from them. Our Western army under Beauregard are fighting at Island No. 10, with what success we know not. The enemy presses us on every side.

29*th*.—After much anxiety, more authentic information from the "Valley" received this morning. We gave them a good fight, but the field was left in the enemy's hand. Poor, noble Winchester, to what degradation is she brought! Our dear W. B. C. was shot through the hip; the wound painful, but not mortal; he was carried to Staunton, and his mother has gone to him. The rest of our own peculiar "boys" are safe, but many lives were lost. It is thought that a great crisis is at hand. The Peninsula is the place appointed by rumour for a great battle. The croakers dread much from their numbers; my trust is in One who can save by many or by few.

April 7.—Just returned from a little trip to the country in time to hear the morning news of a splendid victory yesterday, at Shiloh. No particulars received. Skirmishing near Yorktown reported; nothing definite.

9*th*.—Our victory at Shiloh complete, but General Albert Sydney Johnston was killed. The nation mourns him as one of our most accomplished officers. He fell while commanding in the thickest of the fight. It is an overwhelming loss to the Western army, and to the whole country. Beauregard pursued the enemy, but their General (Grant) having been reinforced very largely, our army had to retreat to Corinth, which they did in good order. This was done by order of General Johnston, should Buell reinforce Grant. They are now at Corinth, awaiting an attack from the combined forces. Van Dorn reinforced Beauregard. We are anxiously awaiting the result.

10*th*.—Spent yesterday in the hospital by the bedside of Nathan Newton, our little Alabamian. I closed his eyes last night at ten o'clock, after an illness of six weeks. His body, by his own request, will be sent to his mother. Poor little boy! He was but fifteen, and should never have left his home. It was sad to pack his knapsack, with his little gray suit, and coloured shirts, so neatly stitched by his poor mother, of whom he so often spoke, calling to us in delirium, "Mother, mother," or, "Mother, come here." He so often called me mother, that I said to him one day, when his mind was clear, "Nathan, do I look like your mother?"

"No, ma'am, not a bit; nobody is like my mother." The packing of his little knapsack reminds me of

THE JACKET OF GRAY.

"Fold it up carefully, lay it aside,
 Tenderly touch it, look on it with pride,
 For dear must it be to our hearts evermore,
 The jacket of gray, our loved soldier-boy wore.

"Can we ever forget when he joined the brave band
 Who rose in defence of our dear Southern land,
 And in his bright youth hurried on to the fray—
 How proudly he donned it, the jacket of gray?

"His fond mother blessed him, and looked up above,
 Commending to Heaven the child of her love;
 What anguish was hers, mortal tongue may not say,
 When he passed from her sight in his jacket of gray.

"But his country had called him, she would not repine,
 Though costly the sacrifice placed on its shrine;
 Her heart's dearest hopes on the altar she lay,
 When she sent out her boy in his jacket of gray.

"Months passed, and war's thunders rolled over the land,
 Unsheathed was the sword, and lighted the brand;
 We heard in the distance the sound of the fray,
 And prayed for our boy in the jacket of gray.

'Ah, vain, all in vain, were our prayers and our tears;
 The glad shout of victory rang in our ears;
 But our treasured one on the battle-field lay,
 While the life-blood oozed out on the jacket of gray.

"Fold it up carefully, lay it aside,
 Tenderly touch it, look on it with pride,

For dear must it be to our hearts evermore,
The jacket of gray our loved soldier-boy wore.

"His young comrades found him, and tenderly bore
The cold lifeless form to his home by the shore:
Oh, dark were our hearts on that terrible day
When we saw our dead boy in the jacket of gray.

"Ah, spotted and tattered, and stained now with gore,
Was the garment which once he so proudly wore;
We bitterly wept as we took it away,
And replaced with death's white robes the jacket of gray.

"We laid him to rest in his cold, narrow bed,
And 'graved on the marble we placed o'er his head,
As the proudest of tributes our sad hearts could pay,
He never disgraced the poor jacket of gray.

"Fold it up carefully, lay it aside,
Tenderly touch it, look on it with pride,
For dear must it be to our hearts evermore,
The jacket of gray our loved soldier-boy wore."

11th.—The "Virginia" went out again to-day. The Federal Monitor would not meet her, but ran to Fortress Monroe, either for protection, or to tempt her under the heavy guns of the fortress; but she contented herself by taking three brigs and one schooner, and carrying them to Norfolk, with their cargoes. Soldiers are constantly passing through town. Every thing seems to be in preparation for the great battle which is anticipated on the Peninsula.

Fort Pulaski has surrendered to the enemy's gun-boats. The garrison fought until several breaches were made. They then surrendered, and are now prisoners. Lord, have them in thy holy keeping!

15th.—A panic prevails lest the enemy should get to Richmond. Many persons are leaving town. I can't believe that they will get here, though it seems to be their end and aim. My mind is much perturbed; we can only go on doing our duty, as quietly as we can.

20th.—On Wednesday we saw eight thousand troops pass through town. We were anxious to see many who were among them. The sidewalks were thronged with ladies, many of them in tears. General C. passed with his brigade, containing the 17th, with its familiar faces. Colonel H. and himself rode to the sidewalk for a shake of the hand, but the rest could only raise their hats in recognition. I knew the cavalry would pass through Franklin Street, and hurried there to see my dear W. B. N. The order "Halt" was given just as he, at the head of his troop, was passing. I called him aloud. Amid the din and tumult of course he could not hear, but as he raised his cap to salute the ladies near him, his quick eye met mine; in an instant he was at my side: "My dear aunt, what are you doing here?" "I came to look for you; where are you going?" "Our orders extend to the steamers at the wharf," he replied; "but don't be uneasy, we are going to the right place." His face glowed with animation, and I meant to appear cheerful to him, but I found, after he was gone, that my face was bathed in tears. They all looked as if the world were bright before them, and we were feeling the appalling uncertainty of all things. A mother stood by, straining her weeping eyes for the parting glance at her first-born; and so many others turned their sad, weary steps homewards, as their dear ones passed from their sight.

21st.—The ladies are now engaged making sand-bags for the fortifications at Yorktown; every lecture-room in town crowded with them, sewing busily, hopefully, prayerfully. Thousands are wanted. No battle, but heavy skirmishing at Yorktown. Our friend, Colonel McKinney, has fallen at the head of a North Carolina regiment. Fredericksburg has been abandoned to the enemy. Troops passing through towards that point. What does it all portend? We are intensely anxious; our conversation, while busily sewing at St. Paul's Lecture-Room, is only of war. We hear of so many horrors committed by the enemy in the Valley—houses searched and robbed, horses taken, sheep, cattle, etc., killed and carried off, servants deserting their homes, *churches desecrated!*

27*th.*—The country is shrouded in gloom because of the fall of New Orleans! It was abandoned by General Lovell—necessarily, it is thought. Such an immense force was sent against the forts which protected it, that they could not be defended. The steamer *Mississippi*, which was nearly finished, had to be burnt. We hoped so much from its protection to the Mississippi River. Oh, it is so hard to see the enemy making such inroads into the heart of our country! it makes the chicken-hearted men and women despondent, but to the true and brave it gives a fresh stimulus for exertion. I met two young Kentuckians to-night who have come out from their homes, leaving family and fortunes behind, to help the South. After many difficulties, running the blockade across the Potomac, they reached Richmond yesterday, just as the news of the fall of New Orleans had overwhelmed the city. They are dreadfully disappointed by the tone of the persons they have met. They came burning with enthusiasm; and anything like depression is a shock to their excited feelings. One said to me that he thought he should return at once, as he had "left every thing which made home desirable to help Virginia, and found her ready to give up." All the blood in my system boiled in an instant. " Where, sir," said I, " have you seen Virginians ready to give up their cause ?" "Why," he replied, "I have been lounging about the Exchange all day, and have heard the sentiments of the people." "Lounging about the Exchange! And do you suppose that Virginians worthy of the name are now seen lounging about the Exchange? There you see the idlers and shirkers of the whole Southern army. No true man under forty-five is to be found there. Virginia, sir, is in the camp. Go there, and find the true men of the South. There they have been for one year, bearing the hardships, and offering their lives, and losing life and limb for the South; it is mournful to say how many! There you will find the chivalry of the South; and if Virginia does not receive you with the shout of enthusiasm which you anticipated, it is because the fire burns steadily and deeply; the surface blaze has long ago passed away. I honour you, and the many noble young Kentuckians who have left their homes for the sake of our country, but it will not do for Kentucky to curl the lip of scorn at Virginia. Virginia blushes, and silently mourns over her recreant daughter, and rejoices over every son of hers who has the disinterestedness to leave her and come to us in this hour of our bitter trial."

I do not believe that this young man really means, or wishes, to return; he only feels disheartened by the gloom caused by our great national loss.

May 2d.—The morning papers contain a most spirited letter by the Mayor of New Orleans, in reply to the Federal commander who demanded the surrender of the city, and that the Confederate flag should be taken down. He refuses to do either, telling him that the city is *his* by *brute force*, but he will never surrender it.

Our young friend, J. S. M., is here, very ill ; I am assisting to nurse him. I feel most anxious about him ; he and his four brothers are nobly defending their country. They have strong motives, personal as well as patriotic. Their venerable father and mother, and two young sisters, were forced to leave their comfortable home in Fairfax a year ago. The mother has sunk into the grave, an early sacrifice, while the father and sisters continue to be homeless. Their house has been burnt to the ground by Federal soldiers—furniture, clothing, important papers, all consumed. Sad as this story is, it is the history of so many families that it has ceased to call forth remark.

3d.—It is distressing to see how many persons are leaving Richmond, apprehending that it is in danger; but it will not—I know it will not—fall. It is said that the President does not fear; he will send his family away, because he thinks it is better for men, on whom the country's weal is so dependent, to be free from private anxiety. General Johnston is falling back from Yorktown, not intending to fight within range of the enemy's gun-boats. This makes us very anxious about Norfolk.

May 5th.—Yesterday we had a blessed Sabbath, undisturbed by rumours; it is generally a day of startling reports set afloat by idlers. The Bishop preached and administered confirmation at St. Paul's. The President was a candidate for confirmation, but was deterred by business. It is such a blessing to have so many of our public men God-fearing, praying Christians!

7th.—Our "peaceful" Sabbath here was one of fearful strife at Williamsburg. We met and whipped the enemy

Oh, that we could drive them from our land forever! Much blood spilt on both sides; our dear W. B. N. is reported "missing"—oh, that heart-sinking word! How short a time since that blessed glimpse of his bright face, as he passed through town, and now he is on his weary way to some Northern prison; at least we *hope so*. His poor wife and mother! Our young friend G. W. was killed! How many bright hopes were crushed in one instant by the fall of that boy! I thank God that he had no mother. General Johnston still falls back, leaving the revered Alma Mater of our fathers to be desecrated, perhaps burned. A party of Yankees landed on Sunday at the White House. That Pamunky country, so fertile, now teeming with grain almost ready for the sickle, is at their mercy; we can only hope that they have no object in destroying it, and that they will not do it wantonly. W. and S. H. and their dear inmates are painfully near them. Richmond, or the *croakers* of Richmond, have been in a panic for two days, because of the appearance of gun-boats on James River. I believe they will not get nearer than they are now. I sat up last night at the hospital with D. L., who is desperately ill—his mother in the Federal lines. My companion during the night was Colonel M., of Maryland. While listening to the ravings of delirium, two gentlemen came in, announcing heavy firing on the river. We had been painfully conscious of the firing before, but remembering that Drury's Bluff was considered impregnable, I felt much more anxious about the patient than about the enemy. The gentlemen, however, were panic-stricken, and one of them seemed to think that "sunrise would find gun-boats at Rocketts." Not believing it possible, I felt no alarm, but the apprehensions of others made me nervous and unhappy. At daybreak I saw loads of furniture passing by, showing that people were taking off their valuables.

12th.—Just returned from a visit to S. H. The family full of patriotism and very bright. While there, dear W's horse and servant came home. His family bore it well, considering imprisonment the least casualty that could have befallen him. If Richmond is invested, that beautiful country will be in the hands of the enemy; the families (except the gentlemen) will remain at home to protect the property as best they may. They are now sending corn, bacon, etc., into Richmond for safety. None but the croakers believe for an instant that it will fall.

Two hours ago we heard of the destruction of the "Virginia" by our own people. It is a dreadful shock to the community. We can only hope that it was wisely done. Poor Norfolk must be given up. I can write no more to-day.

13th.—General Jackson is doing so gloriously in the Valley that we must not let the fate of the "Virginia" depress us too much. On the 9th of May he telegraphed to General Cooper : "God blessed our arms with victory at McDowell yesterday." Nothing more has been given us officially, but private information is received that he is in hot pursuit down the Valley. The croakers roll their gloomy eyes, and say, "Ah, General Jackson is so rash!" and a lady even assured me that he was known to be crazy when under excitement, and that we had every thing to fear from the campaign he was now beginning in the Valley. I would that every officer and soldier in the Southern army was crazed in the same way; how soon we would be free from despotism and invasion !

May 14.—The anxiety of all classes for the safety of

Richmond is now intense, though a strong faith in the goodness of God and the valour of our troops keeps us calm and hopeful. A gentleman, high in position, panic-struck, was heard to exclaim, yesterday : "Norfolk has fallen, Richmond will fall, Virginia is to be given up, and to-morrow I shall leave this city, an exile and a beggar." Others are equally despondent, and, as is too frequently the case in times of trouble, attribute all our disasters to the incompetency and faithlessness of those entrusted with the administration of public affairs. Even General Lee does not escape animadversion, and the President is the subject of the most bitter maledictions. I have been shocked to hear that a counter-revolution, if not openly advocated, has been distinctly foreshadowed, as the only remedy for our ills. The public authorities of Richmond, greatly moved by the defenceless condition of the city, appointed a committee, and appropriated funds to aid in completing the obstructions at Drury's Bluff. The Legislature also appointed a committee to wait upon the President and ascertain the progress of the work. A member of this committee, a near connection of mine, has given me an account of their interview with Mr. Davis. He received them, as is his invariable custom, with marked cordiality and respect. The subject was opened by the chairman of the Senate Committee, who stated the object of the mission, and made appropriate inquiries for information. The President proceeded to give a distinct narrative of the progress of the work, expressed his great desire for its early completion, and regretted that the natural difficulties arising from frequent freshets in the river, which the efforts of man could not overcome, had rendered the progress of the work slow. He said he had just returned from a visit to the Bluff, accompanied by

General Lee; and having heard complaints against the man in charge of the work, he had discharged him, and had appointed another, strongly recommended for efficiency. That the flood was now subsiding, and he thought he could assure the committee that the obstruction of the river would be complete in twenty-four hours. At this point the door-bell rang, and General Lee was announced. "Ask General Lee in," said the President. The servant returned, saying that the General wished to see the President for a few moments in the ante-room. The President retired, met General Lee and the Secretary of the Navy, and soon returned to the committee. The conversation being renewed, some further inquiry was made with regard to Drury's Bluff. The President replied: "I should have given you a very different answer to your question a few moments ago from that which I shall be compelled to give you now. Those traitors at Norfolk, I fear, have defeated our plans." "What traitors?" asked nearly every member of the committee at the same moment. He then proceeded to give a detail of the desertion of the captain and crew of a steamer engaged in transporting guns from Norfolk to Drury's Bluff, who had gone over to the enemy with vessel and cargo, and full information as to the unfinished condition of the works. A member of the committee asked: "Can nothing be done to counteract these traitors?" The President replied: "Every thing will be done, I assure you, which can be done." The member continued: "But, Mr. President, what will be done?" The President politely declined to answer the question, saying there were some things that it was not proper to communicate. The member again pressed for the information, saying: "This is a confidential meeting, and, of course, nothing transpiring here will reach the public." The President, with a smile on his countenance, said: "Mr. ——, I think there was much wisdom in the remark of old John Brown at Harper's Ferry : 'A man who is not capable of keeping his own secrets is not fit to be trusted with the business of other people.'" There was no unpleasant feeling manifested in the committee, and the parting was kind and cordial on both sides ; yet, next morning, it was rumoured on the streets that the President had been rude to the committee, and that the meeting had been extremely unpleasant. On the night of this meeting the river was obstructed by the sinking of the steamer *Patrick Henry*, and other vessels, in the channel. This, it is supposed, was the plan agreed upon by Mr. Davis and General Lee in their short interview. Several days have passed since this interview, and I trust that all is now safe. How thankful I am that I knew nothing of this until the danger was passed!

The Legislature is in almost constant session during these dark days. It contains many gentlemen of great intelligence and of ardent zeal in the public cause. The whole body is as true as steel, and its constant effort is to uphold the hands of the President, to fire the popular heart, and to bring out all the resources of Virginia in defence of the liberty and independence of the South. I am told that day after day, and night after night, "thoughts that breathe and words that burn" are uttered in that hall, which, in other days, has often rung with the eloquence of the noblest statesmen, patriots, and orators of the land. These proceedings are all in secret session, and, for prudential reasons, are withheld from the public ; but are they never to see the light ? Is no one taking note of them? I trust so, indeed, that the civil history of Virginia, during this great struggle, may not be lost to posterity.

15th.—It is now ascertained beyond doubt that my nephew, W. B. N., reported "missing," at Williamsburg, is a prisoner in the enemy's hands. We are very anxious for his exchange, but there seems some difficulty in effecting it. His father, accompanied by Colonel Robertson, of the Fourth Virginia Cavalry, called to see the President a few nights ago, hoping to do something for him. The President had just returned from a long ride to inspect the fortifications. In answer to their card, he desired to see the gentlemen in his study, where he was reclining on a sofa, apparently much fatigued, while Mrs. Davis sat at a table engaged in some fine needle-work. The President immediately arose and received the gentlemen most courteously, introducing them to Mrs. D. Colonel R. stated the object of the visit, saying that Captain N. was one of the very best officers of his rank in the army, and that his services were almost indispensable to his regiment, and urged the President to use every effort to procure his exchange. His father seconded the request with the warmth natural to a parent under such circumstances. The President seemed deeply interested in the subject, and regretted that nothing could then be done, as there was a difficulty pending between the belligerents on the subject of exchange; as soon as that difficulty was removed he would, with pleasure, do all in his power to procure the exchange. Mrs. Davis listened with much interest to the conversation, and her feelings became warmly interested. She said that her husband was a father, and would feel deep sympathy; but if, in the pressure of public business, the subject should pass from his mind, she would certainly remind him of it. She made a very favourable impression on the minds of these gentlemen, who had never seen her before, by her ease of manner, agreeable conversation, and the kindness of heart which she manifested. After a most pleasant interview of an hour, the visitors arose to take leave, but Mrs. Davis invited them with so much cordiality to remain to take a cup of tea with them, which, she said, was then coming up, that they could not decline. The servant brought in the tea-tray, accompanied by some light refreshment. Mrs. D. poured out the tea for the company of four. The scene reminded them of the unpretending and genial hospitality daily witnessed in the families of Virginia.

18th.—The 16th was the day appointed by the President for fasting and prayer. The churches here were filled, as I trust they were all over the land.

27th.—General Jackson's career going on gloriously. After defeating Millroy, and Fremont's advance in the Valley, and driving them back in confusion, so that nothing was to be feared from his threatened union with Banks, he pursued the enemy as far as Franklin, Pendleton County. Then returning, he marched on rapidly, captured Front Royal on the 23d, chasing the enemy through it at more than double-quick. Still pressing hard upon Banks, he gave him no rest night nor day, piercing his main column while retreating from Strasburg to Winchester—the "rear part retreating towards Strasburg. On Sunday, 25th, the other part was routed at Winchester. At last accounts, Brigadier-General George H. Stuart was pursuing them with cavalry and artillery, and capturing many." I quote from the General's own telegram, dated Winchester, May 26th. And now, notwithstanding our condition in Richmond, our hearts and voices are attuned to praise, and our pæans are more loud and bright in contrast to our late distressing trials.

29th.—No official accounts from "Stonewall" and his glorious army, but private accounts are most cheering. In the mean time, the hospitals in and around Richmond are being cleaned, aired, etc., preparatory to the anticipated battles. Oh, it is sickening to know that these preparations are necessary! Every man who is able has gone to his regiment. Country people are sending in all manner of things—shirts, drawers, socks, etc., hams, flour, fresh vegetables, fruits, preserves—for the sick and wounded. It is wonderful how these things can be spared. I suppose, if the truth were known, that they cannot be spared, except that every man and woman is ready to give up every article which is not absolutely necessary; and I dare say that gentlemen's wardrobes, which were wont to be numbered by dozens, are now reduced to couples.

It is said that General Johnston, by an admirable series of manœuvres, is managing to retreat from Williamsburg, all the time concealing the comparative weakness of his troops, and is retarding the advance of the enemy, until troops from other points can be concentrated here.

31st.—The booming of cannon, at no very distant point, thrills us with apprehension. We know that a battle is going on. God help us! Now let every heart be raised to the God of battles.

Evening.—General Johnston brought in wounded, not mortally, but painfully, in the shoulder. Other wounded are being brought in. The fight progressing; but we are driving them.

Night.—We have possession of the camp—the enemy's camp. The place is seven miles from Richmond. General Lee is ordered to take General Johnston's place. The fight may be renewed to-morrow.

June 1.—The loss yesterday comparatively small. General Johnston had managed his command with great success and ability until he received his wound. What a pity that he should have exposed himself! but we are a blessed people to have such a man as General Lee to take his place. He (Gen. J.) is at the house of a gentleman on Church Hill, where he will have the kindest attention, and is free from the heat and dust of the city.

2d.—The battle continued yesterday near the field of the day before. We gained the day! For this victory we are most thankful. The enemy were repulsed with fearful loss; but our loss was great. The wounded were brought until a late hour last night, and to-day the hospitals have been crowded with ladies, offering their services to nurse, and the streets are filled with servants darting about, with waiters covered with snowy napkins, carrying refreshments of all kinds to the wounded. Many of the sick, wounded, and weary are in private houses. The roar of the cannon has ceased. Can we hope that the enemy will now retire? General Pettigrew is missing—it is thought captured. So many others "missing," never, never to be found! Oh, Lord, how long! How long are we to be a prey to the most heartless of foes? Thousands are slain, and yet we seem no nearer the end than when we began!!

7th.—Sad news from the Valley. The brave, gallant, dashing General Ashby has fallen! He was killed yesterday, in a vigorous attack made by the enemy on our rear-guard, at a point between Harrisonburg and Port Republic. The whole country will be shocked by the calamity, for it had a high appreciation of his noble character and achievements. General Jackson valued him very highly, as did both men and officers. His daring was wonderful, and wonderfully did he succeed in his dashing and heroic efforts. "His sagacity in penetrating into the designs of the enemy seemed almost intuitive."* It is so hard, in our weakness, to give up such men!

9*th, Night.*—General Jackson is performing prodigies of valor in the Valley; he has met the forces of Fremont and Shields, and whipped *them in detail*. They fought at Cross Keys and Port Republic yesterday and to-day. I must preserve his last dispatch, it is so characteristic:

"Through God's blessing, the enemy, near Port Republic, was this day routed, with the loss of six pieces of artillery.

"T. J. JACKSON,
"*Major-General Commanding.*"

And now we are awaiting the casualties from the Valley. This feeling of personal anxiety keeps us humble amid the flush of victory. What news may not each mail bring us, of those as dear as our heart's blood? Each telegram that is brought into the hospital makes me blind with apprehension, until it passes me, and other countenances denote the same anxiety; but we dare not say a word which may unnerve the patients; they are rejoicing amid their pain and anguish over our victories. Poor fellows! dearly have they paid for them, with the loss of limb, and other wounds more painful still. They want to be cured that they may be on the field again. "Thank God," said a man, with his leg amputated, "that it was not my right arm, for then I could never have fought

---

* From General Jackson's telegram announcing the death of General Ashby.

again; as soon as this stump is well I shall join Stuart's cavalry; I can ride with a wooden leg as well as a real one."

The "Young Napoleon" does not seem to be dispirited by his late reverses. The *New York Herald* acknowledges the defeat of the 31st, but says they recovered their loss next day; but the whole tone of that and other Northern papers proves that they *know* that their defeat was complete, though they will not acknowledge it. They are marshalling their forces for another "On to Richmond." O God, to Thee, to Thee alone, do we look for deliverance. Thou, who canst do all things, have mercy upon us and help us!

June 12.—We are more successful in Virginia than elsewhere. The whole Mississippi River, except Vicksburg and its environs, is now in the hands of the enemy, and that place must surrender, though it holds out most nobly, amidst the most inveterate efforts to take it. Memphis has fallen! How my spirit chafes and grieves over our losses! O God, let us not be given over a "hissing and a reproach to our enemies."

15*th*.—General Stuart has just returned to camp after a most wonderful and successful raid. He left Richmond two or three days ago with a portion of his command; went to Hanover Court-House, where he found a body of the enemy; repulsed them, killing and wounding several, and losing one gallant man, Captain Latané, of the Essex cavalry; continuing his march by the "Old Church," he broke up their camp and burnt their stores; thence to Tunstall's Station on the York River Railroad; fired into the train, destroying a part of it, and taking some prisoners; thence to Pamunky River; found three transports loaded with provender, which they burned; filled their haversacks with West India fruit, which had been brought on for Federal consumption; then went on towards Charles City Court-House, encountering a train of wagons; took their horses, mules, and drivers, and burnt the wagons and contents; thence they went to a Yankee sutler's stand, took what they wanted, and burnt the rest; thence across the Chickahominy and on to Richmond; bringing 175 prisoners and a number of horses and mules. We are all full of excitement and delight, hoping that he discovered much about the Federal army which may be useful, but which, of course, is kept from the public; and I trust most fervently that our dear ones at S. H. and W. may have been cheered by their presence, for they must have gone very near them, if not immediately by their gates—how the appearance of our men must have excited them! I wish I could see some member of the cavalry who could tell me all about it—where they went, and whom they saw. General Stuart must have gone, it is said, within a few miles, perhaps nearer, of his father-in-law, the Federal General Cooke. I wonder what the old renegade Virginian thinks of his dashing son-in-law? If he has a spark of proper feeling left in his obdurate heart, he must be proud of him.

June 27th.—Yesterday was a day of intense excitement in the city and its surroundings. Early in the morning it was whispered about that some great movement was on foot. Large numbers of troops were seen under arms, evidently waiting for orders to march against the enemy. A. P. Hill's Division occupied the range of hills near "Strawberry Hill," the cherished home of my childhood, overlooking the old "Meadow Bridges." About three o'clock the order *to move*, so long expected, was given. The Division marched steadily and rapidly to the attack—the Fortieth Regiment, under command of my relative, Colonel B., in which are so many of our dear boys, leading the advance. The enemy's pickets were just across the river, and the men supposed they were in heavy force of infantry and artillery, and that the passage of the bridge would be hazardous in the extreme; yet their courage did not falter. The gallant Fortieth, followed by Pegram's Battery, rushed across the bridge at double-quick, and with exultant shouts drove the enemy's pickets from their posts. The enemy was driven rapidly down the river to Mechanicsville, where the battle raged long and fiercely. At nine o'clock all was quiet; the bloody struggle over for the day. Our victory is said to be glorious, but not complete. The fighting is even now renewed, for I hear the firing of heavy artillery. Last night our streets were thronged until a late hour to catch the last accounts from couriers and spectators returning from the field. A bulletin from the Assistant Surgeon of the Fortieth, sent to his anxious father, assured me of the safety of some of those most dear to me; but the sickening sight of the ambulances bringing in the wounded met my eye at every turn. The President, and many others, were on the surrounding hills during the fight, deeply interested spectators. The calmness of the people during the progress of the battle was marvellous. The balloons of the enemy hovering over the battle-field could be distinctly seen from the outskirts of the city, and the sound of musketry as distinctly heard. All were anxious, but none alarmed for the safety of the city. From the firing of the first gun till the close of the battle every spot favourable for observation was crowded. The tops of the Exchange, the Ballard House, the Capitol, and almost every other tall house were covered with human beings; and after nightfall the commanding hills from the President's house to the Alms-House were covered, like a vast amphitheatre, with men, women and children, witnessing the grand display of fireworks—beautiful, yet awful—and sending death amid those whom our hearts hold so dear. I am told (for I did not witness it) that it was a scene of unsurpassed magnificence. The brilliant light of bombs bursting in the air and passing to the ground, the innumerable lesser lights, emitted by thousands and thousands of muskets, together with the roar of artillery and the rattling of small-arms, constituted a scene terrifically grand and imposing. What spell has bound our people? Is their trust in God, and in the valour of our troops, so great that they are unmoved by these terrible demonstrations of our powerful foe? It would seem so, for when the battle was over the crowd dispersed and retired to their respective homes with the seeming tranquility of persons who had been witnessing a panorama of transactions in a far-off country, in which they felt no personal interest; though they knew that their countrymen slept on their arms, only awaiting the dawn to renew the deadly conflict, on the success of which depended not only the fate of our capital, but of that splendid army, containing the material on which our happiness depends. Ah! many full, sorrowful hearts were at home, breathing out prayers for our success; or else were busy in the hospitals, administering to the wounded. Those on the hill-sides and house-tops were too nervous and anxious to stay at home—not that they were apprehensive for the city, but for the fate of those who were defending it, and their feeling was too deep for expression. The same feeling, perhaps, which makes me write so much this morning. But I must go to other duties.

Ten o'Clock at Night.—Another day of great excitement in our beleaguered city. From early dawn the cannon has been roaring around us. Our success has been glorious! The citizens—gentlemen as well as ladies—have been fully occupied in the hospitals. Kent, Paine & Co. have thrown open their spacious building for the use of the wounded. General C., of Texas, volunteer aid to General Hood, came in from the field covered with dust, and slightly wounded; he represents the fight as terrible beyond example. The carnage is frightful. General Jackson has joined General Lee, and nearly the whole army on both sides were engaged. The enemy had retired before our troops to their strong works near Gaines's Mill. Brigade after brigade of our brave men were hurled against them, and repulsed in disorder. General Lee was heard to say to General Jackson, " The fighting is desperate; can our men stand it ?" Jackson replied, "General, I know our boys—they will never give back." In a short time a large part of our force was brought up in one grand attack, and then the enemy was utterly routed. General C. represents the valour of Hood and his brigade in the liveliest colours, and attributes the grand success at the close of the day greatly to their extraordinary gallantry. The works were the strongest ever seen in this country, and General C. says that the armies of the world could not have driven our men from them.

Another bulletin from the young surgeon of the Fortieth. That noble regiment has lost heavily—several of the "Potomac Rifles" among the slain—sons of old friends and acquaintances. E. B., dreadfully wounded, has been brought in, and is tenderly nursed. Our own boys are mercifully spared. Visions of the battle-field have haunted me all day. Our loved ones, whether friends or strangers—all Southern soldiers are dear to us—lying dead and dying; the wounded in the hot sun, the dead being hastily buried. McClellan is said to be retreating. "Praise the Lord, O my soul!"

28th.—The casualties among our friends, so far, not very numerous. My dear R. T. C. is here, slightly wounded; he hopes to return to his command in a few days. Colonel Allen, of the Second Virginia, killed. Major Jones, of the same regiment, desperately wounded. Wood McDonald killed. But what touches me most nearly is the death of my young friend, Clarence Warwick, of this city. Dearly have I loved that warm-hearted, high-minded, brave boy, since his early childhood. To-night I have been indulging sad memories of his earnest manner and affectionate tones, from his boyhood up; and now what must be the shock to his father and brothers, and to those tender sisters, when to-morrow the telegraph shall tell them of their loss! His cousin, Lieutenant-Colonel Warwick, is desperately wounded. Oh, I pray that his life may be spared to his poor father and mother! He is so brave and skilful an officer that we cannot spare him, and how can they? The booming of cannon still heard distinctly, but the sound is more distant.

June 30.—McClellan certainly retreating. We begin to breathe more freely; but he fights as he goes. Oh, that he may be surrounded before he gets to his gun-boats! Rumours are flying about that he is surrounded; but we do not believe it—only hope that he may be before he reaches the river. The city is sad, because of the dead and dying, but our hearts are filled with gratitude and love. The end is not yet—oh that it were!

MECKLENBURG COUNTY, *July* 15.—Mr. —— and myself

summoned here a short time ago to see our daughter, who was very ill. Found her better—she is still improving.

Richmond is disenthralled—the only Yankees there are in the "Libby" and other prisons. McClellan and his "Grand Army," on James River, near Westover, enjoying mosquitoes and bilious fevers. The weather is excessively hot. I dare say the Yankees find the "Sunny South" all that their most fervid imaginations ever depicted it, particularly on the marshes. So may it be, until the whole army melts with fervent heat. The gun-boats are rushing up and down the river, shelling the trees on the banks, afraid to approach Drury's Bluff. The Northern papers and Congress are making every effort to find out to whom the fault of their late reverses is to be traced. Our people think that their whole army might have been captured but for the dilatoriness of some of our generals. General Magruder is relieved, and sent to take command in the West.

21st.—Mr. —— sick, but better to-day. This is the anniversary of the glorious battle of Manassas. Since that time we have had many reverses, but our victories, of late, have atoned for all, except the loss of life.

We have had another naval fight on the Mississippi, just north of Vicksburg. Our large gun-boat, *Arkansas,* ran into the Federal fleet of twelve or thirteen gun-boats and rams, and overcame them completely. Vicksburg stands the bombardment with unflinching gallantry. No news from the Army of the Potomac. It is reported that General Jackson has gone to meet General Pope, who is on this side of the Blue Ridge, marching, it is supposed, to join McClellan.

Mr. —— takes a ride to-day; the first since his sickness. My heart is full of gratitude for public and private blessings.

23d.—Letters and papers to-day. It is reported that Hindman has captured Curtis and his whole command in Arkansas. Delightful, if true. The army in Virginia, and our dear ones, well.

28th.—The report of Hindman's having captured Curtis untrue ; but our army is doing well in the West. Murfreesboro', in Tennessee, has been captured by Confederates—a brigade, two brigadiers, and other officers, taken. " Jack Morgan" is annoying and capturing the Kentucky Yankees. The true Southerners there must endure an almost unbearable thraldom !

A long letter from S. S., describing graphically their troubles when in Federal lines. Now they are breathing freely again. A number of servants from W. and S. H., and indeed from the whole Pamunky River, went off with their Northern friends. I am sorry for them, taken from their comfortable homes to go they know not where, and to be treated they know not how. Our man Nat went, to whom I was very partial, because his mother was the maid and humble friend of my youth, and because I had brought him up. He was a comfort to us as a driver and hostler, but now that we have neither home, carriage, nor horses, it makes but little difference with us ; but how, with his slow habits, he is to support himself, I can't imagine. The wish for freedom is natural, and if he prefers it, so far as I am concerned he is welcome to it. I shall be glad to hear that he is doing well. Mothers went off leaving children—in two instances infants. Lord have mercy upon these poor misguided creatures! I am so thankful that the scurf of the earth, of which the Federal army seems to be composed, has been driven away from Hanover. I would that "Clarke" were as free.

July 29.—No army news. In this quiet nook mail-day is looked forward to with the greatest anxiety, and the newspapers are read with avidity from "Terms" to *finis*—embracing Southern rumours, official statements, army telegrams, Yankee extravaganzas, and the various *et cœteras*. The sick and wounded in the various hospitals are subjects for thought and action in every part of our State which is free to act for them; we all do what we can in our own little way; and surely if we have nothing but prayer to offer, great good must be effected. Yesterday evening, while walking out, a young woman with a baby in her arms passed us rapidly, weeping piteously, and with the wildest expressions of grief; we turned to follow her, but found that another woman was meeting her, whom we recognized as her mother; in another moment all was explained by her father, whom we met, slowly wending his way homeward. He had been to the hospital at Danville to see his son-in-law, whose name appeared among the wounded there. On reaching the place, he found that he had just been buried. On returning he met his daughter walking; in her impatience and anxiety about her husband, she could not sit still in the house; and in her ignorance, she supposed that her father would bring him home to be nursed. Poor thing! she is one of thousands. Oh that the enemy may be driven from our land, with a wholesome dread of encroaching upon our borders again! Our people are suffering too much; they cannot stand it. The family here suffers much anxiety, as each battle approaches, about their young son, the pride and darling of the household. He is a lieutenant in the —— Regiment; but during the fights around Richmond, as his captain was unfit for duty, the first lieutenant killed in the first fight, the command of the company devolved on this dear, fair-haired boy, and many praises have they heard of his bravery during those terrible days. He writes most delightfully encouraging letters, and never seems to know that he is enduring hardships. His last letter, written on a stump near Charles City Court-House, whither they had followed the enemy, was most exultant; and, brave young Christian as he is, he gives the glory to God. He exults in having helped to drive them, and, as it were, *pen them up* on the river; and though they are now desecrating the fair homes of his ancestors, (Berkeley and Westover,) yet, as they dare not unfurl their once proud banner on any other spot in Lower Virginia, and only there because protected by their gun-boats, he seems to think that the proud spirits of the Byrds and Harrisons may submit when they reflect that though their ancestral trees may shelter the direst of all foes, yet their *ancestral* marshes are yielding their malaria and mosquitoes with an unstinting hand, and aiding unsparingly the sword of the South in relieving it of invaders. Dear B., like so many Southern boys, he was summoned by the tocsin of war from the class-room to the camp. His career was most successful in one of the first literary institutions in this country, and if he lives he will return to his studies less of a scholar, but more of a man, in the highest sense of the word, than any collegiate course could have made him. But we can't look forward, for what horrors may come upon us before our independence is achieved it makes my heart ache to dwell upon.

August 4.—The girls just returned from a visit to Mrs. A. of several days, which they enjoyed greatly. Every thing there very bright and cheerful, except the hearts of the parents—they yearn for their sons on the field of danger! A battle is now expected between Jackson and Pope.

August 5.—The papers of last night brought us no news, except that our troops are firing upon the enemy's gun-boats near Coggin's Point. The result not known. A battle between Jackson and Pope still imminent. Major Bailey made a brilliant cavalry raid a few days since upon the enemy in Nicholas County, in which he took the command of a lieutenant-colonel prisoners, burnt their stores, and brought off many horses, mules, and arms. Morgan continues his successful raids in the West. The enemy has abandoned the siege of Vicksburg for the time.

9th.—We hear of a little cavalry fight at Orange Court-House, in which we drove off the enemy. General Pope continues to commit depredations in his district of operations. He seems to have taken Butler as his model, and even to exceed him in ferocity. Our President has just given most sensible orders for retaliation.

The Misses N. are spending the summer here. Their home in Clarke in possession of the enemy, together with their whole property, they are dividing their time among their friends. It is sad to see ladies of their age deprived of home comforts; but, like the rest of the refugees, they bear it very cheerfully. Born and reared at Westover, they are indignant in the highest degree that it should now be desecrated by McClellan's army. They are deeply mourning the death of their noble young cousin, Captain B. Harrison, of Upper Brandon, who was killed at the head of his troop, in one of the battles near Richmond.

LYNCHBURG, *August* 20.—Mr. —— and myself arrived here last night, after a most fatiguing trip, by Clarksville, Buffalo Springs, then to Wolf's Trap Station on the Danville road, and on to the Southside Railroad. The cars were filled with soldiers on furlough. It was pleasant to see how cheerful they were. Poor fellows! it is wonderful when we consider what the next battle may bring forth. They were occupied discussing the late battle at Cedar Run, between General Jackson and a portion of Pope's army, commanded by Banks. It was a very fierce fight, and many casualties on both sides; but we won the day—the Lord be praised! Lynchburg is full of hospitals, to which the ladies are very attentive; and they are said to be very well kept. I have been to a very large one to-day, in which our old home friends, Mrs. R. and Miss E. M., are matrons. Every thing looked beautifully neat and comfortable. As a stranger, and having so much to do for my patient at home, I find I can do nothing for the soldiers, but knit for them all the time, and give them a kind word in passing. I never see one without feeling disposed to extend my hand, and say, "God bless you."

29*th.*—The Richmond papers of yesterday mention two severe skirmishes on the Rappahannock within a week The enemy are retreating through Culpeper, Orange, etc., and our men are driving them on. General Jackson has reached Warrenton. Burnside's army is said to be near Fredericksburg, and Pope retreating towards Manassas. The safe situation of this town makes it a city of refuge to many. Several of our old friends are here. Mr. and Mrs. D., of Alexandria, are just across the passage from us; the J's are keeping house, and Mrs. M. is boarding very near us. This evening our friends the S's arrived. None but persons similarly situated can know the heartfelt pleasure of meeting with home friends, and talking of home scenes—of going back, as we did this evening, to the dear old times when we met together in our own parlours, with none to make us afraid. We see very little of Lynchburg society, but in this pleasant boarding-house, with *refugee society*, we want nothing more. The warmest feelings of my heart have been called forth, by meeting with one of the most intimate friends of my youth—now Mrs. Judge D. We met the other day in the church-door, for the first time for many, many years. Time has done its work with us both, but we instantly recognized each other. Since that time, not a day has passed without some affectionate demonstration on her part towards us. At her beautiful home, more than a mile from town, I found her mother, my venerable and venerated friend Mrs. Judge C., still the elegant, accomplished lady, the cheerful, warm-hearted, Christian Virginian woman. At four-score, the fire kindles in her eye as she speaks of our wrongs. "What would your father and my husband have thought of these times," she said to me—"men who loved and revered the *Union*, who would have yielded up their lives to support the Constitution, in its purity, but who could never have given up their cherished doctrines of State rights, nor have yielded one jot or tittle of their independence to the aggressions of the North?" She glories in having sons and grandsons fighting for the South. Two of the latter have already fallen in the great cause; I trust that the rest may be spared to her.

I see that the Northern papers, though at first claiming a victory at "Cedar Run," now confess that they lost three thousand killed and wounded, two generals wounded, sundry colonels and other officers. The *Times* is severe upon Pope—thinks it extraordinary that, as he knew two days before that the battle must take place, he did not have a larger force at hand; and rather "*strange*" that he should have been within six miles of the battle-field, and did not reach it until the fight was nearly over! They say, as usual, that they were greatly outnumbered! Strange, that with their *myriads*, they should be so frequently outnumbered on the battle-field! It is certain that our loss there was comparatively very small; though we have to mourn General Winder of the glorious Stonewall Brigade, and about two hundred others, all valuable lives.

August 30th.—A package arrived last night from our sisters, with my sister M's diary, for my amusement. It was kept while our dear ones of W. and S. H. were surrounded by McClellan's army. I shall use my leisure here in copying it, that our children's children may know all that our family suffered during this cruel war. During the six weeks that they were surrounded by the foe, we only heard from them through letters written to their husbands in Richmond. These letters were captured by the enemy, and published in a New York paper; and one was republished in the Richmond *Enquirer*, where we were most delighted to find it. In that way W. B. N., then incarcerated in the walls of Fort Delaware, heard from his mother, wife, and children, for the first time since he was captured, in March.

Mrs. N's diary begins: "*May* 18*th.*—S. H., Hanover County, Va. C. M. and myself set off yesterday morning for church. At my brother's gate we met Dr. N., who told us that there were rumours of the approach of the enemy from the White House. We then determined not to go to our own church, but in another direction, to the Presbyterian church. After waiting there until the hour for service had arrived, an elder came in and announced to us that the minister thought it prudent not to come, but to have the congregation dismissed at once, as the enemy were certainly approaching. We returned home in a most perturbed state, and found that my husband had just arrived, with several of our sons and nephews, to spend a day or two with us. In a short time a servant announced that he had seen the Yankees that morning at the "Old Church." Then there was no time to be lost; our gentlemen must go. We began our hurried preparations, and sent for the carriage and buggy. We were told that the driver had gone to the Yankees. After some discussion, one of the gentlemen determined to drive, and they were soon off. It was then eleven o'clock at night, and the blackness of darkness reigned over the earth. It was the most anxious night of my life. Surrounded by an implacable foe, our gentlemen all gone, we knew not how long we should be separated, or what might not happen before we met, and the want of confidence in our servants, which was now for the first time shaken, made us very nervous. This morning we went to W., and took leave of our sister, Mrs. C., and daughters. Her sons are in the army, and being a refugee, she says she must follow the army, and go where she can reach them if they are wounded. We found C. busily dividing her year's supply of bacon among the servants, that each may take care of his own. As the enemy never regards locks, she knows that her meat-house will be unsafe; we secreted two guns, which had been inadvertently left, and returned, feeling desolate, but thankful that our gentlemen were safely off.

"22*d*.—Papers from Richmond to-day. We are not yet in the enemy's lines.

"23*d*.—The enemy's pickets gradually encroaching upon us. A squad of their cavalry has been in the Hanover Town lane all day; five or six lancers, with their red streamers, rode slowly by our gate this evening. C. encountered them in her walk home, and had a conversation with an officer, Major Doyle, who made many *professions of friendship!*

"24*th*.—We were aroused this morning at an early hour, by the servants rushing in, exclaiming : "The house is surrounded by Yankees, and they are coming into the house." I rushed to the window, and there they were. An officer in the front porch, and a squad of cut-throat-looking fellows on the steps; while a number, with their red streamers and lances, were dashing hither and thither; some at the stable, some at the kitchen, others around the servants' quarters and at the barn, while the lane was filled with them. Dr. T. had spent the night with little L., who is ill with scarlet fever. I knocked at his door, and asked him to go down and see what the people wanted. We dressed as rapidly as possible. C. and M. had been up all night with L., and were soon ready to go down. They quickly returned, to say that the officer was Colonel Rush, of Philadelphia, and demanded that my little son Edward should be sent down immediately. It was in vain that they told him that E. was a mere child—he had evidently heard that he was a young man, and demanded his presence. The child was aroused from his sleep, and hastily dressed himself, but not quickly enough for our impatient Colonel, who walked to the staircase and began to ascend, when C. called to him, "Colonel R., do you mean to go to a lady's chamber before she is dressed? The boy is in his mother's room." Somewhat abashed, he stepped back. I soon descended, accompanied by E. N. and W. S. There on the mat before me stood a live Yankee colonel, with an aid on either side. I approached; he pointed to W. S., saying, "Is that Edward N?" "No," said I; "that is my grandson ; this is E. N." He said, "I want the boys to go with me." Looking him full in the eye, I said, "Sir, will you take these children prisoners?" His eye fell, and with many grimaces he replied, " Oh, no; I only want to ask the boys a few questions." He then took them across the lawn, I all the time watching them; asked them many questions, but finding that he could get nothing out of them, he sent them back, calling them "little rebels," etc. The Colonel had seen defiant looks enough while in the house, and did not return. He asked M. to let him give her a remedy for scarlet fever, which Mrs. *Colonel* Huger had given him. "Mrs. *General* Huger you mean?" replied M. "Thank you, I have perfect confidence in Dr. T." In the mean time his commissary went to the meat-house, demanded the key, and looking in, said, " I want three hundred pounds of this bacon, and shall send for it this evening." Another man went to the stable, took Dr. T's horse, saddle, and bridle, and went off with them. The Colonel was immediately informed of it, *seemed* shocked, and said, "Impossible;" but on ordering it to be brought back, it was soon returned. Presently the Quartermaster rode up to the door, calling out, " Mrs. N., three horses were in your stable last night, and they are not there now; the Colonel wishes their absence accounted for." " Perhaps, sir," replied M., " they have been stolen, as the other was; but as you get your information from the servants, I refer you to them." He rode off, and the whole party returned to their camp.

"*Monday*, 26*th*.—A cry of " Yankees," this morning, sent us to the windows; there we saw a regiment of Lancers, one of regulars, one of rifles, and another of zouaves, composed of the most dreadful-looking creatures I ever beheld, with red caps and trowsers ; also two guns. They were on their way to the Wyoming bridge, which they destroyed, and then made a reconnoissance of the Court House road. On their return they called here, boasting that they had killed one of our men; they advised M. to hang out a white flag to protect her house, which she, of course, declined doing.

"*27th.*—Last night I could not sleep, in consequence of a threat made by one of the Yankee soldiers in our kitchen. He said that 30,000 soldiers had been ordered to the Court-House to-day, to "wipe out" our people. Were our people ignorant of this, and how should we let them know of it? These were questions that haunted me all night. Before day I formed my plan, and awakened S. to consult her on the subject. It was this: To send W. S. to the Court-House, *as usual*, for our letters and papers. If the Yankee pickets stopped him, he could return; if he could reach our pickets, he could give the alarm. She agreed to it, and as soon as it was day we aroused the child, communicated to him our plan, (for we dared not write;) he entered into the spirit of it, and by light he was off. I got up and went down to the yard, for I could not sit still; but what was my consternation, after a short time had elapsed, to see at the gate, and all along the road, the hated red streamers of our enemy, going towards the Court-House! S. and myself were miserable about W. M. and C. gave us no comfort; they thought it very rash in us to send him—he would be captured, and "Fax" (the horse) would certainly be taken. We told them that it was worth the risk to put our people on their guard; but, nevertheless, we were unhappy beyond expression. Presently a man with a wretched countenance, and, from his conversation, an abolitionist of the deepest dye, rode in to inquire if the artillery had passed along. My fears about

W. induced me to assume a bland countenance and manner, and I told him of having sent a little boy for the mail, and I wanted him to see that he came home safely; he said that the boy would not be allowed to pass, and promised, gruffly, to do what he could for him; but at the same time made such remarks as made our blood boil; but, remembering W's danger, we made no reply. He said he was aid to General Warren. Before he left our gate, what was our relief to see W. ride in, escorted by fourteen lancers, he and his horse unmolested! The child had gone ahead of the Yankees, reached our picket, told his story, and a vidette had immediately been sent with the information to head-quarters. I then for the first time took my seat, with my heart full of gratitude for W's safety, and feeling greatly relieved that I had done what I could. At three o'clock the firing commenced; it was very heavy for some hours; we knew they were fighting, and knew, too, that our force at the Court-House was not large. Oh, what anxious moments we have experienced this day! The firing has now ceased, and the Yankees are constantly straggling in, claiming a great victory; but we have learned to believe nothing they say.

"28*th*.—Now our mail is broken up, and we feel that we are indeed in the hands of the enemy. Oh, how forsaken and forlorn we are! yet we do what we can to cheer each other, and get on right well.

"30*th*.—This morning two horsemen rode up, and seeing our cold looks, said, "Ladies, do you take us for Yankees?" "Of course we do—are you not Yankees?" "Oh, no; we belong to the Augusta troop, and want to hear something of the movements of the enemy." We pointed to their pickets, and implored them to go at once. We, of course, filled their haversacks, and they were scouting about the woods for some time. Oh, how our hearts go out towards our own people!

"*June 1st.*—We heard very heavy firing all day yesterday, and again to-day. At one time the roar was so continuous that I almost fancied I heard the shouts of the combatants; the firing became less about twelve o'clock, and now (night) it has ceased entirely. Dr. N. and Dr. T. have been accused by the Yankees of having informed our people of their meditated attack the other day. They were cross-examined on the subject, and of course denied it positively. They were threatened very harshly, the Yankees contending that there was no one else in the neighbourhood that could have done it. Poor little W. was not suspected at all—they little know what women and children can do.

"*7th.*—We have been now surrounded by the enemy for two weeks, cut off from every relative except our two households. Our male relations, who are young enough, are all in the army, and we have no means of hearing one word from them. The roar of artillery we hear almost every day, but have no means of hearing the result. We see the picket-fires of the enemy every night, but have, so far, been less injured by them than we anticipated. They sometimes surround our houses, but have never yet searched them.

"*8th.*—The *New York Herald* reports a bloody fight on the 31st of May and 1st of June. They acknowledge from 3,000 to 4,000 killed and wounded—give us credit for the victory on the first day, but say that they recovered on the second day what they lost on the first. I have no doubt, from their own account, that they were badly whipped; but how long shall this bloody work continue?

Thousands and thousands of our men are slain, and we seem to be no nearer the end than at first.

"9*th*.—Yankee wagons about all day, looking for corn and fodder. I am thankful to say that M. has none for them, the flood of last year having destroyed W's corn crop. I felt to-day our short-sightedness; what they considered a calamity when the flood came, we feel now to be a blessing, as we are not able to furnish food for our foes. God forgive me for my feelings towards them; but when I see insolent fellows riding around and around our dwellings, seeking what they may devour, every evil feeling of my heart is kindled against them and their whole nation. They, the murderers of our husbands, sons, fathers, thinking themselves at liberty to riot over our homesteads! They got their wagons filled from my brother's barn, and in return pretended to give a bond, which they know is not worth the paper on which it is written. One had the assurance to tell C. that her husband would be paid if he took the oath of allegiance. She told him that he would not do that for all the corn in the Southern Confederacy. Within two or three days they have become very bold; they ride up and demand the key of the corn-house or meat-house, and if it is not immediately given, they break open the door and help themselves.

"11*th*.—Yesterday evening we had another visit from the Lancers: they fed their horses at M's barn, ripping off the planks that the corn might roll out. The door was opened by the overseer, but that was too slow a way for thieves and robbers. They encamped for the night in front of W. C. was detained here yesterday by rain, and was not at home all day, and they took that opportunity for searching every thing. While they were filling the wagons at the barn, four officers went over every part of the house, even the drawers and trunks. They were moderate in their robberies, only taking some damask towels and napkins from the drawers, and a cooked ham and a plate of rolls from the pantry. These men wore the trappings of officers! While I write, I have six wagons in view at my brother's barn, taking off his corn, and the choice spirits accompanying them are catching the sheep and carrying them off. This robbery now goes on every day. The worst part of our thraldom is, that we can hear nothing from our own army

"13th.—Good news at last. Four letters were received last night by way of Ashland. We learn that we certainly whipped the Yankees on the 31st of May and 1st of June, and that Jackson has had a most glorious campaign in the Valley. We are grieved to hear that the gallant Ashby has been killed, and trust that it is a mere rumour, and that God has spared his valuable life. My sons were not in the late fight, but are stationed at Strawberry Hill, the home of my childhood. Every thing is being stolen on these two places and elsewhere. A lieutenant on General Porter's staff rode up this evening to ask M. to sell him butter, fowls, eggs, etc. She told him that her poultry-yard had been robbed the night before by some of his men. He professed great horror, but had not gone fifty yards when we heard the report of a pistol, and this wonderfully proper lieutenant of a moment before had shot the hog of an old negro woman who lives here.

"14th.—While quietly sitting on the porch yesterday evening, I saw a young man rapidly approaching the house, on foot; at first we took it for granted that he was a Yankee, but soon found from his dress that he was one of our soldiers, and from his excited manner that there was something unusual the matter. He was Lieutenant Latané, of Stuart's Brigade. They had been fighting on the road from Hanover Court-House to the Old Church, and his brother, the captain of the Essex Troop, had been killed about two miles from W. The mill-cart from W. soon after passed along, and he put his brother's body into it, and brought it to W. There he found a Yankee picket stationed. C. immediately took the dead soldier into her care, promising to bury him as tenderly as if he were her brother ; and having no horse left on the place, (the enemy had taken them all,) sent him here, by a private way, to elude the vigilance of the picket, to get M's only remaining horse—for the poor fellow had given up his to a soldier whose horse had been killed. The horse was soon ready, and as soon as we saw him safely off, we went over to W. to assist in preparing the body for the burial. Oh, what a sad office ! This dear young soldier, so precious to many hearts, now in the hands of sorrowing, sympathizing friends, yet, personally, strangers to him ! He looked so young—not more than twenty years of age. He was shot in four places ; one ball had entered the region of his heart and passed out at the back. We cut a large lock of his hair, as the only thing we could do for his mother. We have sent for Mr. Carraway to perform the funeral services, and shall bury him by our dear Willie Phelps, another victim to this unholy war.

"15th.—Yesterday was the only day for three weeks that we have been free from the hated presence of Yankees. Aaron, whom we sent for Mr. C., was not allowed to pass the picket-post, so we took the body of our poor young captain and buried it ourselves in the S. H. grave-yard, with no one to interrupt us. The girls covered his honoured grave with flowers. He and our precious W. lie side by side, martyrs to a holy cause.

"We have heard nothing from General Stuart; he had 5,000 men and three guns. The pickets have disappeared from around us. The servant we sent for Mr. C. says that General S. burnt the encampment near the Old Church, on Saturday evening, killed many horses, and severely wounded a captain, who refused to surrender; the men scampered into the woods. He represents the Yankees as very much infuriated, vowing vengeance upon our people, from which we hope that they have been badly used. We feel intensely anxious about our brigade.

"*16th.*—Yesterday we sent letters to the Court-House to be mailed, presuming, as we had not seen an enemy for twenty-four hours, that the coast would be clear for awhile; but Bartlett rode into a detachment of them in Taliaferro's Lane. The poor old man, in his anxiety to save his letters, betrayed himself by putting his hand on his pocket. They were, of course, taken from him. [The letters I mentioned as having been published in the New York papers.] They are heartily welcome to mine; I hope the perusal may do them good, but C. is annoyed. It was the first letter she had written to her husband since the depredations at W., and she had expressed herself very freely.

"*June* 17.—The Yankees have returned upon us. They came this morning early, and caught J. W's horse, which they took off. We can hear nothing of General S. We presume he has returned to Richmond. We shall have to pay for it, I dare say, by being robbed, etc.; but if it has done good to the great cause, we do not mind personal loss. We are now honoured with a guard of twenty-five men—why, we are at a loss to conjecture, unless our intercepted letters may have convinced them that we are dangerous characters. We doubtless have the will to do them harm enough, but, surrounded and watched as we are, the power is wanting. Our guard is composed of regulars, who are much more decent men than the volunteers.

"C. commenced harvest yesterday, in a small way, but so many servants are gone to the Yankees, that much of the wheat must be lost, and the corn cannot be worked. The milkmaid amused herself at their remarks to them: *"Ladies, why do you work for white people? You are all free now,"* etc., etc.

"18*th*.—Our guard in full force to-day. It is so absurd to see the great fellows on their horses, armed from head to foot, with their faces turned towards us, standing at our yard-gate, guarding women and children, occasionally riding about on the gravel-walks, plucking roses, with which they decorate their horses' heads. A poor woman came to-day in a buggy, in pursuit of corn. She had been robbed by the enemy of every grain. This is the case with many others, particularly with soldiers' wives. I asked an officer to-day, what had become of General Stuart? He said he was a 'smart fellow,' and he 'guessed' he had returned to Richmond, but he 'ought to have paid a visit to his father-in-law, General Cooke, commanding the United States cavalry not many miles distant.'

"20*th*.—Our guard withdrew to-day, and we walked to W., a privilege we had not enjoyed for many days. We received a Richmond *Dispatch* by *underground railroad*. General Stuart's raid was like a story in the 'Arabian Nights' Entertainments.' He passed down from Hanover Court-House, behind the whole of McClellan's army, in many places so near as to hear the pickets, capturing and burning every thing which they could not take with them. They then crossed the Lower Chickahominy, and got back to camp before the enemy had recovered from their surprise; losing but one man, Captain Latané, whom we had the honour of burying. The man who shot him, a Federal officer, was immediately killed by a private in his (Captain L's) company. The raiders burned two transports at the White House, destroyed any number of wagons, mules, stores, etc., and carried back 200 prisoners. The Yankees have been making vast preparations for surrounding them as they returned; but they were too wise to be caught in that trap. Their masked batteries will be of no avail this time. At New Kent Court-House our men refreshed themselves with all manner of good things, at the expense of the enemy, providing themselves with clothing, boots, etc., and taking the sleek proprietor of the establishment prisoner.

"*21st.*—Yesterday we heard firing all day—heavy guns in the morning, and musketry during the day, and heavy guns again in the evening. Oh, that we could know the result! This morning is as calm and beautiful as though all was peace on the earth. O God, with whom all things are possible, dispel the dark clouds that surround us, and permit us once more to return to our homes, and collect the scattered members of our flock around our family altar in peace and safety! Not a word from my husband or sons.

"*22d.*—Dr. T. called to-day, to say that the firing we heard on Friday was from our guns shelling the enemy, to drive them lower down the Chickahominy. Letters, by underground railroad, from our dear William, at Fort Delaware. He complains of nothing but his anxiety to be exchanged, and the impossibility of hearing from home.

C., at the same time, got a letter from my brother. He writes in good spirits about our affairs. Jackson's career is glorious. The sick and wounded are doing well ; hospitals are in good order, and the ladies indefatigable in nursing. Surgeon-like, he tells more of the wounded than any thing else. Rev. Mr. C. came up to-day, and gave us some amusing incidents of Stuart's raid. As some of our men rode by Mr. B's gate, several of them went in with Mr. B's sons for a few moments. A dead Yankee lay at the gate. Mrs. W. (Mrs. B's daughter) supposing he was only wounded, ran out with restoratives to his assistance. While standing there, two Yankees came up. Mrs. W. ordered them to surrender, which one did without the slightest hesitation, giving up his arms, which she immediately carried in to her younger brother, who was badly armed. The other escaped, but her prisoner went along with the crowd. Yankee wagons are again taking off corn from W. The men are very impertinent to C.

" 24*th*.—Yankee scouts are very busy around us to-day. They watch this river, and are evidently fearing a flank movement upon them. Wagons passing to Dr. N's for corn, guarded by Lancers, who are decidedly the worst specimens we have seen. Compared with them, the regulars are welcome guests. It is so strange that Colonel Rush, the son of a distinguished man, whose mother belonged to one of the first families in Maryland, the first-cousin of James M. Mason, and Captain Mason of our navy, of Mrs. General Cooper and Mrs. S. S. Lee, should consent to come among his nearest of kin, at the head of ruffians like the Lancers, to despoil and destroy our country ! I suppose that living in Philadelphia has hardened his heart against us, for the city of Brotherly Love is certainly more fierce towards us than any other. Boston cannot compare with it. This is mortifying, because many of us had friends in Philadelphia, whom we loved and admired. We hope and believe that the Quaker element there is at the foundation of their ill-will.

"25th.—I got by chance a Philadelphia paper of the 20th. Very little bragging, but an earnest appeal to their men to be united, to forget that there will be any more presidential elections, and to let squabbling among themselves alone; that the critical time is at hand, etc.

"*Friday*, 27th.—The roar of cannon and musketry has been incessant to-day; now as I sit in the yard it is terrific. I doubt not that a general engagement is going on. O God! be with us now; nerve the hearts and strengthen the arms of our men! Give wisdom and skill to our commanders, and grant us victory for thy great name's sake!

"28th.—We have just heard of our success, and that Jackson and Ewell have come from the Valley, and have flanked the enemy on the Chickahominy. Two of our troopers called in this morning.

"*July* 1st.—Firing continues, but lower and lower down. No news from my dear boys. I wish, but dread, to hear.

"2d.—My boys and nephews safe, God be praised! McClellan in full retreat. C. and M. are sending off a wagon with ice, chickens, bread, eggs, vegetables, etc., to our hospital at Cold Harbor.

"*July* 4th.—A beautiful, glorious day, and one which the Yankees expected confidently to spend triumphantly in Richmond. Last Fourth of July old General Scott expected to be there, to tread in triumph the fallen fortunes of his quondam friends, and to-day McClellan has been obliged to yield his visions of glory. 'Man proposes, but God disposes.' Many of their companions in arms are there, in the Libby and other prisons, wounded in the hospitals, and dead in the swamps and marshes, or buried on the battle-fields while the 'Grand Army' and the 'Young Napoleon' are struggling desperately to get out of the bogs of the Chickahominy to his gunboats on James River. I sent the carriage to Richmond a day or two ago for Mr. N., but he writes that he is sending it backwards and forwards to the battle-fields for the wounded. It is a season of wide-spread distress; parties are going by constantly to seek their husbands, brothers, sons, about whose fate they are uncertain. Some old gentlemen passed yesterday, *walking* all the way from Lancaster County. All the boats and bridges have been destroyed on the rivers, and conveyances can't be put across. Ladies are sent from river to river by those persons who have conveyances and horses left to them. Oh, I trust that blood enough has been spilled now! Dr. S. has just arrived; he has been twenty miles below Richmond. He says the Yankee dead still lie unburied in many places—our men are too much worn out to undertake to bury them. The Yankee hospitals, as well as our own, are all along the roads; their hospital flag is red; ours is orange. They have their own surgeons, and, of course, many delicacies that our men can't have. The Northern papers speak of this retreat of McClellan's as a 'strategic movement.' The bloody fights of eight days, the retreat of thirty miles, attended by immense loss of life, thousands of prisoners, many guns, stores of all kinds, etc., a 'strategic movement!' But our loss is heavy—so many valuable lives, and such suffering among the wounded. O God! interpose and stop this cruel war!"

I quote no further from Mrs. N's diary, as the next page

was devoted to the visits of those dear ones whom God had preserved amid strife and carnage. She mentions the return of our dear W. B. N. from Fort Delaware on the 5th of August, where he had been for several months. He asked but five days' furlough to be with his family, and then returned to his regiment, (Fourth Cavalry.) His reception by his company was most gratifying. As soon as he got to camp, it drew up in line, and requested him to come to the *front,* when the "Orderly" came up, leading a very handsome bay horse, elegantly equipped, which he presented to his "Captain," in the name of the company.

LYNCHBURG, *September* 2.—The papers to-day give glorious news of a victory to our arms on the plains of Manassas, on the 28th, 29th, and 30th. I will give General Lee's telegram:

"ARMY OF NORTHERN VIRGINIA,
GROVETON, *August* 30—10 P.M.
Via RAPIDAN.

"To PRESIDENT DAVIS :—This army achieved to-day, on the plains of Manassas, a signal victory over the combined forces of McClellan and Pope. On the 28th and 29th, each wing, under Generals Longstreet and Jackson, repulsed with valour attacks made on them separately. We mourn the loss of our gallant dead in every conflict, yet our gratitude to Almighty God for his mercies rises higher each day. To Him and to the valour of our troops a nation's gratitude is due.

(Signed) "R. E. LEE."

Nothing more to-day—my heart is full. The papers give no news of the dead and wounded. The dreaded black-list yet to come. In the mean time we must let no evil forebodings mar our joy and thankfulness.

3d.—Wild stories on the street this morning, of the capture of prisoners, killing of generals, etc. Burnside and staff captured, they say. This last too good to be true.

4th.—Our victory at Manassas complete; the fight lasted four days. General Kearney was killed in a cavalry fight at Chantilly. Beautiful Chantilly has become a glorious battle-field. The splendid trees and other lovely surroundings all gone; but it is classic ground from this time. In those fights I had eight nephews! Are they all safe? I have heard from two, who fought gallantly, and are unscathed. It is said that our army is to go to Maryland.

5th.—Our son J. arrived last night with quite a party, his health greatly suffering from over-work in Richmond during these exciting times. One of the party told me an anecdote of General J. E. B. Stuart, which pleased me greatly. Mrs. S. was in the cars, and near her sat a youth, in all the pride of his first Confederate uniform, who had attended General S. during his late raid as one of his guides through his native county of Hanover. At one of the water stations he was interesting the passengers by an animated account of their hair-breadth escapes by flood and field, and concluded by saying, "In all the tight places we got into, I never heard the General swear an oath, and I never saw him drink a drop." Mrs. S. was an amused auditor of the excited narrative, and after the cars were in motion she leaned forward, introduced herself to the boy, and asked him if he knew the reason why General S. never swears nor drinks; adding, "It is because he is a Christian and loves God, and nothing will induce him to do what he thinks wrong, and I want you and all his soldiers to follow his example."

September 12.—No news from the army, except a letter in the morning's paper speaking of General Lee's being pleased with his reception in Maryland, and that our troops are foraging in Pennsylvania. I hope so; I like the idea of our army subsisting on the enemy; they certainly have subsisted on us enough to be willing that we should return the compliment. Took leave of our nephew, B. H. M., this morning; he has been here on sick-leave, and has gone in pursuit of his regiment, which is now across the Potomac. Poor child! it was hard to see him go off alone, with his child-like countenance and slender figure; but he is already a veteran in the service, and has a most unflinching, undaunted spirit.

Took a ride this evening with Mrs. D. through the beautiful environs of this city. After getting beyond the hospitals, there was nothing to remind us of war; all was peaceful loveliness; we talked of days long passed, and almost forgot that our land was the scene of bitter strife. Sometimes I almost fancy that we are taking one of our usual summer trips, with power to return when it terminates; and then I am aroused, as from a sweet dream, to find myself a homeless wanderer, surrounded by horrors of which my wildest fancy had never conceived a possibility, in this Christian land and enlightened day.

Sunday.—Just returned from church. Mr. K. gave us a delightful sermon on our dependence on God as a people. "When Moses held up his hand, then Israel prevailed; and when he let down his hand, then Amalek prevailed." Oh, that our hands may always be "held up" for our cause and armies! Next Thursday (18th) is the day appointed by our

President as a day of thanksgiving for our successes. His proclamation is so beautiful that I will copy it:

"To the People of the Confederate States:

"Once more upon the plains of Manassas have our armies been blessed by the Lord of Hosts with a triumph over our enemies. It is my privilege to invite you once more to His footstool, not now in the garb of fasting and sorrow, but with joy and gladness, to render thanks for the great mercies received at His hands. A few months since our enemies poured forth their invading legions upon our soil. They laid waste our fields, polluted our altars, and violated the sanctity of our homes. Around our capital they gathered their forces, and with boastful threats claimed it as already their prize. The brave troops which rallied to its defence have extinguished their vain hopes, and under the guidance of the same Almighty hand, have scattered our enemies and driven them back in dismay. Uniting those defeated forces and the various armies which had been ravaging our coasts with the army of invasion in Northern Virginia, our enemies have renewed their attempt to subjugate us at the very place where their first effort was defeated, and the vengeance of retributive justice has overtaken their entire host in a second and complete overthrow. To this signal success accorded to our arms in the East has been graciously added another, equally brilliant, in the West. On the very day on which our forces were led to victory on the plains of Manassas, in Virginia, the same Almighty arm assisted us to overcome our enemies at Richmond, in Kentucky. Thus, at one and the same time, have two great hostile armies been stricken down, and the wicked designs of our enemies set at naught. In such circumstances it is meet and right that, as a people, we should bow down in adoring thankfulness to that gracious God who has been our bulwark and defence, and to offer unto Him the tribute of thanksgiving and praise. In His hand is the issue of all events, and to Him should we in a special manner ascribe the honour of this great deliverance. Now, therefore, I, Jefferson Davis, President of the Confederate States, do issue this, my proclamation setting apart Thursday, the 18th day of September, as a day of thanksgiving and prayer to Almighty God, for the great mercies vouchsafed to our people, and more especially for the triumph of our arms at Richmond and Manassas, in Virginia, and at Richmond in Kentucky; and I do hereby invite the people of the Confederate States to meet on that day, at their respective places of public worship, and to unite in rendering thanks and praise to God for these great mercies, and to implore Him to conduct our country safely through the perils which surround us, to the final attainment of the blessings of peace and security.

"Given under my hand and the seal of the Confederate States, at Richmond, this fourth day of September, A. D. 1862.

"JEFF. DAVIS, *Pres. of the C. S.*
'J. P. BENJAMIN, *Sec. of State.*"

Tuesday, September 16*th*.—The papers to-day give no account of our army in Maryland. General Loring has been successful in the Kanawha Valley, in driving the enemy, taking prisoners, and 5,000 stand of arms, etc. Our success in the West still continues. Kentucky is represented to be in a flame of excitement. General Kirby Smith asks for 20,000 stand of arms to be sent him to arm Kentuckians, who are rushing to his standard. Cincinnati preparing for defence, etc.

Yesterday I was surprised and delighted to see my nephew, W. B. C. After passing through the bloody fight at Manassas, he found he could not march into Maryland, in consequence of the soreness of his wound received last spring at Kernstown. He gives a graphic account of our army's trials, tribulations, and successes at Manassas. Our dear ones all passed safely through the fights.

Winchester once more disenthralled. My dear S. B. S. about to return to her home there—but in what state will she find it? When Jackson drove Banks down the Valley, Dr. S., in passing through Winchester, stepped into the open door of his house; found it had been Banks's headquarters; the floors covered with papers torn up in haste; the remnant of the General's breakfast on the dining-room table, and other unmistakable signs of a recent and *very* hurried departure.

September 18*th.*—Thanksgiving-day for our victories! We went to church this morning and heard Mr. K's admirable sermon from 1st Sam., chap. vii., v. 12: "Then Samuel took a stone, and set it between Mizpeh and Shen, and called the name of it Ebenezer, saying, Hitherto hath the Lord helped us." Oh! I trust that this day has been observed throughout the Confederacy. If all our duties were as easily performed, we should be very good Christians; but, alas! our hearts are often heavy, and do not cheerfully respond to the calls of duty. In prosperity, praise and thanksgiving seem to rise spontaneously to our lips, but to humble ourselves, and feel our entire dependence, is a much more difficult duty.

Saturday, September 20*th.*—An official account in the morning's paper of the surrender of Harper's Ferry to our men on Sunday last. Colonel Miles, the Federal commander, surrendered, unconditionally, to General Jackson, 11,000 prisoners, 50 pieces of artillery, 12,000 stand of arms, ammunition, quartermaster and commissary stores in large quantities. McClellan attempted to come to the rescue of Harper's Ferry. A courier was captured, sent by him to Miles, imploring him to hold out until he could bring him reinforcements. General Lee ordered General D. H. Hill to keep McClellan in check, and, for this purpose, placed him on the road near Boonesborough. It is said that McClellan had a force of 80,000 men, and that General Hill, on Saturday and Sunday, kept him in check all day—General Longstreet getting up at night. Next day they attacked him, repulsed and drove him five miles. The details of the battle have not yet appeared. We have further rumours of fighting, but nothing definite. It is impossible for me to say how miserable we are about our dear boys.

The body of Brigadier-General Garland was brought to this, his native city, and his home, yesterday for interment. He was killed in the battle near Boonesborough. This event was a great shock to the community, where he was loved, admired, and respected. His funeral yesterday evening was attended by an immense concourse of mourning friends. It made my heart ache, as a soldier's funeral always does. I did not know him, but I know that he was "the only child of his mother, and she is a widow;" and I know, moreover, that the country cannot spare her chivalric sons.

Monday Night, September 22d.—Probably the most desperate battle of the war was fought last Wednesday near Sharpsburg, Maryland. Great loss on both sides. The Yankees claim a great victory, while our men do the same. We were left in possession of the field on Wednesday night, and buried our dead on Thursday. Want of food and other stores compelled our generals to remove our forces to the Virginia side of the river, which they did on Thursday night, without molestation. This is all I can gather from the confused and contradictory accounts of the newspapers.

24th.—Still no official account of the Sharpsburg fight, and no list of casualties. The Yankee loss in generals very great—they must have fought desperately. Reno, Mansfield, and Miles were killed; others badly wounded. The Yankee papers say that their loss of "field officers is unaccountable;" and add, that but for the wounding of General Hooker, they would have driven us *into the Potomac!*

25th.—The tables were turned on Saturday, as we succeeded in driving a good many of them into the Potomac. Ten thousand Yankees crossed at Shepherdstown, but unfortunately for them, they found the glorious Stonewall there. A fight ensued at Boteler's Mill, in which General Jackson totally routed General Pleasanton and his command. The account of the Yankee slaughter is fearful. As they were recrossing the river our cannon was suddenly turned upon them. They were fording. The river is represented as being blocked up with the dead and dying, and crimsoned with blood. Horrible to think of! But why will they have it so? At any time they might stop fighting, and return to their own homes. We do not want their blood, but only to be separated from them as a people, eternally and everlastingly. Mr. ——, Mrs. D., and myself, went to church this evening, and after an address from Mr. K. we took a delightful ride.

A letter from B. H. M., the first she has been able to write for six months, except by "underground railroad," with every danger of having them read, and perhaps published by the enemy. How, in the still beautiful but much injured Valley, they do rejoice in their freedom! Their captivity—for surrounded as they were by implacable enemies, is captivity of the most trying kind—has been very oppressive to them. Their cattle, grain, and every thing else, have been taken from them. The gentlemen are actually keeping their horses in their cellars to protect them. Now they are rejoicing in having their own Southern soldiers around them; they are busily engaged nursing the wounded; hospitals are established in Winchester, Berryville, and other places.

Letters from my nephews, W. B. N. and W. N. The first describes the fights of Boonesborough, Sharpsburg, and Shepherdstown. He says the first of these was the severest hand-to-hand cavalry fight of the war. All were terrific. W. speaks of his feelings the day of the surrender of Harper's Ferry. As they were about to charge the enemy's intrenchments, he felt as if he were marching into the jaws of death, with scarcely a hope of escape. The position was very strong, and the charge would be up a tremendous hill over felled timber, which lay thickly upon it—the enemy's guns, supported by infantry in intrenchments, playing upon them all the while. What was their relief, therefore, to descry the *white flag* waving from the battlements! He thinks that, in the hands of resolute men, the position would have been impregnable. Thank God, the Yankees thought differently, and surrendered, thus saving many valuable lives, and giving us a grand success. May they ever be thus minded!

30*th.*—The *Richmond Examiner* of yesterday contains Lincoln's Proclamation, declaring all the negroes free from the 1st of January next! The Abolition papers are in ecstasies; as if they did not know that it can only be carried out *within their* lines, and there they have been practically free from the moment we were invaded. The *New York Tribune* is greatly incensed at the capture of Harper's Ferry; acknowledges that the battle of Sharpsburg was a disaster to them—Sumner's corps alone having lost 5,000 men in killed and wounded. It says it was the " fiercest, bloodiest, and most indecisive battle of the war." Oh, that their losses could convince them of the wickedness of this contest! but their appetite seems to grow on what it feeds upon. Blood, blood, is still their cry. My heart sickens at the thought of what our dear soldiers have yet to pass through. Arise, O God, in thy strength, and save us from our relentless foes, for thy great name's sake!

Mr. —— has improved so much in health that we return in a few days to Richmond, that he may again enter upon the duties of his office. Ashland is our destiny for next year; the difficulty of obtaining a house or board in Richmond has induced us to join a party of refugee friends in taking a cottage there. Our children are already there, and write that a comfortable room is awaiting us. Last night we received a message from Mrs. and Miss S., of Alexandria, that they were in this place, having run the *blockade*, from their oppressed home, during the battles around Richmond, when many of the soldiers had been withdrawn, and of course the surveillance of the old town had become less severe. Mrs. D., of Alexandria, and myself went directly after breakfast to see them. They had much to tell of the reign of terror through which they had gone, and nothing very satisfactory of our homes. Mrs. D's house was occupied as barracks, and ours as a hospital. Miss —— had accompanied our friend Mrs. —— there one day during the last winter; it was used as a hospital, except the front rooms, which were occupied by General N. (a renegade Virginian) as headquarters. Can it be that any native of Virginia can be untrue to her now? Let General Scott, General Newton, and Captain Fairfax answer! General N. married a Northern wife, which must account for his defection. The ladies drove up to our poor old home, the road winding among stumps of trees, which had been our beautiful oak grove; but one tree was left to show where it had been; they inquired for Mrs. N. She was out, and they determined to walk over the house, that they might see the state of our furniture, etc. They went up-stairs, but, on opening the door of our daughter's room, they found a lady standing at a bed, cutting out work. Mrs. —— closed the door and turned to my chamber; this she found occupied by a family, children running about the room, etc.; these she afterwards found were the families of the surgeons. With no very *amiable* feelings she closed that door and went to another room, which, to her relief, was unoccupied; the old familiar furniture stood in its place, and hanging over the mantel was my husband's portrait. We left it put away with other pictures. The wardrobe, which we had left packed with valuables, stood open and empty; just by it was a large travelling-trunk filled with clothing, which, she supposed, was about to be transferred to the wardrobe. She turned away, and on going down-stairs met Mrs. N., who politely invited her into her (!) parlour. The piano, sofas, etc., were arranged precisely as she had been accustomed to see them arranged, she supposed by our servants, some of whom were still there. This furniture we had left carefully rolled together, and covered, in another room. The weather was cold, and the floor was covered with matting, but no carpet. Mrs. N. apologized, saying that she had lately arrived, and did not know that there was a carpet in the house until, the day before, she was "exploring" the third story, and found in a locked room some very nice ones, which the soldiers were now shaking, and "she should make herself comfortable." She had just before been expressing holy horror at the soldiers in Alexandria having injured and appropriated the property of others. Mrs. —— looked at her wonderingly! Does she consider these carpets her own? Our parlour curtains were upon the passage-table, ready to be put up. She found them, no doubt, while exploring the third story, for there we left them securely wrapped up to protect them from moths. Ah! there are some species of moths (bipeds) from which bars and bolts could not protect them. This we did not anticipate. We thought that Federal officers were gentlemen!

October 1*st*.—Letters from Winchester, giving cheering accounts of our army. It is stationed at Bunker's Hill, twelve miles from Winchester, greatly increased since our recent fights, and in fine spirits. We leave Lynchburg to-morrow, and after spending a few days with our friends at the University, proceed to Richmond and Ashland.

3*d*.—UNIVERSITY OF VIRGINIA.—Arrived here yesterday, and met with a glowing reception from the friends of my youth, Professor and Mrs. Maupin. My sister, Mrs. C., and daughters, staying next door, at Professor Minor's. In less than five minutes we were all together—the first time for many anxious months. They are refugees, and can only hear from home when our army finds it convenient to clear "The Valley" of invaders. One of her sons, dear R., was ordered last winter, by General Jackson, to command a body of soldiers, whom he sent to break the dam in the Potomac, which at that point supplied the Ohio and Chesapeake Canal with water, and which, if effectually broken, would prevent the Yankees using it for transportation—(this dam also worked his mother's mill.) This dangerous project was undertaken most cheerfully, and was most thoroughly effected. It was necessarily done in the night, to elude the vigilance of the Yankees on the Maryland shore. In the dead hour of the winter's night did some of the first gentlemen's sons in the South, who happened to belong to that portion of the army, work up to their waists in water, silently, quietly, until the work was finished; nor were they discovered until day dawned, and revealed them retiring; then shot and shell began to fall among them furiously. One of the brave band fell! Notwithstanding their danger, his companions could not leave him, but lifted him tenderly, and carried him to a place of safety, where he might at least have Christian burial by sympathizing friends. The large old mill, which had for many years sent its hundreds and thousands of barrels of flour to the Baltimore and Georgetown markets, still stood, though its wheels were hushed by the daring act of the night before. It had been used of late by the Yankees for their own purposes. The enemy seemed to have forgotten to destroy it, but the Union men could not allow their old friend and neighbour, though the widow of one whom they had once delighted to honour, to have such valuable property left to her; they immediately communicated to the Yankees that it belonged to the mother of the leader of the party who broke the dam. It was, of course, shelled and burned to the ground, except its old stone walls, which defied their fury; but if it helped the *cause*, the loss of the property did not weigh a feather with the family. This son has just been promoted to the lieutenant-colonelcy of the Second Regiment. His mother expressed her gratification, but added, that he had been so successful as captain of the company which he had raised, drilled, and led out from his own county, that she dreaded a change; besides, in that Second Regiment so many field-officers had fallen, that she had almost a superstitious dread of it. My dear R., his heart is so bound up in the cause, that self-preservation is the last thing that ever occurs to him. Oh! I trust that all evil may be averted from him.

It is sad to see these elegant University buildings, and that beautiful lawn, which I have always seen teeming with life and animation, now almost deserted. Two of the Professors are on the field; the Professors of Medicine and Surgery are surgeons in the neighbouring hospitals, and Dr. B. is Assistant Secretary of War. Others, unfitted by age and other circumstances for the service, are here pursuing their usual avocations with assiduity, but through many difficulties. The students are mere boys, not arrived at military age, or, in a few instances, wounded soldiers unfit for service. The hospitals at Charlottesville are very large, and said to be admirably managed. Every lady at this place, or in town, seems to be actively engaged in making the patients comfortable. The kitchens are presided over by ladies; each lady knows her own day to go to a particular kitchen to see that the food is properly prepared and served to the patients—I mean those who are confined to their beds or wards—the regular "matrons" do every thing else. This rich country supplies milk, butter, fruit, vegetables, fresh meat, etc.; and all kinds of delicacies are prepared by the ladies. Our friends, Dr. and Mrs. M., have sons in the field. The elder, though not of military age at the time, shouldered his musket at the first tap of the drum; he would not be restrained. When I saw him, with his slight figure and boyish look, in his uniform and soldier's trappings, my heart sank within me, as I remembered that 'twas but as yesterday that this child, with his pictured beauty, was the pet of the household. Now he is quite a veteran; has fought on many a field; scorns the idea of danger; prides himself on being a good soldier; never unnecessarily asking for furloughs, and always being present at roll-call. The second son, but sixteen, as his father would not allow him to enlist, has gone as an independent in a cavalry company, merely, he said, for the "summer campaign." Ah! in this "summer campaign," scarcely equalled in the annals of history, what horrors might have come! But he has passed through safely, and his father has recalled him to his college duties. Their mother bears the separation from them, as women of the South invariably do, calmly and quietly, with a humble trust in God, and an unwavering confidence in the justice and righteousness of our cause.

W., HANOVER COUNTY, *October 6th.*—We left the University on the 4th, and finding J. B. N. on the cars, on "sick-leave," I determined to stop with him here to spend a few days with my sisters, while Mr. —— went on to Richmond and Ashland. I do nothing but listen—for my life during the last three months has been quiet, compared with that of others. J. gives most interesting accounts of all he has seen, from the time he came up the Peninsula with the army in May, until he was broken down, and had to leave it, in Maryland, after the battle of Sharpsburg. As a surgeon, his personal danger has not been so great as that of others, but he has passed through scenes the most trying and the most glorious. My sisters and M. give graphic descriptions of troubles while in the enemy's lines, but, with the exception of loss of property, our whole family has passed through the summer unscathed. Many friends have fallen, and one noble young relative, E. B., of Richmond County; and I often ask myself, in deep humility of soul, why we have been thus blessed, for since our dear W. P. and General McIntosh fell, the one in December, the other in March, we have been singularly blessed. Can this last, when we have so many exposed to danger? O, God, spare our sons! Our friend, Dr. T., of this neighbourhood, lost *two* sons at Sharpsburg! Poor old gentleman! it is so sad to see his deeply-furrowed, resigned face.

McClellan's troops were very *well-behaved* while in this neighbourhood; they took nothing but what they considered contraband, such as grain, horses, cattle, sheep, etc., and induced the servants to go off. Many have gone—it is only wonderful that more did not go, considering the inducements that were offered. No houses were burned, and not much fencing. The ladies' rooms were not entered except when a house was searched, which always occurred to unoccupied houses; but I do not think that much was stolen from them. Of course, silver, jewelry, watches, etc., were not put in their way. Our man Nat, and some others who went off, have returned—the reason they assign is, that the Yankees made them work too hard! It is so hard to find both families without carriage horses, and with only some mules which happened to be in Richmond when the place was surrounded. A wagon, drawn by mules, was sent to the depot for us. So many of us are now together that we feel more like quiet enjoyment than we have done for months.

8th.—Mr. N. joined us this morning, and we all gathered

here for the day. It seemed so much like old times, that C. broke a war rule, and gave us pound-cake for supper.

9th.—A very pleasant day at S. H. The ladies all busily knitting for our soldiers—oh, that we could make them comfortable for the winter!

10th.—Bad news! The papers bring an account of the defeat of our army at Corinth. It was commanded by General Van Dorn—the Federals by Rosecranz. They fought Friday, Saturday, and Sunday. The fight said to have been very bloody—great loss on both sides. The first two days we had the advantage, but on Sunday the Yankees "brought up reinforcements," and our men had to retire to Ripley. The Northern papers do not brag quite so much as usual; they say their loss was very great, particularly in officers; from which, I hope it was not quite so bad with us as our first accounts represent. This bringing up of reinforcements, which the Yankees do in such numbers, is ruinous to us. Ah! if we could only fight them on an equal footing, we could expunge them from the face of the earth; but we have to put forth every energy to get rid of them, while they come like the frogs, the flies, the locusts, and the rest of the vermin which infested the land of Egypt, to destroy our peace.

RICHMOND, *October 15th.*—Yesterday morning my sister M., J. W., and myself, drove up from W. to the depot, seven miles, in a wagon, with four mules. It was a charming morning, and we had a delightful ride; took the accommodation cars at twelve and arrived here at two. We drove to the Exchange, and were delighted to find there our dear J. McI. and her little Bessie, on her way to W. to spend the winter. Poor thing, her lot is a sad one! She was excited by seeing us, and was more cheerful than I expected to see her; though she spoke constantly of her husband, and dwelt on her last days with him. She was in Memphis; her little Jemmie was excessively ill; she telegraphed for her husband in Arkansas. He came at once, and determined that it would be better to take the little boy to the house of his aunt in Louisiana, that J. might be with her sister. They took the boat, and after a few hours arrived at Mr. K.'s house. The child grew gradually worse, and was dying, when a telegram came to General McIntosh from General Price, "Come at once—a battle is imminent." He did not hesitate; the next steamer bore him from his dying child and sorrowing wife to the field of battle, Pea Ridge. He wrote to her, immediately on his arrival at camp, the most beautifully resigned letter, full of sorrow for her and for his child, but expressing the most noble, Christian sentiments. Oh, how she treasures it! The lovely boy died the day after his father left him! The mother said, "For a week H. and myself did nothing but decorate my little grave, and I took a melancholy pleasure in it; but darker days came, and I could not go even to that spot." She dreamed, a few nights after little Jemmie's death, of being at Fort Smith, her home before the war; standing on the balcony of her husband's quarters, her attention was arrested by a procession—an officer's funeral. As it passed under the balcony she called to a passer-by : "Whose funeral is that?" "General McIntosh's, madam." She was at once aroused, and ran to her sister's room in agony. She did what she could to comfort her, but the dream haunted her imagination. A few days afterwards she saw a servant ride into the yard, with a note for Mrs. K. Though no circumstance was more common, she at once exclaimed, "It is about my husband." She did not know that the battle had taken place; but it was the fatal telegram. The soldiers carried his body to Fort Smith, and buried it there. To-morrow she returns, with her aunt, to W. She wishes to get to her mother's home in Kentucky, but it is impossible for her to run the blockade with her baby, and there is no other way open to her.

ASHLAND, *October* 19.—We are now snugly fixed in Ashland. Our mess consists of Bishop J. and family, Major J. and wife, Lieutenant J. J. and wife (our daughter,) Mrs. S. and daughter, of Chantilly, Mr. ——, myself, and our two young daughters—a goodly number for a cottage with eight small rooms; but we are very comfortable. All from one neighbourhood, all refugees, and *none able to do better*, we are determined to take every thing cheerfully. Many remarks are jestingly made suggestive of unpleasant collisions among so many families in one house; but we anticipate no evils of that kind; each has her own place, and her own duties to perform; the young married ladies of the establishment are by common consent to have the housekeeping troubles; their husbands are to be masters, with the onerous duties of caterers, treasurers, etc. We old ladies have promised to give our sage advice and experience, whenever it is desired. The girls will assist their sisters, with their nimble fingers, in cases of emergency; and the *clerical* gentlemen are to have their own way, and to do their own work without let or hindrance. All that is *required* of them is, that they shall be household chaplains, and that Mr. —— shall have service every Sunday at the neglected village church. With these discreet regulations, we confidently expect a most pleasant and harmonious establishment. Our young gentlemen are officers stationed in Richmond. Mr. —— and themselves go in every morning in the cars, after an early breakfast, and return to dinner at five o'clock. J. J. and myself have free tickets to go on the cars to attend to our hospital duties. I go in twice a week for that purpose.

A dispatch just received from General Bragg, claiming a signal victory at Perryville; but in consequence of the arrival of large reinforcements to the enemy, he had fallen back to Cumberland Gap. These victories without permanent results do us no good, and so much blood is spilled. There seems to be a revolution going on at the North. Ohio, Indiana, and Pennsylvania have given the Democrats a large majority for Congress! So may it be!

November 4.—A letter from my dear S. at Winchester. She says she is wearing herself down in the Confederate service; but there are so many soldiers in the hospitals that she is too much interested to give up nursing them even for a day. Our army still at Bunker's Hill. We are expecting daily to hear that it is falling back. When they leave the Valley all the sick that can be moved will be brought down to the Richmond hospitals, which are now comparatively empty.

November 7.—The snow falling rapidly—the trees and shrubs in full leaf, and the rose-bushes, in bright bloom, are borne down by the snow. Our poor soldiers! What are they to do to-night, without shelter, and without blankets? Everybody seems to be doing what they can to supply their wants; many persons are having carpets made into soldiers' blankets. My brother J. told me that he had every chamber carpet in the house, except one, converted into coverlets; and this is by no means a singular instance. A number of coverlets, made of the most elegant Brussels carpeting, were sent by Mr. B., of Halifax County, the other day, to our hospital, with a request to Miss T. that blankets should be given from the hospital to the camp, as more easily transported from place to place, and the carpeting retained in the hospital. This was immediately done. The blankets that could be spared from private houses were given last winter. How it gladdens my heart when I see that a vessel has run the blockade, and arrived safely at some Southern port, laden with ammunition, arms, and clothing for the army! The Bishop and J. have just left us, for the council of the Southern Church, to meet at Augusta, Georgia. Oh that their proceedings may be directed by the All-wise Counsellor!

12*th.*—Spent yesterday at the hospital—very few patients. Our army in the Valley falling back; and the two armies said to be very near each other, and much skirmishing. Our dear W. B. N. had his horse shot under him a few days ago. This is fearful. Our country is greatly afflicted, and our dear ones in great peril; but the Lord reigneth—He, who stilleth the raging of the seas, can surely save us from our enemies and all that hate us—to Him do we look for help.

A Baltimore paper of the 11th gives an account of McClellan having been superseded by Burnside. We are delighted at this, for we believe McC. to be the better general of the two. It is said that he was complained of by Halleck for not pushing the army on, and preventing the capture of Harper's Ferry and the 11,000. McC. knew it could not be done, for he had General Jackson to oppose him! His removal was an unexpected blow to the North, producing great excitement. Oh that the parties there would fight among themselves! The Northern papers are insisting upon another "On to Richmond," and hint that

McC. was too slow about every thing. The "Young Napoleon" has fallen from his high estate, and returns to his family at Trenton! The Yankees are surely an absurd race, to say the least of them. At one moment extolling their generals as demi-gods, the next hurling them to the dust—none so poor as to do them reverence. "General McClellan is *believed* to have passed through Washington last night," is the announcement of a late Yankee paper, of the idol of last week.

18*th*.—Another raid upon Fredericksburg; much mischief done! They are preparing for a second evacuation of the town! The number of refugees will be greatly increased, and where are they to go? Poor homeless wanderers, leaving business and the means of support to the mercy of a vindictive soldiery!

Letters from our Valley friends taking leave of us, written some time ago, when the enemy were again closing around them. We are very anxious about them. Their situation is becoming pitiable; every new set of troops help themselves to whatever suits their fancy—stock of all sorts, grain, meat, every thing valuable and portable! Silver, glass, china, has to be buried, and very adroitly, or it is found. Some of the servants are very unfaithful, and let the enemy in to the most private places. There are some honourable exceptions to this last remark. Our relative, Mr. P., has moved below the mountains for security; but he was in the habit, when at home, of intrusting every thing to his house-servant, including his wine and ardent spirits—and it was all kept sacredly—the master knew not where; but on each departure of the enemy every thing would be returned to its accustomed place, in good order.

November 23.—Poor Fredericksburg! The enemy on

the Stafford side of the river in force ; their cannon planted on the hills. Day before yesterday they demanded the surrender of the town, which was declined by General Lee. They then threatened to shell it, at nine o'clock this morning; but it is now night and it has not been done. It is hourly expected, however, and women and children are being hurried off, leaving every thing behind, except what they can get off in bundles, boxes, etc. There is no transportation for heavy articles. The Vandals threw a shell at a train of cars filled with women and children. It burst very near them, but they were providentially protected. A battle is daily expected. In the mean time the sufferings of wandering women and children are very great.

November 25.—Just from the depot. The cars have gone to Richmond, filled with non-combatants from Fredericksburg—ladies, with their children, many of whom know not where to go. They will get to Richmond after dark, and many propose staying in the cars this cold night, and seeking a resting-place to-morrow. The feeling of desolation among them is dreadful. Oh, how I wish that I had even one room to offer! The bombardment has not commenced, but General Lee requested last night that the women and children who had not gone should go without delay. This seems to portend hot work.

29*th.*—Nothing of importance from the army. The people of Fredericksburg suffering greatly from the sudden move. I know a family, accustomed to every luxury at home, now in a damp basement-room in Richmond. The mother and three young daughters cooking, washing, etc.; the father, a merchant, is sick and cut off from business, friends, and every thing else. Another family, consisting of mother and four daughters, in one room, supported by the work of one of the daughters who has an office in the Note-Signing Department. To keep starvation from the house is all that they can do; their supplies in Fredericksburg can't be brought to them—no transportation. I cannot mention the numbers who are similarly situated; the country is filled with them. Country houses, as usual, show a marvellous degree of elasticity. A small house accommodating any number who may apply; pallets spread on the floor; every sofa and couch *sheeted* for visitors of whom they never heard before. If the city people would do more in that way, there would be less suffering. Every cottage in this village is full; and now families are looking with wistful eyes at the ball-room belonging to the hotel, which, it seems to me, might be partitioned off to accommodate several families. The billiard-rooms are taken, it is said, though not yet occupied. But how everybody is to be supported is a difficult question to decide. Luxuries have been given up long ago, by many persons. Coffee is $4 per pound, and good tea from $18 to $20; butter ranges from $1.50 to $2 per pound; lard 50 cents; corn $15 per barrel; and wheat $4.50 per bushel. We can't get a muslin dress for less than $6 or $8 per yard; calico $1.75, etc. This last is no great hardship, for we will all resort to homespun. We are knitting our own stockings, and regret that we did not learn to spin and weave. The North Carolina homespun is exceedingly pretty, and makes a genteel dress; the only difficulty is in the dye; the colours are pretty, but we have not learned the art of *setting* the wood colours; but we are improving in that art too, and when the first dye fades, we can dip them again in the dye.

30*th*.—The Yankee army ravaging Stafford County dreadfully, but they do not cross the river. Burnside, with the "greatest army on the planet," is quietly waiting and watching our little band on the opposite side. Is he afraid to venture over? His "On to Richmond" seems slow.

December 10.—Just returned from a visit of a week to my old friend Mrs. C. Her home in Richmond is the very picture of comfort and hospitality; having wealth, she uses it freely, in these troublous times, for the comfort of others. If all hearts were as *large* as hers, there would be no refugees in garrets and cellars. I was touched by her attention to Mr. ——, whom she had always seen engaged in his duties as a minister of the Gospel. She seemed to think it a kind of sacrilege to see him employed from nine until four o'clock in the duties of his secular office, and "to think of his reverend and hoary head bending over a clerk's desk;" she would say: "Oh, what awful times!" I told her that she must not think of it in that light; that he had been greatly blessed to get the office, which supported us so much better than many other refugees. While talking this way, she would be suiting the action to the word, by rolling up a most delightful chair to the fire, placing a small table before it, ready for some nice refreshment when he returned. It is trying to see him work so hard for our support, in his delicate state of health. The girls and myself are very anxious to get work from Government, signing notes, copying—any thing to assist in supporting ourselves; but we have tried in vain, and I suppose it is right, for there are so many widows and orphans who have a much higher claim to any thing that Government can do for them. We have heard heavy firing to-day. The car passengers report that there is skirmishing near Port Royal.

13*th*.—Our hearts are full of apprehension! A battle is going on at or near Fredericksburg. The Federal army passed over the river on their pontoons night before last. They attempted to throw the bridges over it at three places; from two of these they were driven back with much slaughter; at the third they crossed. Our army was too small to guard all points. The firing is very heavy and incessant. We hear it with terrible distinctness from our portico. God of mercy, be with our people, and drive back the invaders! I ask not for their destruction; but that they may be driven to their own homes, never more to put foot on our soil again; that we may enjoy the sweets of peace and security once more. Our dear boys—now as ever—I commit them into Thy hands!

Night.—Passengers report heavy skirmishing before they left Fredericksburg this morning, but cannonading tells us of bloody work since. A few wounded men were carried by to-night. We went to the depot to see if there were any particular friends among them, but found none.

14*th.*—Firing in the direction of Fredericksburg renewed this morning, but at irregular intervals. Telegraph wires are cut. No news except from passengers in the trains. The cars are not allowed to go to the town, but stop at a point some miles below. They report that every thing goes on well for us, of which we were sure, from the receding sound of the cannon. Praise the Lord, O my soul, and all that is within me praise His holy name! How can we be thankful enough for such men as General Lee, General Jackson, and our glorious army, rank and file!

Nine o'Clock at Night.—A sad, sad train passed down a short time ago, bearing the bodies of Generals Cobb, of Georgia, and Maxcy Gregg, of South Carolina. Two noble spirits have thus passed away from us. Peace to their honoured remains! The gentlemen report many wounded on the train, but not very severely. I fear it has been another bloody Sabbath. The host of wounded will pass to-morrow; we must be up early to prepare to administer to their comfort. The sound of cannon this evening was much more distant, and not constant enough for a regular fight. We are victorious again! Will they now go from our shores forever? We dread to hear of the casualties. Who may not be among the wounded to-morrow?

15*th.*—An exciting day. Trains have been constantly passing with the wounded for the Richmond hospitals. Every lady, every child, every servant in the village, has been engaged preparing and carrying food to the wounded as the cars stopped at the depot—coffee, tea, soup, milk, and every thing we could obtain. With eager eyes and beating hearts we watched for those most dear to us. Sometimes they were so slightly injured as to sit at the windows and answer our questions, which they were eager to do. They exult in the victory. I saw several poor fellows shot through the mouth—they only wanted milk; it was soothing and cooling to their lacerated flesh. One, whom I did not see, had both eyes shot out. But I cannot write of the horrors of this day. Nothing but an undying effort to administer to their comfort could have kept us up. The Bishop was with us all day, and the few gentlemen who remained in the village. When our gentlemen came home at five o'clock they joined us, and were enabled to do what we could not—walk through each car, giving comfort as they went. The gratitude of those who were able to express it was so touching! They said that the ladies were at every depot with refreshments. As the cars would move off, those who were able would *shout* their blessings on the ladies of Virginia: "We will fight, we will protect the ladies of Virginia." Ah, poor fellows, what can the ladies of Virginia ever do to compensate them for all they have done and suffered for us? As a train approached late this evening, we saw comparatively very few sitting up. It was immediately surmised that it contained the desperately wounded—perhaps many of the dead. With eager eyes we watched, and before it stopped I saw Surgeon J. P. Smith (my connection) spring from the platform, and come towards me; my heart stood still. "What is it, Doctor? Tell me at once." "Your nephews, Major B. and Captain C., are both on the train, dangerously wounded." "Mortally?" "We hope not. You will not be allowed to enter the car; come to Richmond to-morrow morning; B. will be there for you to nurse. I shall carry W. C. on the morning cars to his mother at the University. We will do our best for both." In a moment he was gone. Of course I shall go down in the early cars, and devote my life to B. until his parents arrive. I am writing now because I can't sleep, and must be occupied. The cars passed on, and we filled our pitchers, bowls and baskets, to be ready for others. We cannot yield to private feelings now; they may surge up and rush through our hearts until they almost burst them, but they must not overwhelm us. We must do our duty to our country, and it can't be done by nursing our own sorrows.

1863.

January 8th.—On the 16th of December, the day after the last entry in my diary, I went to Richmond, and found B. B. at the house of Mr. P., on Grace Street, surrounded by luxury, and the recipient of unnumbered kindnesses; but so desperately ill ! The surgeons had been up all night in the various hospitals, and, as numerous as they were, they were sadly deficient in numbers that night. The benevolent Dr. Bolton had taken his wife and her sister, who had learned the art of binding up wounds, to his hospital, and all night long they had been engaged most efficiently in their labour of love. Other ladies were engaged in offices of mercy. Women who had been brought up surrounded by the delicacies and refinements of the most polished society, and who would have paled at the sight of blood under other circumstances, were bathing the most frightful gashes, while others were placing the bandages. I found B. suffering the most intense agony, and Mrs. P. agitated and anxious. No surgeon could be obtained for private houses. I sent for one, who was not an army surgeon, to come at once. He sent me word that he had been up all night, and had just retired. Again I sent to implore him to come; in five minutes he was there. He told me at once that his situation was critical in the extreme; the Minié ball had not been extracted; he must die, if not soon relieved. He wanted assistance—another surgeon. To send in pursuit of Dr. Gibson for my brother, then stationed at Camp

JANUARY, 1863.

Winder, and to telegraph for his father, occupied but a few moments; but the surgeons could not come. Hour after hour I sat by him. To *cut* off his bloody clothes, and replace them by fresh ones, and to administer the immense doses of morphine, was all that Mrs. P. and myself could do. At dark, Surgeons G. and B., accompanied by my brother, arrived. They did what they could, but considered the case hopeless. His uncle, General C., arrived, to our great relief. He joined us in nursing him during the night. The cars were constantly coming in. Shouts of victory and wails for the dead were strangely blended. I was glad that I did not hear during that dreadful night that the body of that bright, beautiful boy, that young Christian hero, Randolph Fairfax, had been brought to town. The father, mother, sisters!—can they bear the blighting stroke? The hope, the pride, almost the idol of the family, thus suddenly cut down! We, too, mourn him dead, as we had loved and admired him living. We had watched his boyhood and youth, the gradual development of that brilliant mind and lofty character. His Christian parents are bowed down, but not crushed; their future on earth is clouded; but by faith they see his abundant entrance into the kingdom of heaven, his glorious future, and are comforted. Another young Christian soldier of the same battery was shot down about the same moment—our young friend David Barton, of Winchester. Three months ago his parents buried their oldest son, who fell nobly defending his native town, and now their second has passed into heaven. The Church mourns him as one who was about to devote his life to her sacred cause, but who felt it his duty to defend her against the hosts who are desecrating her hallowed precincts. How many, oh, how many of the young soldiers of the Cross are obliged to take up carnal weapons, to "save from spoil that sacred place!" Poor fellows! their life's blood oozes out in a great cause. But our church!

> "Will she ever lift her head
> From dust, and darkness, and the dead?"

Yes, the time is at hand when she, our Southern Church, shall

> "Put all her beauteous garments on,
> And let her excellence be known.
> Decked in the robes of righteousness,
> The world her glory shall confess.
>
> "No more shall foes unclean invade
> And fill her hallowed walls with dread;
> No more shall hell's insulting host
> Their victory and thy sorrows boast."

The churches of Fredericksburg suffered dreadfully during the bombardment. Some were torn to pieces. Our dear old St. George's suffered very little; but a shell burst through her revered walls, and her steeple was broken by a passing shot. She stands a monument of Vandalism, though still a Christian chapel, from which the Gospel will, I trust, be poured forth for many years, when we shall no longer be surrounded by those who cry, "Raze it, raze it, even to the foundations thereof."

But to return to my patient. After days and nights of watching, I left him improving, and in the hands of his parents. The physicians seem still doubtful of the result, but I am full of hope. The ball, after much difficulty, was extracted, since which time he has gradually improved; but his sufferings have been indescribable. W. B. C. is also slowly convalescing. One night while sitting up with B., together with a surgeon and General C., when we had not been able to raise him up for two days, we were startled by his springing from the bed in agony, and running to the fire; the surgeon (his uncle) gently put his arm around him and laid him on the couch. I hastened to the bed to make it comfortable; but it was so large that I could not raise it up; at last I called out, "General, help me to make up this bed; come quickly!" In an instant the large feather bed was grasped by him with strength and skill, turned over and beaten thoroughly, the mattrass replaced; then to help me to spread the sheets, smooth the pillows, etc., was the work of a moment. The patient was replaced in bed and soothed to sleep. Not till then did I remember that my companion in making the bed was one who but a short time before had led his brigade in the hottest of the fight, and would, perhaps, do it again and again. I complimented him on his versatility of talent, and a pleasant laugh ensued. During the Christmas holidays, while most anxious about our wounded, a letter from Kentucky reached us, announcing the death of my lovely niece, Mrs. K. As soon as her home on the Mississippi became surrounded by the enemy, she was obliged to leave it. She then joined her husband, who is on General Breckinridge's staff, and stationed near Knoxville. As her health was very delicate, she determined, as soon as General B. was ordered off, to attempt to get to her mother in Kentucky; her husband placed her in the care of an elderly physician and friend, who accompanied her in a carriage across the mountains, as the public conveyances between those hostile regions are, of course, discontinued. Before she had travelled many days she was compelled to stop at a small house on the roadside, and there, with much kindness from the hostess, and from her travelling companion, but none of the comforts to which she had been accustomed, she suffered intensely for many days, and then attempted to go on. She reached Georgetown, Kentucky, which was her summer home; her mother was telegraphed for, and reached her just three days before she breathed her last. Dear H.! another victim of the war; as much so as was her brother, who received his mortal wound at Dranesville, or her brother-in-law, who was shot through the heart at Pea Ridge. Her poor mother deemed it a blessed privilege to be able to be with her in her dying hour; a comfort which she did not experience after her long trip to see her son. I fear she will sink under accumulated misfortunes; cut off as she is from all that makes life bearable under such circumstances. During the campaign of last summer around Richmond, she describes her feelings as being anxious and nervous beyond expression. She heard nothing but threats against us, and braggadocio, until she believed that we must be crushed; the many Southerners around her could not express their feelings except in subdued whispers. The Cincinnati and Covington papers expressed their confidence of success. Each day she would go to Cincinnati to hear the news, and come back depressed; but on the sixth day after the battles commenced, as she took her usual morning walk, she observed that the crowd around the telegraph office was more quiet than usual. As she approached, "curses, not loud, but deep," reached her ear. Hope dawned upon her subdued spirit. "Is there any thing the matter?" she asked, meekly, of the first gentlemanly-looking man she saw. "The matter!" he exclaimed. "Oh! madam, we are defeated. McClellan is retreating down the river towards Harrison's Landing. I don't know *where* that is, but we are shamefully beaten." She did not allow herself to speak, but rapidly wended her way home, her face bathed in tears of thankfulness, and singing the *Gloria in Excelsis*.

Several days ago General Bragg reported a victory at Murfreesboro', Tennessee. There was certainly a victory on the first day, as 4,000 prisoners were secured, with thirty-one pieces of cannon, and sent to Chattanooga. On the third day the enemy were reinforced, and our army was obliged to fall back. A friend remarked that the Bragg victories never seem to do us much good. The truth is, the Western Yankees fight much better than the Eastern, and outnumber us fearfully. They claim the victory, but acknowledge the loss of 30,000 men. It must have been a most severe conflict. At Vicksburg they have made another attack, and been repulsed; and yet another misfortune for them was the sinking of their brag gun-boat *Monitor*. It went down off Cape Hatteras. In Philadelphia the negroes and Abolitionists celebrated the 1st of January with mad demonstrations of delight, as the day on which Lincoln's proclamation to abolish slavery would take effect. In Norfolk the negroes were deluded by the Abolitionists into great excitement. Speeches were made, encouraging them to take up arms against their masters! Hale has offered a resolution in the Northern Congress to raise two hundred regiments of negroes! The valiant knight, I hope, will be generalissimo of the corps. He is worthy of the position!

16*th*.—Just returned from Richmond. B's situation still precarious, and I am obliged to stay with him a great deal. I see a number of officers and other gentlemen in his room; they seem to be in fine spirits about the country. Our President's Message has been enthusiastically received. It is a noble production, worthy of its great author. I think the European public must contrast it with the Northern "Message" most favourably to us.

Several friends have just arrived from Yankeedom in a vessel fitted out by the Northern Government to receive the exchanged prisoners. About six hundred women and children were allowed to come in it from Washington. They submitted to the most humiliating search, before they left the wharf, from men and women. The former searched their trunks, the latter their persons. Mrs. Hale, of California, and the wife of Senator Harlan, of Iowa, *presided* at the search. Dignified and lady-like! One young friend of mine was bringing five pairs of shoes to her sisters; they were taken as contraband. A friend brought me one pound of tea; this she was allowed to do; but woe betide the bundle of more than one pound! Some trunks were sadly pillaged if they happened to contain more clothes than the Northern Government thought proper for a rebel to possess. No material was allowed to come which was not made into garments. My friend brought me some pocket-handkerchiefs and stockings, scattered in various parts of the trunk, so as not to seem to have too many. She brought her son, who is in our service, a suit of clothes made into a cloak which she wore. Many a gray cloth travelling-dress and petticoat which was on that boat is now in camp, decking the person of a Confederate soldier; having undergone a transformation into jackets and pants. The searchers found it a troublesome business; not the least assistance did they get from the searched. The ladies would take their seats, and put out first one foot and then the other to the Yankee woman, who would pull off the shoes and stockings—not a pin would they remove, not a string untie. The fare of the boat was miserable, served in tin plates and cups; but, as it was served gratis, the "*Rebs*" had no right to complain, and they reached Dixie in safety, bringing many a contraband article, notwithstanding the search.

The hated vessel "Harriet Lane," which, like the *Pawnee*, seemed to be ubiquitous, has been captured near Galveston by General Magruder. Its commander, Captain Wainwright, and others were killed. Captain W. was most intimately connected with our relatives in the "Valley," having married in Clarke County. He wrote to them in the beginning of the war, to give them warning of their danger. He spoke of the power of the North and the impotency of the South. He thought that we would be subjugated in a few months—little did he anticipate his own fate, or that of his devoted fleet.

19*th*.—Colonel Bradley Johnson has been with us for some days. He is nephew to Bishop J., and as bright and agreeable in private as he is bold and dashing in the field. Our little cottage has many pleasant visitors, and I think we are as cheerful a family circle as the Confederacy can boast. We are very much occupied by our Sunday-schools—*white* in the morning, and coloured in the afternoon. In the week we are often busy, like the "cotter's" wife, in making "auld claes look amaist as weel as new." "*New claes*" are not attainable at present high prices; we are therefore likely to become very ingenious in fixing up "auld anes." My friend who lately arrived from Washington looked on very wonderingly when she saw us all ready for church. "Why, how genteel you look!" at last broke from her; "I had no idea of it. We all thought of you as suffering in every respect." I told her that the Southern women were as ingenious as the men were brave; and while we cared little for dress during such anxious times, yet when our husbands and sons returned from the field we preferred that their homes should be made attractive, and that they should not be pained by the indifferent appearance of their wives, sisters, and mothers. She was still more surprised by the neatly fitting, prettily made dresses of Southern manufacture. "Are they of Virginia cloth?" she asked. No, poor old Virginia has no time or opportunity for improving her manufactures, while almost her whole surface is scarred and furrowed by armies; but Georgia and North Carolina are doing much towards clothing the first ladies in the land. Sister M. has just improved my wardrobe by sending me a black alpaca dress, bought from a Potomac blockade-runner. We, ever and anon, are assisted in that way: sometimes a pound of tea, sometimes a pair of gloves, is snugged away in a friendly pocket, and after many dangers reaches us, and meets a hearty welcome; and what is more important still, medicine is brought in the same way, having escaped the eagle eyes of Federal watchers. A lady in Richmond said laughingly to a friend who was about to make an effort to go to Baltimore, "Bring me a pound of tea and a hoop-skirt;" and after a very short absence he appeared before her, with the tea in one hand and the skirt in the other. It is pleasant to see how cheerfully the girls fall into habits of economy, and occupy themselves in a way of which we never dreamed before.

January 23.—The gentlemen had their friend, General Lovell, to spend last night with them. I was sorry not to be able to see more of him, as I was too sick to remain in the parlour, having been occupied night and day with my dear B., who has been again very dangerously ill, with erysipelas in his wound. We are troubled about our son J., who has just been ordered to North Carolina; but we have no right to complain, as his health is good, and his position has hitherto been very pleasant.

31st.—We are in *statu quo*, and our armies quiet. The Northern army seems to be in commotion. Burnside has resigned, and "fighting Joe Hooker" has been put in his place. Sumner and Franklin have also resigned their "grand divisions." *Pourquoi?* Won't the men advance? Perhaps the Stafford mud has been more than a match for them. Burnside had issued but a few days ago an address to his men, saying they were about to "strike the final blow at the rebellion." All was in readiness, and the "Grand Army" moved forward; just then the "rain descended and the floods came," and, attempting to cross the Rappahannock ten miles above Fredericksburg, ambulances, wagons, big guns and all stuck in the mud; the order, "To your tents, O Israel," had to be given, and the "rebellion" still flourishes.

February 11.—For ten days past I have been at the bedside of my patient in Richmond. The physicians for the third time despaired of his life; by the goodness of God he is again convalescent. Our wounded are suffering excessively for tonics, and I believe that many valuable lives are lost for the want of a few bottles of porter. One day a surgeon standing by B's bedside said to me, "He must sink in a day or two; he retains neither brandy nor milk, and his life is passing away for want of nourishment." In a state bordering on despair, I went out to houses and stores, to beg or buy porter; not a bottle was in town. At last a lady told me that a blockade-runner, it was said, had brought ale, and it was at the medical purveyor's. I went back to Mr. P's instantly, and told my brother (B's father) of the rumour. To get a surgeon's requisition and go off to the purveyor's was the work of a moment. In a short time he returned, with a dozen bottles of India ale. It was administered cautiously at first, and when I found that he retained it, and feebly asked for more, tears of joy and thankfulness ran down my cheeks. " Give him as much as he will take during the night," was the order of the physician. The order was obeyed, and life seemed to return to his system; in twenty-four hours he had drank *four bottles;* he began then to take milk, and I never witnessed any thing like the reanimation of the whole man, physical and mental. The hospitals are now supplied with this life-giving beverage, and all have it who "absolutely require it," though great care is taken of it, for the supply is limited. Oh, how cruel it is that the Northern Government should have made medicines, and the necessaries of life to the sick and wounded, contraband articles !

12*th.*—We have lately had a little fight on the Blackwater. The Yankees intended to take General Pryor by surprise, but he was wide awake, and ready to receive and repulse them handsomely. The late democratic majorities at the North seem to have given the people courage; denunciations are heard against the despotism of the Government. Gold has gone up to 160, causing a ferment. Oh that they would " bite and devour one another !" Since I have been so occupied in nursing B. I have not had as much time for the hospital, but go when I can. A few days ago, on going there in the morning, I found Miss T. deeply interested about a soldier who had been brought in the evening before. The gentleman who accompanied him had found him in the pouring rain, wandering about the streets, shivering with cold, and utterly unable to tell his own story. The attendants quickly replaced his wet clothes by dry ones, and put him into a warm bed ; rubbing and warm applications were resorted to, and a surgeon administered restoratives. Physical reaction took place, but no clearing of the mind. When soothingly asked about his name, his home, and his regiment, he would look up and speak incoherently, but no light was thrown on the questions. He was watched and nursed during the night. His pulse gradually weakened, and by the break of day he was no more. That morning I found the nameless, homeless boy on the couch which I had so often seen similarly occupied. The wind had raised one corner of the sheet, and as I approached to replace it a face was revealed which riveted me to the spot. It was young, almost boyish, and though disease and death had made sad ravages, they could not conceal delicately-carved features, a high, fair forehead, and light hair, which had been well cared for. He looked like one of gentle blood. All seemed so mysterious, my heart yearned over him, and my tears fell fast. Father, mother, sisters, brothers—where are they ? The morning papers represented the case, and called for information. He may have escaped in delirium from one of the hospitals ! That evening, kind, gentle hands placed him in his soldier's coffin, and he had Christian burial at "Hollywood," with the lonely word "Stranger" carved upon the headboard. We trust that the sad story in the papers may meet some eye of which he had once been the light, for he was surely "Somebody's Darling." Sweet lines have been written, of which this sad case reminds me :—

"Into a ward of the whitewashed walls,
    Where the dead and dying lay—

Wounded by bayonets, shells, and balls—
    Somebody's darling was borne one day :—
Somebody's darling! so young and brave,
    Wearing yet on his sweet, pale face—
Soon to be hid in the dust of the grave—
    The lingering light of his boyhood's grace.

"Matted and damp are the curls of gold,
    Kissing the snow of that fair young brow;
Pale are the lips of delicate mould—
    Somebody's darling is dying now.
Back from the beautiful, blue-veined brow,
    Brush his wandering waves of gold;
Cross his hand on his bosom now—
    Somebody's darling is still and cold.

"Kiss him once for somebody's sake;
    Murmur a prayer soft and low;
One bright curl from its fair mates take,—
    They were somebody's pride, you know
Somebody's hand hath rested there;
    Was it a mother's, soft and white?
Or have the lips of a sister fair
    Been baptized in their waves of light?

"God knows best! He has somebody's love·
    Somebody's heart enshrined him there;
Somebody wafted his name above,
    Night and morn, on wings of prayer.
Somebody wept when he marched away,
    Looking so handsome, brave, and grand!
Somebody's kiss on his forehead lay;
    Somebody clung to his parting hand.

"Somebody's watching and waiting for him,
    Yearning to hold him again to her heart;
And there he lies with his blue eyes dim,
    And the smiling, childlike lips apart.

> Tenderly bury the fair young dead,
>   Pausing to drop on his grave a tear;
> Carve on a wooden slab o'er his head—
>   'Somebody's darling slumbers here!'"

13*th.*—Still in Richmond, nursing B. He was wounded this day two months ago; but such fluctuations I have never witnessed in any case. We have more hope now, because his appetite has returned. I sent over to market this morning for partridges and eggs for him, and gave 75 cents apiece for the one, and $1.50 per dozen for the other. I am afraid that our currency is rapidly depreciating, and the time is approaching when, as in the old Revolution, a man had to give $300 for a breakfast. Mrs. P. came in to scold me for my breach of good manners in *buying* any thing in her house. I confessed myself ashamed of it, but that I would be more ashamed to disturb her whenever B's capricious appetite required indulgence. I have never seen more overflowing hospitality than that of this household. Many sick men are constantly refreshed from the bounties of the table; and supplies from the larder seem to be at the command of every soldier. One of the elegant parlours is still in the occupancy of the wounded soldier brought here with B.; his wound was considered slight, but he suffers excessively from nervous debility, and is still unfit for service. I did feel uncomfortable that we should give Mrs. P. so much trouble, until she told me that, having no sons old enough for service, and her husband being unable to serve the country personally, except as a member of the "Ambulance Committee," they had determined that their house should be at the service of the soldiers. Last summer, during the campaigns around Richmond, they took in seven wounded men, some of whom had to be nursed for months.

20th.—A letter this morning from Sister M., who has returned to her home on the Potomac. She gives me an account of many "excitements" to which they are exposed from the landing of Yankees, and the pleasure they take in receiving and entertaining Marylanders coming over to join us, and others who go to their house to "bide their time" for running the blockade to Maryland. "Among others," she says, "we have lately been honoured by two sprigs of English nobility, the Marquis of Hastings and Colonel Leslie of the British army. The Marquis is the future Duke of Devonshire. They only spent the evening, as they hoped to cross the river last night. They are gentlemanly men, having no airs about them; but 'my lord' is excessively awkward. They don't compare at all in ease or elegance of manner or appearance with our educated men of the South. They wore travelling suits of very coarse cloth—a kind of pea-jacket, such as sailors wear. As it was raining, the boots of the Colonel were worn over his pantaloons. They were extremely tall, and might have passed very well at first sight for Western wagoners! We have also had the Rev. Dr. Joseph Wilmer with us for some days. He is going to Europe, and came down with a party, the Englishmen included, to cross the river. The Doctor is too High Church for my views, but exceedingly agreeable, and an elegant gentleman. They crossed safely last night, and are now *en route* for New York, where they hope to take the steamer on Weduesday next." She does not finish her letter until the 17th, and gives an account of a pillaging raid through her neighbourhood. She writes on the 14th: "There had been rumours of Yankees for some days, and this morning they came in good earnest. They took our carriage horses, and two others, in spite of our remonstrances; demanded the key of the meat-house, and took as many of our sugar-cured hams as they wanted; to-night they broke open our barn, and fed their horses, and are even now prowling around the servants' houses in search of eggs, poultry, etc. They have taken many prisoners, and all the horses they could find in the neighbourhood. We have a rumour that an infantry force is coming up from Heathsville, where they landed yesterday. We now see many camp-fires, and what we suppose to be a picket-fire, between this and the Rectory. My daughters, children and myself are here alone; not a man in the house. Our trust is in God. We pray not only that we may be delivered from our enemies, but from the fear of them. It requires much firmness to face the creatures, and to talk with them. The Eighth New York is the regiment with which we are cursed. The officers are *polite* enough, but are determined to steal every thing they fancy." On the 15th she says: "This morning our enemies took their departure, promising to return in a few days. They visited our stable again, and took our little mare 'Virginia.' The servants behaved remarkably well, though they were told again and again that they were free." Again, on the 17th, she writes: "I saw many of the neighbours yesterday, and compared losses. We are all pretty severely pillaged. The infantry regiment from Heathsville took their departure on Sunday morning, in the '*Alice Price*,' stopped at Bushfield, and about twelve took breakfast there. Mr. B. says the vessel was loaded with plunder, and many negroes. They took off all the negroes from the Mantua estate; broke up the beautiful furniture at Summerfield, and committed depredations everywhere. A company of them came up as far as Cary's on Saturday evening, and met the cavalry. They stole horses enough on their way to be pretty well mounted. They will blazon forth this invasion of a country of women, children, and old men, as a brilliant feat! Now that they are gone, we breathe more freely, but for how long a time?" We feel very anxious about our friends between the Rappahannock and Potomac, both rivers filled with belligerent vessels; but they have not yet suffered at all, when compared with the lower Valley, the Piedmont country, poor old Fairfax, the country around Richmond, the Peninsula; and, indeed, wherever the Yankee army has been, it has left desolation behind it, and there is utter terror and dismay during its presence.

ASHLAND, *February* 22*d.*—A very deep snow this morning. The cars are moving slowly on the road, with two engines attached to each train. Our gentlemen could not go to Richmond to-day. Washington's birthday is forgotten, or only remembered with a sigh by his own Virginia. Had he been gifted with prophetic vision, in addition to his great powers, we would still remain a British colony; or, at least, he would never have fought and suffered for seven long years to have placed his native South in a situation far more humiliating than the colonies ever were towards the mother-country; or to have embroiled her in a war compared to which the old Revolution was but child's play.

26*th*.—In the city again yesterday. B. improving. The morning papers report firing upon Vicksburg. Several steamers have arrived lately, laden for the Confederacy. Blockade-running seems to be attended with less danger than it was, though we have lately lost a most valuable cargo by the capture of the "Princess Royal." The "Alabama" continues to perform the most miraculous feats, and the "Florida" seems disposed to rival her in brilliant exploits. They "walk the water," capturing every thing in their way, and know no fear, though many vessels are in pursuit. I am grieved to hear that my dear little J. P. has been ordered to Charleston. While he was on James River, I felt that I could be with him if he were wounded; but he is in God's hands :

> "Be still, my heart; these anxious cares
> To thee are burdens, thorns, and snares."

The papers full of the probable, or rather *hoped for*, intervention of France. The proposition of the Emperor, contained in a letter from the Minister to Seward, and his artful, wily, Seward-like reply, are in a late paper. We pause to see what will be the next step of the Emperor. Oh that he would recognize us, and let fanatical England pursue her own cold, selfish course!

28*th*.—To-day we are all at home. It is amusing to see, as each lady walks into the parlour, where we gather around the centre-table at night, that her work-basket is filled with *clothes to be repaired*. We are a cheerful set, notwithstanding. Our winding "*reel*," too, is generally busy. L. has a very nice one, which is always in the hands of one or the other, preparing cotton for knitting. We are equal to German women in that line. Howitt says that throughout Germany, wherever you see a woman, you see the "everlasting knitting;" so it is with Confederate women. I only wish it was "everlasting," for our poor soldiers in their long marches strew the way with their wornout socks.

March 5th.—Spent last night in Richmond with my friend Mrs. R. This morning we attended Dr. Minnegerode's prayer-meeting at seven o'clock. It is a blessed privilege enjoyed by people in town, that of attending religious services so often, particularly those social prayer-meetings, now that we feel our dependence on an Almighty arm, and our need of prayer more than we ever did in our lives. The President has issued another proclamation, setting aside the 27th of this month for fasting and prayer.

Again I have applied for an office, which seems necessary to the support of the family. If I fail, I shall try to think that it is not right for me to have it. Mr. ——'s salary is not much more than is necessary to pay our share of the expenses of the mess. Several of us are engaged in making soap, and selling it, to buy things which seem essential to our wardrobes. A lady who has been perfectly independent in her circumstances, finding it necessary to do something of the kind for her support, has been very successful in making pickles and catsups for the restaurants. Another, like Mrs. Primrose, rejoices in her success in making gooseberry wine, which sparkles like champagne, and is the best domestic wine I ever drank ; this is designed for the highest bidder. The exercise of this kind of industry works two ways : it supplies our wants, and gives comfort to the public. Almost every girl plaits her own hat, and that of her father, brother, and lover, if she has the bad taste to have a lover out of the army, which no girl of spirit would do unless he is incapacitated by sickness or wounds. But these hats are beautifully plaited of rye straw, and the ladies' hats are shaped so becomingly, that though a Parisian milliner might pronounce them old-fashioned, and laugh them to scorn, yet our Confederate girls look fresh and lovely in them, with their gentle countenances and bright, enthusiastic eyes; and what do we care for Parisian style, particularly as it would have to come to us through Yankee-land? The blockade has taught our people their own resources; but I often think that when the great veil is removed, and reveals us to the world, we will, in some respects, be a precious set of antiques. The ladies occasionally contrive to get a fashion-plate "direct from France," by way of Nassau; yet when one of them, with a laudable zeal for enhancing her own charms by embellishments from abroad, sends gold to Nassau, which should be kept in our own country, and receives in return a trunk of foreign fabrics, she will appear on the street immediately afterwards in a costume which seems to us so new and fantastic, that we are forced to the opinion that we would appear to the world ludicrously *passé*. A gentleman, lately from Columbia, tells me that the South Carolina girls pride themselves on their palmetto hats; and the belle of large fortune, who used to think no bonnet presentable but one made by the first New York or Parisian milliner, now glories in her palmetto. The balmoral, too, the product of our own spinning-wheel and loom, would show well with the prettiest imported ones. I have seen several, which the young wearers told me were "dyed in the wool, spun, and woven by the *poor* of our own neighbourhood. The dye-stuffs were from our own woods." These are little things, but, proving the independence of our people, I rejoice in them. The croakers are now indulging themselves with fears of famine; they elongate their gloomy visages, and tell us, in sad accents, that butter was $3.50 per pound in market this morning, and other things in proportion. I am sorry to say that it is true, and that it is evident we must have scarcity, particularly of such things as butter, for the cattle must go to feed the army. The soldiers must be fed; our gardens will give us vegetables; God will give us the fruits of the earth abundantly, as in days past, and if we are reduced, which I do not anticipate, to bread and water, we will bear it cheerfully, thank God, and take courage:

"Brought safely by his hand thus far,
Why should we now give place to fear?"

The *poor*, being well supplied with Government work, are better off than usual.

All quiet in the army. This may portend a storm. Several pieces of cannon passed this morning on the Fredericksburg train. Raids still continue in the Northern Neck, keeping us very uneasy about our friends there.

March 15*th*.—Weather dark and cloudy. We had a good congregation in our little church. Mr. —— read the service. The Bishop preached on "Repentance." Richmond was greatly shocked on Friday, by the blowing up of the Laboratory, in which women, girls, and boys were employed making cartridges; ten women and girls were killed on the spot, and many more will probably die from their wounds. May God have mercy upon them! Our dear friend Mrs. S. has just heard of the burning of her house, at beautiful Chantilly. The Yankee officers had occupied it as head-quarters, and on leaving it, set fire to every house on the land, except the overseer's house and one of the servants' quarters. Such ruthless Vandalism do they commit wherever they go! I expressed my surprise to Mrs. S. that she was enabled to bear it so well. She calmly replied, "God has spared my sons through so many battles, that I should be ungrateful indeed to complain of any thing else." This lovely spot has been her home from her marriage, and the native place of her many children, and when

I remember it as I saw it two years ago, I feel that it is too hard for her to be thus deprived of it. An officer (Federal) quartered there last winter, describing it in a letter to the New York *Herald,* says the furniture had been " removed," except a large old-fashioned sideboard; he had been indulging his curiosity by reading the many private letters which he found scattered about the house; some of which, he says, were written by General Washington, " with whom the family seems to have been connected." In this last surmise he was right, and he must have read letters from which he derived the idea, or he may have gotten it from the servants, who are always proud of the aristocracy of their owners; but not a letter written by General Washington did he see, for Mrs. S. was always careful of them, and brought them away with her; they are now in this house. The officer took occasion to sneer at the pride and aristocracy of Virginia, and winds up by asserting that " this establishment belongs to the mother of General J. E. B. Stuart," to whom she is not at all related.

March 18*th.*—This evening, when leaving Richmond, we were most unexpectedly joined at the cars by our friend N. P. Dear child, we had not seen her since her father's family left their home, some weeks before we left ours. Well do I remember the feeling of misery which I experienced at seeing them go off. We have all suffered since that time, but none of us can compare with them in that respect. They are living in desolated Fauquier. There they have buried their lovely little Kate, and N's principal object in visiting this country now is to see the grave of her eldest brother, a victim of the war, and to see the lady at whose house he died, and who nursed him as though he had been her son We enjoy her society exceedingly, and linger long over our reminiscences of the past, and of home scenes. Sadly enough do we talk, but there is a fascination about it which is irresistible. It seems marvellous that, in the chances and changes of war, so many of our "Seminary Hill" circle should be collected within the walls of this little cottage. Mrs. P. has once been, by permission of the military authorities, to visit her old home; she found it *used as a bakery* for the troops stationed around it. After passing through rooms which she scarcely recognized, and seeing furniture, once her own, broken and defaced, she found her way to her chamber. There was her wardrobe in its old place; she had left it packed with house-linen and other valuables, and advanced towards it, key in hand, for the purpose of removing some of its contents, when she was roughly told by a woman sitting in the room not to open that wardrobe, "there was nothing in it that belonged to her." Oh, how my blood would have boiled, and how I should have opened it, unless put aside by force of arms, just to have peeped in to see if my own things were still there, and to take them if they were! But Mrs. P., more prudently, used a gentle remonstrance, and finding that nothing could be effected, and that rudeness would ensue, quietly left the room. We bide our time.

19*th*.—My birthday. While in Richmond, this morning, brother J. and myself called on some friends, among others our relative Mrs. H., who has lately been celebrating the marriage of her only son, and took us into the next room for a lunch of wine and fruit-cake. We had never, during two years, thought of fruit-cake, and found it delightful. The fruit consisted of dried currants and cherries from her garden, at her elegant James River home, Brandon, now necessarily deserted. She fortunately was enabled to bring her furniture to Richmond, and is the only refugee that I know who is surrounded by home comforts.

March 20*th*.—Severe snow-storm. This will retard the attack upon Fredericksburg, if the enemy designed it. We spent the morning in the parlour. N. P. read aloud the old-fashioned but amusing novel, " Pride and Prejudice," in very spirited style. The event of the day was the arrival from Alexandria of a bundle, filled with useful articles for a lady, who, not wanting them all herself, allowed us to help ourselves at the price which they cost her in Alexandria. It was amusing to see with what avidity the girls seized on a calico dress at only seventy-five cents per yard (Confederate money); every thing was in such demand, that I only got a tooth-brush, at one dollar; they are two dollars and fifty cents in Richmond.

27*th*.—To-day was set apart by the President as a day of fasting and prayer. Some of us went to Richmond, and joined in the services at St. Paul's. The churches were all crowded with worshippers, who, I trust, felt their dependence on God in this great struggle. The President was in church, and, I believe, most of the dignitaries. One of the ladies of the hospital, seeing this morning two rough-looking convalescent soldiers sitting by the stove, exhorted them to observe the day by prayer and fasting. They seemed to have no objection to the praying, but could not see the " good of fasting," and doubted very much whether " Marse Jeff fasted all day himself—do you reckon he does ?" The lady laughingly told him that she would inquire and let them know, but she *reckoned* that such was his habit. In the course of the morning she met with Mrs. Davis, and told her the anecdote. " Tell them from me," said Mrs. D., " that Mr. Davis never eats on fast-day, and that as soon as he returns from church he shuts himself up in his study, and is never interrupted during the day, except on public business." Of course this was soon given as an example, not only to the two convalescents, but to the whole hospital.

March 28*th*.—A letter from ——. She tells me that W. B. N. and E. C. both passed through the fierce fight at Kelly's Ford uninjured. How can we be grateful enough for all our mercies? Letters also from B., by underground railroad. That sweet child and her whole family surrounded and roughly treated by the Yankees; and so it will be as long as Millroy is allowed to be the scourge of the Valley.

Sunday Night.—Very sweet services in our little church to-day. The subject of the sermon was, "Woe to them who are at ease in Zion." Mr. —— found a note on the pulpit from a Georgia soldier, asking the prayers of the congregation for himself and his family at home. The extemporaneous prayer after the sermon, offered for him, was most earnestly and tearfully joined in by all.

April 1*st*.—"All quiet on the Rappahannock to-night," and we are almost as still as in days gone by. The girls got up a little merriment this morning by their "April fools." The remainder of the day passed in our usual way.

April 2*d*.—We were shocked when the gentlemen returned, to hear of the riot which occurred in Richmond to-day. A mob, principally of women, appeared in the streets, attacking the stores. Their object seemed to be to get any thing they could; dry-goods, shoes, brooms, meat, glassware, jewelry, were caught up by them. The military was called out—the Governor dispersed them from one part of the town, telling them that unless they disappeared in five minutes, the soldiers should fire among them. This he said, holding his watch in his hand. Mr. Munford, the President of the Young Men's Christian Association, quieted them on another street by inviting them to come to the rooms of the Association, and their wants should be supplied; many followed him—I suppose those who were really in want. Others there were, of the very worst class of women, and a great many who were not in want at all, which they proved by only supplying themselves with jewelry and other finery. The President was out speaking to them, and trying to secure order. The Mayor made them a speech, and seemed to influence them, but I dare say that the bayonets of the soldiers produced the most decided effect. It is the first time that such a thing has ever darkened the annals of Richmond. God grant it may be the last. I fear that the poor suffer very much; meal was selling to-day at $16 per bushel. It has been bought up by speculators. Oh that these hard-hearted creatures could be made to suffer! Strange that men with human hearts can, in these dreadful times, thus grind the poor.

Good-Friday.—The Bishop preached for us to-day most delightfully from the text: "Jesus Christ and Him crucified." In the afternoon Mrs. S. had the inexpressible pleasure of welcoming her son, Mr. A. S., from the Western Army. He thinks that Vicksburg and Port Hudson are both impregnable. God grant that it may be so!

April 4th.—Spent to-day in Richmond, attending on the wounded. The mob of women came out yesterday, but in smaller numbers, and was easily put down by military authority. To-day a repetition was expected, and the cannon was in place to rake the streets, but they thought discretion the better part of valour, and staid at home. The riot, it is ascertained, was not caused by want; it was no doubt set on foot by Union influences. I saw the Rev. Mr. Peterkin, who is perhaps more thoroughly acquainted with the state of the poor than any man in the city. He says that they are admirably attended to. Large sums of money are put in the hands of the clergy for their benefit; this money is disbursed by ladies, whose duty and pleasure it is to relieve the suffering. One gentleman gave as much as $5,000 last winter. Besides this, the industrious poor are supplied with work by the Government, and regularly paid for it.

The Bishop set off this morning for his spring visitations, which are becoming, alas! very circumscribed—so much of the diocese is in the hands of the enemy.

Mr. C., of Georgetown, Captain Norton, of New Orleans, and Mr. A. S. are with us. The first of these gentlemen ran the blockade from his home some months ago, finding he was to be arrested for opinion's sake, and now holds a Confederate office in Richmond. He very rarely hears from his wife and children. Flag-of-truce letters seldom reach their destination, and when they do, letters of one page, written to be inspected by strangers, are very unsatisfactory. An occasional "underground" communication comes to him, like water in a thirsty land. I often look at his calm countenance with sympathy, knowing that there must be deep sorrow and anxiety underneath.

9th.—On Monday saw B. removed from the bed of suffering, on which he had been lying four months, put on a stretcher, and carried to the canal-boat. His countenance was full of joyful anticipations of home. His arm, which should have been amputated on the field, hangs lifeless by his side; and yet he expects to return to his post, that of Major of artillery, as soon as he is strong enough. Poor fellow, it is well for him to amuse himself with the idea, but he will never again be fit for any duty but that at a post. He has been the recipient of kindnesses from Mr. and Mrs. P. and others, which could only be experienced in this dear, warm-hearted Southern country of ours, and which he can never forget to his dying day. That night I spent with my kind friend Mrs. R., and next morning made such purchases as were absolutely necessary for our comfort. I gave for bleached cotton, which used to be sold for $12\frac{1}{2}$ cents, $3.50 per yard; towelling $1.25 per yard; cotton 50 cents a spool, etc. Nothing reconciled me to this extravagance but that I had sold my soap for $1 per pound!!

The enemy has retired from Vicksburg, their canal having proved a failure. Where they will reappear nobody knows. Another ineffectual attempt upon Charleston on the 7th and 8th.

Sunday Night, April 12th.—Mr. —— administered the Sacrament here to-day, the first time it was ever administered by Episcopalians in Ashland. There were fifty communicants, the large majority of them refugees. Our society here has been greatly improved by the refugees from Fredericksburg. The hotel is full. The G's have rented the last vacant cottage, and are boarding others. The R's, with their three pretty young daughters and son, occupy the ball-room of the hotel. The dressing-room makes a pleasant chamber, and the long dancing-room, partitioned off into rooms by the suspension of their handsome crimson damask curtains, is very pretty, and, for spring and summer use, makes very comfortable apartments. They saved some of their furniture, and are nicely fixed for refugees, who must do the best they can, and be thankful it is no worse. The C's seem very happy in the old billiard-rooms; the large room answers the double purpose of dining-room and parlour, and the smaller rooms, which I am afraid were once used for card-playing when this place was a summer resort, are now put to a better use, as sleeping apartments and kitchen for three most agreeable families. One family in the opposite cottage has interested us very much. Mr. Wade (the husband) was an Englishman, who had been in office in Washington; he resigned and came South on the breaking out of the war, placed his family in Richmond, and joined our army; he was not young or healthy, and soon was broken down by the service; he was then made clerk in the Quartermaster's Department, and removed his family to Ashland for cheapness. He was very highly educated and gentlemanly, and his coming here seems to me very mysterious. Soon after his removal to this place he grew worse and died. His wife and five children were left penniless and friendless. They seemed to have no acquaintances, however slight. The villagers, from their limited resources, raised a sum for her present support, and after much difficulty procured her a situation in the Note-signing Department. She goes into the city every morning on the cars, as do several other ladies to the duties of their offices, leaving her children to the care of a faithful coloured nurse, whom she never saw until two months ago. We have taught her the art of making soap of concentrated ley, and often when she gets on the train, a basket may be seen in the freight-train filled with soap, which she sells to the grocers or commissaries. She is an interesting-looking woman, Northern born and educated. Her father, she says, is a Colonel in the Yankee army. She wrote to him again and again, and one of our gentlemen did the same, representing her case. After long silence he has written to her a short letter, which she showed me, inviting her, in rather an indifferent manner, to come to Georgetown, where her mother is now staying, but remits her no money to pay her passage or to support her here. Our gentlemen have interested Mr. Lawley, an Englishman of some note in Richmond, in her case; and her husband having been a British subject, he may be enabled to get her a passport and a free passage on the flag-of-truce boat.

15*th.*—Spent yesterday in the hospital. I am particularly interested in two very ill men. One is a youth of seventeen years, who has been seventeen months in service. Poor boy! he is now sinking with consumption, and has lately been brought to our hospital from another. His case elicits great sympathy and kindness. His name is Stansberry, and he is from Baltimore. We have reason to hope that he is prepared to meet his God.

Letters (underground) from the Valley to-day. Millroy is doing his worst among the dear people there. It is grievous to think how much of Virginia is down-trodden and lying in ruins. The old State has bared her breast to the destroyer, and borne the brunt of battle for the good of the Confederacy, and this too after long and vain efforts for peace. Her citizens, young and old, are doing what they can. Her sons have bled and died, and are still offering themselves willing sacrifices on the country's altar. Her daughters are striving in their vocation in this hallowed cause, all looking to God for his blessing upon our efforts.

17*th.*—On going to the hospital yesterday, I found

that young Stansberry had died, surrounded by sympathizing friends, and having a bright hope of a blessed immortality. We are anxious about our armies everywhere, from the Mississippi to the seaboard. Rumours are rife about General Longstreet having thrown his forces between Norfolk and the Yankee army at Suffolk. In the mean time we must possess our souls in patience.

18th.—A letter from our son J. to-day; full of pleasant feeling at finding himself again in the Army of Northern Virginia. He is just established near General Jackson's head-quarters, as Surgeon of the First Virginia Battalion; had just breakfasted with Stonewall, and is filled with enthusiastic admiration for the great Christian soldier and patriot.

The enemy seems to have left Charleston. The Northern papers, after much circumlocution, prevarication, and boasting of a successful reconnoissance, acknowledge that they were greatly injured by their last attack on it. "All quiet on the Rappahannock," continues to be reported. God grant that it may continue so!

Yesterday spent in the hospital; some of the men are very ill. I go back to-morrow.

Wednesday Night, April 29.—On Saturday Mr. —— and myself went up to Cedar Hill, and he attempted to go to Fredericksburg; when he reached Hamilton's Crossings he found it impossible to go on—conveyances were so scarce and the roads so terrible. He had the pleasure to dine, by invitation, at General Jackson's head-quarters. That night he spent with his old friend, Mr. M. Garnett. Once having every luxury which could be desired, he now lives in his desolated house, surrounded by down-trodden fields, without fences, trees, or vegetation of any sort. His servants, except a few faithful ones, have deserted him; his horses and stock of all kinds have been swept away; his sons in the army; and he is cheerful and buoyed with hope, not for himself, but for the cause : good old patriot as he is, forgetting his own privations in zeal for his country. On Sunday Mr. ——— heard an admirable sermon at head-quarters (General Jackson's) from the Rev. Mr. Lacy, a Presbyterian chaplain, and returned home on Monday, having found it impossible to fulfil the object of his trip, that of preaching to the soldiers in Fredericksburg.

Saturday Night, May 9.—So much has happened since I last wrote in my diary, that I can scarcely collect my thoughts to give a plain detail of facts as they occurred. Ten days ago, Mr. ——— and myself went in to spend two days with our children who are living in Richmond. It soon became apparent that we could not return, as the Government had taken the cars for the purpose of transporting soldiers to Fredericksburg. Hooker was making immense demonstrations, and was crossing 159,000 men. They fought on Saturday, Sunday, and Monday, at different points, principally at Chancellorsville, and the enemy was repulsed at all points. Hooker and his host retired to the Rappahannock, and recrossed, I think, on Wednesday. It is said that General Lee would have followed him, but for the dreadful storm of Monday night and Tuesday. General Lee in his official report speaks of it as a "signal victory." Our army was smaller than usual, as Longstreet was still near Suffolk, and could not get up in time. It is pretty certain that Hooker—fighting Joe !!—had two to Lee's one, and was defeated. But General Jackson was wounded severely. The great Stonewall is lost to us for a time; his left arm has been amputated, and there is a severe wound in his right hand. Oh, I pray that God may raise him up to be a continued blessing to the country. His wife has gone to him. The best surgical skill of the army, the sympathy and anxiety of the whole South, and the prayers of the country, are his. General Paxton, of the Stonewall Brigade, was killed, and many, ah, how many, valuable lives were lost! it is impossible for us yet to know, as the telegraphic wires are cut, and mail communication very uncertain. From my own family boys we have not heard, and we are willing to believe that "no news is good news." Two more of the dear ones over whose youth we so anxiously watched have fallen—Hill Carter, of Shirley, and Benjamin White, of Charlestown, Jefferson County. Thank God, they were both Christians! My heart aches for their parents. The last was an only son, and justly the pride and joy of his household. His parents are in the enemy's lines. O Lord, uphold that tender mother when the withering stroke is known to her! Major Channing Price and Colonel Thomas Garnett are gone! God help our country! We can't afford to lose such men.

While our army was busily engaged last Sunday, the Yankees took occasion to send out a raiding party of their superfluous numbers. A party of several hundred came here about three o'clock in the afternoon. They knew that the cars containing the wounded from the battle-field would be here. The cars arrived, and were immediately surrounded and the soldiers paroled. The ladies all the while were in the cars administering comfort to the wounded. They remained about three hours, took off every horse they could find, and every servant that they could induce to go, which was very few, and then rode off without burning the houses or offering other injury to the villagers. They belonged to

Stoneman's command. They went over this county, Goochland, Louisa, and a part of Fluvanna, without molestation. They became alarmed, however, and cut their career short. They went to Columbia for the purpose of destroying the canal, but in their haste did it very little injury. The injury to the railroads was slight, and easily repaired. To individuals they did some mischief; at W. they fed four hundred horses at my brother's barn, took his buggy horse, and rode off. His neighbours, and others in their route, fared very much in the same way. In Richmond the excitement was terrible. The alarm-bell pealed out its startling notes; citizens were armed, and sent out to man the batteries; extemporaneous cavalry companies were formed and sent out; women were seen crying and wringing their hands on the streets; wild rumours were afloat; but it all ended in the raiders not attempting to get to the Richmond batteries, and the city in a few hours became perfectly quiet.

Sunday, May 10.—Sad, sad tidings were brought to our cottage this morning! Washington, the youngest and darling son of our dear friend, Mrs. Stuart, has fallen. The mother and sisters are overwhelmed, while our whole household is shrouded in sorrow. He was young, brave, and a Christian. He fell while nobly fighting with his company, the famous Rockbridge Battery, on Marye's Hill. We have heard no other particulars. The brave boy had scarcely recovered from a most severe wound received last summer near Winchester. To God we commend his afflicted, though quietly submissive, mother. He alone can soothe the sorrow which He has seen fit to permit.

Tuesday Evening, May 12*th.*—How can I record the sorrow which has befallen our country! General T. J. Jackson is no more. The good, the great, the glorious Stonewall Jackson is numbered with the dead! Humanly speaking, we cannot do without him; but the same God who raised him up, took him from us, and He who has so miraculously prospered our cause, can lead us on without him. Perhaps we have trusted too much to an arm of flesh; for he was the nation's idol. His soldiers almost worshipped him, and it may be that God has therefore removed him. We bow in meek submission to the great Ruler of events. May his blessed example be followed by officers and men, even to the gates of heaven! He died on Sunday the 10th, at a quarter past three, P. M. His body was carried by yesterday, in a car, to Richmond. Almost every lady in Ashland visited the car, with a wreath or a cross of the most beautiful flowers, as a tribute to the illustrious dead. An immense concourse had assembled in Richmond, as the solitary car containing the body of the great soldier, accompanied by a suitable escort, slowly and solemnly approached the depot. The body lies in state to-day at the Capitol, wrapped in the Confederate flag, and literally covered with lilies of the valley and other beautiful Spring flowers. To-morrow the sad *cortège* will wend its way to Lexington, where he will be buried, according to his dying request, in the "Valley of Virginia." As a warrior, we may appropriately quote from Byron:

> "His spirit wraps the dusky mountain,
> His memory sparkles o'er the fountain,
> The meanest rill, the mightiest river,
> Rolls mingling with his fame forever."

As a Christian, in the words of St. Paul, I thank God to be able to say, "He has fought the good fight, he has finished his course, he has kept the faith. Henceforth there is laid up for him a crown of righteousness, which the Lord, the righteous Judge, shall give him at the last day."

Wednesday, 13*th.*—I have just heard that my dear nephew, Will'by N., was wounded at Chancellorsville, and that his left leg has been amputated. He is at Mr. Marye's, near Hamilton's Crossings, receiving the warm-hearted hospitality of that house, now so widely known. His mother has reached him, and he is doing well. I pray that God may have mercy upon him, and raise him up speedily, for the Saviour's sake.

May 16*th.*—We were aroused this morning before daylight, by reports that the Yankees were making a raid, and were very near this place. We all dressed hastily, and the gentlemen went out to devise means to stop the trains which were to pass through. Though within five miles of us, they became aware that notice had been given of their purpose, and they immediately turned their steps to some more private place, where they might rob and plunder without molestation. The miserable poltroons, when on one of their raids, will become frightened by the sudden rising of a covey of partridges, and be diverted from their course ; then they will ride bravely to a house, where they know they will only find women and children; order meals to be prepared; search the house; take the valuables; feed their horses at the barns; take off the horses from the stables; shoot the pigs, sheep, and other stock, and leave them dead in the fields; rob the poultry-yards; then, after regaling themselves on the meals which have been prepared by force, with the threats of bayonets and pistols, they ride off, having pocketed the silver spoons and forks, which may have unwittingly been left in their way.

I have been in Richmond for two days past, nursing the

wounded of our little hospital. Some of them are very severely injured, yet they are the most cheerful invalids I ever saw. It is remarked in all the hospitals that the cheerfulness of the wounded in proportion to their suffering is much greater than that of the sick. Under my care, yesterday, was one poor fellow, with a ball embedded in his neck; another with an amputated leg; one with a hole in his breast, through which a bullet had passed; another with a shattered arm; and others with slighter wounds; yet all showed indomitable spirit; evinced a readiness to be amused or interested in every thing around them; asked that the morning papers might be read to them, and gloried in their late victory; and expressed an anxiety to get well, that they may have another "*chance at them fellows.*" The Yankees are said to have landed at West Point, and are thence sending out raiding parties over the country. Colonel Davis, who led the party here on the third, has been severely wounded by a scouting party, sent out by General Wise towards Tunstall's Station. It is said he has lost his leg. So may it be!

Monday, May 18*th.*—This morning we had the gratification of a short visit from General Lee. He called and breakfasted with us, while the other passengers in the cars breakfasted at the hotel. We were very glad to see that great and good man look so well and so cheerful. His beard is very long, and painfully gray, which makes him appear much older than he really is. One of the ladies at table, with whom he is closely connected, rallied him on allowing his beard to grow, saying, "Cousin R., it makes you look too venerable for your years." He was amused, and pleaded as his excuse the inconvenience of shaving in camp. "Well," she replied, "if I were in Cousin Mary's place

(Mrs. L's) I would allow it to remain now, but I would take it off as soon as the war is over." He answered, while a shade passed over his bright countenance, "When the war is over, my dear L., she may take my beard off, and my head with it, if she chooses." This he said as the whistle summoned him to his seat in the cars, not meaning to depress us, or imagining for an instant that we would think of it again; but it proved to us that he *knew* that the end was not yet, and disappointed us, for after every great victory we cannot help hoping that the Federal Government may be tired of war and bloodshed, rapine and murder, and withdraw its myriads to more innocent pursuits.

Yesterday evening we were agreeably surprised by a call from W. B. C., just recovered from his dreadful wound, received at Fredericksburg last winter. He is an infantry captain of the Stonewall Brigade, and is just returning to his company. Alas! alas! his great Captain has passed away during his absence, which makes his return very sad. He thinks that General Ewell is the man of all others to put in his place, though no man can fill it. General Ewell, he says, is one of General Jackson's most enthusiastic admirers, believing him to have been almost an inspired man. General E. relates an incident of him, when on their victorious march through the Valley last summer, which is beautifully characteristic of General J. One night, when it was evident that there must be a battle next day, he (General E.) went to General Jackson for his plans. General J. replied that he would give them to him next morning, as they had not yet been formed. General E. felt uneasy and restless, and could not sleep. About midnight he arose, and, passing through the sleeping multitudes, he reached General Jackson's tent, and was about to raise the curtain to enter it, when his attention was arrested by the voice of prayer. General Jackson was praying fervently for guidance through the coming day. General E. remarked to a friend that he had never before heard a prayer so devout and beautiful; he then, for the first time, felt the desire to be a Christian. He retired to his tent quietly, without disturbing General J., feeling assured that all would be well. The next morning a fight came off, replete with victory. General Ewell was subsequently wounded at the second battle of Manassas, and it is said that he has since become a Christian. God grant that it may be so !

May 20*th*.—I feel depressed to-night. Army news from the South bad. General Pemberton has been repulsed between Jackson and Vicksburg. General Johnston is there; I hope, by the mercy of God, he may be able to keep the enemy out of Vicksburg. Besides the depressing news, the day has been distressing in the hospital—so much suffering among the wounded. One fine young man has the appearance and manner of imbecility, from having been struck on the head by a piece of shell. No relief can be given him, and the surgeons say that he must die.

Mr. —— staid in town to attend the Church " Council," as it is now called. This new name may be more appropriate to an ecclesiastical meeting, yet " Virginia Convention" has a sweet, hallowed sound to me.

23*d*.—We tremble for Vicksburg; an immense army has been sent against it; we await its fate with breathless anxiety.

25*th*.—The enemy repulsed at Vicksburg, though it is still in a state of siege. General Johnston is there, and we hope that the best means will be used to save that heroic little city; and we pray that God may bless the means used.

A friend called this morning, and told us of the fall of another of those dear youths, over whose boyish sojourn with us memory loves to linger. Kennedy Groghan, of Baltimore, who, in the very beginning of the war, came over to help us, fell in a skirmish in the Valley, a short time ago. The only account given us is, that the men were forced to retreat hastily, and were only able to place his loved body under the spreading branches of a tree. Oh! I trust that some kindly hand has put him beneath God's own earth, free from the din of war, from the strife of man, and from the curse of sin forever. I remember so well when, during our stay in Winchester, the first summer of the war, while General Johnston's army was stationed near there, how he, and so many others, would come in to see us, with their yet unfaded suits of gray—already sunburnt and soldier-like, but bright and cheerful. Alas! alas! how many now fill the graves of heroes—their young lives crushed out by the unscrupulous hand of an invading foe!

27*th.*—The news from Vicksburg by the morning's papers is very delightful, if authentic. We pause for confirmation of it. The young people among the villagers and refugees have been amusing themselves, during the past two evenings, with tableaux. I am too old to enjoy such things in these troubled times, but one picture I regretted not seeing. It represented the young Confederacy. The whole bright galaxy was there—South Carolina in scarlet, restive and fiery; Virginia, grave and dignified, yet bright with hope, seemed to be beckoning Kentucky on, who stood beyond the threshold, her eyes cast down with shame and suffering; Maryland was at the threshold, but held back by a strong hand; all the rest of the fair sisters were there in their appropriate places, forming a beautiful picture.

I am amused to see how the Democrats of the North are speechifying and exciting themselves about the arrest of Vallandigham, and how Lincoln will soon make them *back down*.

May 28.—Hospital day. The wounded cheerful and doing well. I read, distributed books, and talked with them. They are always ready to be amused, or to be instructed. I have never but in one instance had an unpleasant word or look from any whom I endeavoured to treat with kindness in any way. Bible reading is always kindly received. J. J. has returned home, as usual much interested in hospital work.

June 1.—L. and B. went up to Mr. Marye's near Fredericksburg to-day, to visit their brother's grave. They took flowers with which to adorn it. It is a sweet, though sad office, to plant flowers on a Christian's grave. They saw my sister, who is there, nursing her wounded son.

News from Vicksburg cheering.

5*th*.—Our household circle has been broken to-day, by Mrs. S. and her daughter B. leaving it for South Carolina. We are grieved to give them up.

6*th*.—We have been greatly interested lately by a visit to the village of our old friend, Mrs. T., of Rappahannock County. She gives most graphic descriptions of her sojourn of seven weeks among the Yankees last summer. Sixty thousand surrounded her house, under command of General Siegel. On one occasion, he and his staff rode up and announced that they would *take tea with her*. Entirely alone, that elegant old lady retained her composure, and with unruffled countenance rang her bell; when the servant appeared, she said to him, "John, tea for fourteen." She quietly retained her seat, conversing with them with dignified politeness, and submitting as best she could to the General's very free manner of walking about her beautiful establishment, pronouncing it "baronial," and regretting, in her presence, that he had not known of its elegancies and comforts in time, that he might have brought on Mrs. Siegel, and have made it his head-quarters. Tea being announced, Mrs. T., before proceeding to the dining-room, requested the servant to call a soldier in, who had been guarding her house for weeks, and who had sought occasion to do her many kindnesses. When the man entered, the General demurred: "No, no, madam, he will not go to table with us." Mrs. T. replied, "General, I must beg that you will allow this *gentleman* to come to *my table*, for *he* has been a friend to me when I have sadly wanted one." The General objected no farther; the *man* took tea with the master. After tea, the General proposed music, asking Mrs. T. if she had ever played; she replied that "such was still her habit." The piano being opened, she said if she sang at all she must sing the songs of her own land, and then, with her uncommonly fine voice, she sang "The Bonnie Blue Flag," "Dixie," and other Southern songs, with great spirit. They listened with apparent pleasure. One of the staff then suggested that the General was a musician. Upon her vacating the seat he took it, and played in grand style; with so much beauty and *accuracy*, she added, with a twinkle of her eye, that I strongly suspected him of having been a music-master. Since that time she has heard that he was once master of that beautiful art in Mobile. Well, he was at least a more innocent man then than now. Almost every woman of the South, or at least of Virginia, will have her tale to tell when this "cruel war is over." The life of too many will be, alas! as a "tale that is told;" its interest, its charm, even its hope, as far as this world is concerned, having passed away. Their crown of rejoicing will be in the public weal, which their loved and lost have fought, bled, and died to establish; but their own hearts will be withered, their hearths deserted.

Mrs. G. D., of Fredericksburg, has been giving some amusing incidents of her sudden departure from her home. She had determined to remain, but when, on the night of the bombardment, a shell burst very near her house, her husband aroused her to say that she must go. They had no means of conveyance, and her two children were both under three years of age, and but one servant, (the others having gone to the Yankees,) a girl twelve years old. It so happened that they had access to three straw carriages, used by her own children and those of her neighbours. They quickly determined to put a child in each of two carriages, and to bundle up as many clothes as would fill the third. The father drew the carriage containing one child, the mother the other child, and the little girl drew the bundle of clothes. They thus set out, to go they knew not whither, only to get out of the way of danger. It was about midnight, a dark, cold night. They went on and on, to the outskirts of the town, encountering a confused multitude rushing pell-mell, with ever and anon a shell bursting at no great distance, sent as a threat of what they might expect on the morrow. They were presently overtaken by a respectable shoemaker whom they knew, rolling a wheelbarrow containing a large bundle of clothes, and *the baby*. They were attracted by the poor little child rolling off from its elevated place on the bundle, and as Mrs. D. stopped, with motherly solicitude for the child, the poor man told his story. In the darkness and confusion he had become separated from his wife and other children, and knew not where to find them; he thought he might find them but for anxiety about the baby. Mrs. D. then proposed that he should take her bundle of clothes with his in the wheelbarrow, and put his child into the third straw carriage. This being agreed to, the party passed on. When they came to our encampment, a soldier ran out to offer to draw one carriage, and thus rest the mother; having gone as far as he dared from his regiment, then another soldier took his place to the end of his line, and so on from one soldier to another until our encampment was passed. Then she drew on her little charge about two miles farther, to the house of an acquaintance, which was wide open to the homeless. Until late the next day the shoemaker's baby was under their care, but he at last came, bringing the bundle in safety. As the day progressed the cannon roared and the shells whistled, and it was thought advisable for them to go on to Chancellorsville. The journey of several miles was performed on foot, still with the straw carriages, for no horse nor vehicle could be found in that desolated country. They remained at Chancellorsville until the 2d or 3d of May, when that house became within range of cannon. Again she gathered up her little flock, and came on to Ashland. Her little three-years old boy explored the boarding-house as soon as he got to it, and finding no cellar he became alarmed, and running to his mother, exclaimed, "This house won't do, mother; we all have no cellar to go into when they shell it!" Thus our children are born and reared amid war and bloodshed! It seemed so sad to me to see a bright little girl, a few days ago, of four years old, stop in the midst of her play, when she heard distant thunder, exclaiming, "Let me run home, they are firing!" Poor little child, her father had been a sacrifice; no wonder that she wanted to run to her mother when she thought she heard firing. Tales far more sad than that of Mrs. D. are told, of the poor assembled by hundreds on the roadside in groups, having no shelter to cover them, and often nothing to eat, on that dark winter's night.

June 7.—We are living in fear of a Yankee raid. They have a large force on York River, and are continually sending parties up the Pamunky and Mattapony Rivers, to devastate the country and annoy the inhabitants. Not long ago a party rode to the house of a gentleman on Mattapony; meeting him on the lawn, the commander accosted him: "Mr. R., I understand you have the finest horses in King William County?" "Perhaps, sir, I have," replied Mr. R. "Well, sir," said the officer, "I want those horses immediately." "They are not yours," replied Mr. R, "and you can't get them." The officer began to curse, and said he would burn every house on the place if the horses were not produced. Suiting the action to the word, he handed a box of matches to a subordinate, saying, "Burn!" In half an hour Mr. R. saw fourteen of his houses in a light blaze, including the dwelling, the kitchen, corn-houses and barn filled with grain, meat-house filled with meat, and servants' houses. Scarcely any thing was saved, not even the family clothes. But he did not get the horses, which were the objects of his peculiar wishes; the faithful servants had carried them away to a place of safety. How strange it is that we can be so calm, surrounded as we are by danger!

8*th.*—We have had a cavalry fight near Culpeper Court-House. We drove the enemy back, but I am afraid that our men won no laurels, for we were certainly surprised most shamefully.

16*th.*—The morning papers gave a telegram from General

Lee, announcing that General Early's Brigade had taken Winchester by storm. So again Winchester and all that beautiful country, Clarke, etc., are disenthralled.

It is said that our army will go to Pennsylvania. This I dread ; but it is in God's hands, I believe, for good and not for evil.

21st.—We hear of fights and rumours of fights. It is said that Ewell's Division captured 6,000 prisoners at Winchester, and that General Edward Johnson went to Berryville and captured 2,000 that were on their way to reinforce Millroy. They have driven the enemy out of the Valley, so that now we have possession of it once more. Our cavalry has been as far as Chambersburg, Pennsylvania, but I do not know what they have accomplished.

26th.—While in the midst of preparation to visit my sisters at W. and S. H., we have been startled by the account of Yankees approaching. They have landed in considerable force at the White House, and are riding over the country to burn and destroy. They have burned the South Anna Bridge on the Central Railroad, and this evening were advancing on the bridge over the South Anna, on this railroad, which is but four miles above us. We have a small force there, and a North Carolina regiment has gone up to-night to reinforce them. We are, of course, in considerable excitement. I am afraid they are ruining the splendid wheat harvests which are now being gathered on the Pamunky. Trusting in the Lord, who hath hitherto been our help, we are going quietly to bed, though we believe that they are very near us. From our army we can hear nothing. No one can go farther than Culpeper Court-House in that direction. Why this has been ordered I know not, but for some good military reason, I have no doubt. It is said that Stuart's cavalry have been fighting along the line of the Manassas Gap Railroad with great success. We can hear no particulars.

Saturday Evening.—Just heard from W. and S. H.; both terribly robbed by the raiders in the last three days. All of my brother's horses and mules taken. Some of the servants were forced off, who staid so faithfully by them, and resisted all the Yankee entreaties twice before. They attempted to burn the wheat, which is shocked in the field, but an opportune rain made it too wet to burn. The raiders came up the river, destroying crops, carriages, etc., stealing horses and cattle, and carrying off the servants from every plantation, until they got to Hickory Hill, (Mr. W. F. Wickham's,) where they found a prize in the person of General W. F. Lee, who was wounded at the cavalry fight of Beverley's Ford, and was at Mr. W's, unable to move. Notwithstanding the remonstrances of his wife and mother, they took him out of his bed, placed him in Mr. Wickham's carriage, and drove off with him. I can't conceive greater hardness of heart than it required to resist the entreaties of that beautiful young wife and infirm mother. F. has just received a note from the former, written in sorrow and loneliness. She fears that the wound may suffer greatly by locomotion; beyond that, she has much to dread, but she scarcely knows what.

Wednesday.—Many exciting rumours to-day about the Yankees being at Hanover Court-House, within a few miles of us. They can be traced everywhere by the devastation which marks their track. There are also rumours that our army is in Pennsylvania. So may it be! We are harassed to death with their ruinous raids, and why should not the North feel it in its homes? Nothing but their personal suffering will shorten the war. I don't want their women and children to suffer; nor that our men should follow their example, and break through and steal. I want our warfare carried on in a more honourable way; but I do want our men and horses to be fed on the good things of Pennsylvania; I want the fine dairies, pantries, granaries, meadows, and orchards belonging to the rich farmers of Pennsylvania, to be laid open to our army; and I want it all paid for with our *Confederate money, which will be good at some future day.* I want their horses taken for our cavalry and wagons, in return for the hundreds of thousands that they have taken from us; and I want their fat cattle driven into Virginia to feed our army. It amuses me to think how the Dutch farmers' wives will be concealing the golden products of their dairies, to say nothing of their apple-butter, peach-butter, and their wealth of apple-pies.

July 3.—The scarcity of blank-books, and the very high prices, make them unattainable to me ; therefore I have determined to begin another volume of my Diary on some nice wrapping-paper which I happen to have ; and though not very pleasant to write on, yet it is one of the least of my privations.

We are still worried by reports that the Yankees are very near us, and we are constantly expecting them to raid upon Ashland. We have a good force at "The Junction," and at the bridge just above us, which they may respect, as they are dreadfully afraid of our forces.

Spent yesterday in the hospital; the wounded are getting on well. The city was put into a blaze of excitement by the report that General Dix was marching on it from the White House. I dare say they think that General Lee has left it undefended, in which surmise they are vastly

10*

mistaken. Our troops seem to be walking over Pennsylvania without let or hindrance. They have taken possession of Chambersburg, Carlisle, and other smaller towns. They surrendered without firing a gun. I am glad to see that General Lee orders his soldiers to respect private property; but it will be difficult to make an incensed soldiery, whose houses have in many instances been burned, crops wantonly destroyed, horses stolen, negroes persuaded off, hogs and sheep shot down and left in the field in warm weather—it will be difficult to make such sufferers remember the Christian precept of returning good for evil. The soldiers in the hospital seem to think that many a private torch will be applied "just for revenge." It was in vain that I quoted to them, " Vengeance is mine; I will repay, saith the Lord." One stoutly maintained that he would like to go North "just to burn two good houses: one in return for my own house on Mississippi River; the other for that of my brother-in-law, both of which they burned just after landing from their boat, with no pretence at an excuse for it; and when I think of my wife and children homeless, I feel as if I could set all Yankeedom in a blaze." Poor fellow! he became so excited that he arose in his bed, as if impatient to be off and at his work of vengeance. I am glad to hear that quantities of horses and fat cattle are driven into Virginia.

July 4.—Our celebration of this day is more serious than in days gone by. Our military have no time for dressparades and barbecues. The gentlemen could not get home yesterday evening; the trains were all used for carrying soldiers to the bridge on this railroad just above us, upon which the Yankees are making demonstrations. The morning papers report that General D. H. Hill had a skirmish near

Tunstall's Station on Thursday evening, and repulsed the enemy. Nothing from our armies in Pennsylvania or Vicksburg.

July 4, Eleven o' Clock P. M.—Heavy musketry to-night, for two hours, at the bridge above this place. It has ceased, and we hope that the enemy are driven back.

Mr. —— came home this evening; the other gentlemen are absent. We are going to bed, feeling that we are in God's hands. The wires are cut between this and "The Junction," and there is every indication that the Yankees are near. The telegraph operator has gone off, and great anxiety is felt about the village. There are no Government stores here of any sort; I trust that the Yankees know that, and will not think us worth the trouble of looking after.

Monday Morning.—The hope I expressed in my last line on Saturday night was delusive. About one o'clock I was awakened by E. leaning over me, and saying in a low, tremulous tone, "Mother, get up, the Yankees are come." We sprang up, and there they were at the telegraph office, immediately opposite. In an instant the door was broken down with a crash, and the battery and other things thrown out. Axes were at work cutting down the telegraph-poles, while busy hands were tearing up the railroad. A sentinel sat on his horse at our gate as motionless as if both man and horse had been cut from a block of Yankee granite. We expected every moment that they would come to the house, or at least go into the hotel opposite to us; but they went off to the depot. There was a dead silence, except an occasional order, "Be quick," "Keep a sharp look-out," etc., etc. The night was moonlight, but we dressed ourselves and sat in the dark; we were afraid to open the window-shutters or to light a lamp, lest they might be attracted to the house. We remained in this way perhaps two hours, when the flames suddenly burst from the depot. All parts of the building seemed to be burning at once; also immense piles of wood and of plank. The conflagration was brilliant. As soon as the whole was fairly blazing the pickets were called in, and the whole party dashed off, with demoniac yells. Soon after, as the dawn began to break upon us, doors were thrown open, and the villagers began to sally forth to the fire. In a short time all of us were there, from every house—even the babies; and as it became daylight, an amusing group was revealed. Every one had dressed in the dark, and all manner of costumes were to be seen—dressing-gowns, cravatless old gentlemen, young ladies in curl-papers, collars pinned awry, etc. Some ladies presented themselves in full costume—handsome dresses, lace collars, ear-rings and breastpins, watches, etc.—giving as a reason, that, if they were burnt out, they would at least save their best clothes—forgetting, the while, that a Yankee soldier has an irresistible *penchant* for watches and other jewelry. Some of us were more cautious, and had put all our valuables in *unapproachable* pockets—the pockets to a lady's dress not having proved on all occasions a place of safety. The loss to the railroad company will be considerable; to the public very small, for they are already replacing the broken rails, and the telegraph was put in operation yesterday.

The morning papers give the Northern account of a battle in Gettysburg, Pennsylvania. It gives the victory to the Federals, though it admits a very heavy loss on their side; announces the loss of Major-General Reynolds and Brigadier-General Paul by death. We pause for the truth.

8th.—Accounts from Gettysburg very confused. Nothing seems to be known certainly; but Vicksburg has fallen! So says rumour, and we are afraid not to believe. It is a terrible loss to us; but God has been so good to us heretofore that we can only say, "It is the Lord." A victory is announced to the War Department gained by General Loring in the West; and another gained by General Richard Taylor over Banks. For these successes I thank God from my heart. Many troops have passed here to-day, for what point we know not. Our anxiety is very great. Our home is blessed with health and comfort.

July 11.—Vicksburg was surrendered on the 4th of July. The terms of capitulation seem marvellously generous for such a foe. What can the meaning be?

General Lee has had a most bloody battle near Gettysburg. Our loss was fearful. We have heard of no casualties except in general officers. General Richard Garnett, our friend and connection, has yielded up his brave spirit on a foreign field. He was shot through the head while standing on the fortifications, encouraging his men and waving them on to the fight. How my heart bleeds to think of his hoary-headed father, of whom he was the stay! General Barksdale, of Mississippi, is another martyr. Also General Armstead, of Virginia. Generals Kemper and Pender wounded. I dread to hear of others. Who of our nearest kin may have ceased to live? When I think of probabilities and possibilities, I am almost crazy. Some of our men are reported wounded and in the enemy's hands. They took many prisoners. The cars are rushing up and down with soldiers. Two trains with pontoons have gone up within the last two days. What does it all portend?

July 12. — The enemy is again before Charleston.

Lord, have mercy on the efforts of our people! I am miserable about my poor little J. P., who is on board the *Chicora*, in Charleston harbor.

14th.—To-day spent in the hospital; a number of wounded there from the fatal field of Gettysburg. They are not severely wounded, or they could not have been brought so far. Port Hudson has fallen! It could not be retained after losing Vicksburg. General Lee's army is near Hagerstown. Some of the casualties of the Gettysburg fight which have reached me are very distressing. The death of James Maupin, of the University of Virginia—so young, so gentle, so brave! He fell at his gun, as member of the Second Howitzers of Richmond. My heart goes out in warmest sympathy for his parents and devoted grandmother. Colonel James Marshall, of Fauquier, has fallen. He is yet another of those dear ones over whose youth we so fondly watched. Yet another was Westwood McCreery, formerly of Richmond. Another was Valentine Southall. They all went with bright hope, remembering that every blow that was struck was for their own South. Alas! alas! the South now weeps some of her bravest sons. But, trying as it is to record the death of those dear boys, it is harder still to speak of those of our own house and blood. Lieutenant B. H. McGuire, our nephew, the bright, fair-haired boy, from whom we parted last summer at Lynchburg as he went on his way to the field, full of buoyancy and hope, is among the dead at Gettysburg. Also, Captain Austin Brockenbrough, of Essex County. Virginia had no son to whom a brighter future opened. His talents, his education, his social qualities, his affectionate sympathy with all around him, are all laid low. Oh, may God be with those of whose life they seemed a part! It is hard to think of so many of our warm-hearted, whole-souled, brave, ardent Southern youths, now sleeping beneath the cold clods of Pennsylvania. We can only hope that the day is not far distant when we may bring their dear bodies back to their native soil.

15th.—In Richmond, to-day, I saw my old friend, Mrs. E. R. C., looking after her sons. One was reported "wounded;" the other "missing." This sad word may mean that he is a prisoner; it may mean worse. She can get no clue to him. His company has not come, and she is very miserable. Two mothers, one from Georgia, another from Florida, have come on in pursuit of their sons, and are searching the hospitals for them. They were not in our hospital, and we could give them no information, so they went on to others. There is more unhappiness abroad among our people than I have ever seen before. Sometimes I wish I could sleep until it is over—a selfish wish enough; but it is hard to witness so much sorrow which you cannot alleviate.

July 18.—This day two years ago the battle of Bull Run was fought, a kind of prelude to that of Manassas, on the 21st. Since that time what scenes have been enacted! Battles have been fought by scores, and lives, precious lives, have been sacrificed by thousands, and that, too, of the very flower of our country. Again I have heard of the death of one of our dear E. H. S. boys—William H. Robb, of Westmoreland. He was with us for four years, and was very, very dear to us all. He died of wounds received in a cavalry fight at Brandy Station. We thought he had recovered, but this evening brought the fatal tidings. The news of the New York riots, which they got up in opposition to the draft, is cheering! Oh! that they could not get up another army, and would fight each other! Fitz Lee's cavalry had a fight yesterday at Shepherdstown, and repulsed the enemy handsomely. All eyes turn gloomily to Charleston. It is greatly feared that it will have to succumb to Federal force. I trust that our Heavenly Father may avert so dire a calamity!

19*th*.—When shall we recover from this fatal trip into Pennsylvania? General Pettigrew, of North Carolina, fell on the retreat, at a little skirmish near the Falling Waters. Thus our best men seem to be falling on the right hand and on the left. When speaking of General P's death, a friend related a circumstance which interested me. General P. was severely wounded at the battle of "Seven Pines." He was lying in a helpless condition, when a young soldier of another command saw him, and, immediately stooping to the ground, assisted him in getting on his back, and was bearing him to a place of safety, when he (the soldier) was struck by a ball and instantly killed. The General fell to the ground, and remained there, unable to move, until he was captured by the enemy. He was subsequently incarcerated in Fort Delaware. Having learned from the soldier, while on his back, that his name was White, from Westmoreland County, Virginia, as soon as the General was exchanged he inquired for the family, and found that the mother was a respectable widow who had had five sons on the field, but one of whom survived. He immediately wrote to her, expressing his deep sense of obligation to her son for his gracious effort to save his life, delicately inquired into her circumstances, and offered, if necessary, to make a liberal provision for her. I did not learn the widow's reply.

We have had this week a visit of two days from Mrs.

General Lee. She was on her way to the Hot Springs in pursuit of health, of which she stands greatly in need. She is a great sufferer from rheumatism, but is cheerful, notwithstanding her sufferings, bodily and mentally. She is, of course, unhappy about her imprisoned son, and, I should suppose, about the overpowering responsibilities of her noble husband; but of that you never hear a word from her. She left us this morning, in a box car, fitted up to suit an invalid, with a bed, chairs, etc. She was accompanied by the lovely wife of her captive son, also travelling in pursuit of health. Greater beauty and sweetness rarely fall to the lot of woman; and as I looked at the sad, delicate lineaments of her young face, I could but inwardly pray that the terrible threats denounced against her husband by Yankee authority might never reach her ear; for, though we do not believe that they will dare to offer him violence, yet the mere suggestion would be enough to make her very miserable.

Yesterday morning we had quite a pleasant diversion, in attending a marriage in the village. Mr. —— performed the ceremony, and we afterwards breakfasted with the bridal party. We then proceeded to Richmond—they to spend their honeymoon in and around the city, and we to our duties there.

July 23.—Spent the day at the hospital. Mr. —— has just received a post chaplaincy from Government, and is assigned to the Officers' Hospital on Tenth Street. For this we are very thankful, as the performance of the duties of the ministerial office is in all respects congenial to his taste and feeling. I pray that God may give him health and strength for the office!

28*th*.—The girls are in Richmond, staying at Dr. G's.

They went in to attend a tournament to be given to-day by General Jenkins's Brigade, stationed near Richmond; but this morning the brigade was ordered to go South, and great was the disappointment of the young people. They cannot feel as we do during these gloomy times, but are always ready to catch the "passing pleasure as it flies," forgetting that, in the best times,

> "Pleasures are like poppies spread:
> You seize the flower, the bloom is shed."

And how much more uncertain are they now, when we literally cannot tell what a day may bring forth, and none of us know, when we arise in the morning, that we may not hear before noonday that we have been shorn of all that makes life dear!

July 29.—A letter of farewell from the Valley, written as the enemy's lines were closing around our loved ones there. It is painful to think of their situation, but they are in God's hands.

It is said that Lee's army and Meade's are approaching each other. Oh, I trust that a battle is not at hand! I feel unnerved, as if I could not stand the suspense of another engagement. Not that I fear the result, for I cannot believe that Meade could whip General Lee, under any circumstances; but the dread casualties! The fearful list of killed and wounded, when so many of our nearest and dearest are engaged, is too full of anguish to anticipate without a sinking of heart which I have never known before.

There was a little fight some days ago, near Brandy Station—the enemy driven across the river. Fredericksburg and Culpeper Court-House are both occupied by our troops. This is very gratifying to our Fredericksburg refugees, who are going up to see if they can recover their property. All movables, such as household furniture, books, etc., of any value, have been carried off. Their houses, in some instances, have been battered down.

I was in Richmond this morning, and bought a calico dress, for which I gave $2.50 per yard, and considered it a bargain; the new importations have run up to $3.50; and $4 per yard. To what are we coming?

30th.—Our good President has again appointed a day for fasting and prayer.

The *Florida* and *Alabama* are performing wonderful feats, and are worrying the North excessively. Many a cargo has been lost to the Northern merchant princes by their skill, and I trust that the Government vessels feel their power.

Several members of our household have gone to the mountains in pursuit of health—Mr. —— among the rest. Mrs. P., of Amelia, is here, cheering the house by her sprightliness; and last night we had Mr. Randolph Tucker, who is a delightful companion—so intellectual, cheerful, and God-fearing!

The army is unusually quiet at all points. Does it portend a storm? Many changes are going on in " our village." The half-English, half-Yankee Wades are gone at last, to our great relief. I dare say she shakes the dust from her feet, as a testimony against the South; for she certainly has suffered very much here, and she will not have as many difficulties there, with her Yankee Colonel father. She professes to outrebel the rebels, and to be the most intense Southern woman of us all; but I rather think that she deceives herself, and unless I mistake her character very much indeed, I think when she gets among her own people she will tell them all she knows of our hopes, fears, and difficulties. Poor thing! I am glad she is gone to those persons on whom she has a natural claim for protection.

August 10.—Spent this morning in the house of mourning. Our neighbour Mrs. S. has lost her eldest son. The disease was " that most fatal of Pandora's train," consumption. He contracted it in the Western Army. His poor mother has watched the ebbing of his life for several months, and last night he died most suddenly. That young soldier related to me an anecdote, some weeks ago, with his short, oppressed breathing and broken sentences, which showed the horrors of this fratricidal war. He said that the day after a battle in Missouri, in the Fall of 1861, he, among others, was detailed to bury the dead. Some Yankee soldiers were on the field doing the same thing. As they turned over a dead man, he saw a Yankee stop, look intently, and then run to the spot with an exclamation of horror. In a moment he was on his knees by the body, in a paroxysm of grief. It was his brother. They were Missourians. The brother now dead had emigrated South some years before. He said that before the war communication had been kept up between them, and he had strongly suspected that he was in the army; he had consequently been in constant search of his brother. The Northern and Southern soldier then united in burying him, who was brother in arms of the one, and the mother's son of the other!

The Bishop and Mrs. J. returned home to-day from their long trip in the South-west. They travelled with great comfort, but barely escaped a raid at Wytheville. We welcomed them gladly. So many of our family party are wandering about, that our little cottage has become lonely.

Mr. C. has come out, and reports a furious bombardment of Sumter. This has been going on so long, that I begin to feel that it is indeed impregnable.

Wednesday.—We are all pursuing the even tenor of our way, as if there were no war. An order from General Lee is in to-day's paper, exhorting officers and soldiers to a strict observance of fast-day, which is on Friday. In the mean time the enemy is storming Charleston with unprecedented fury. It is an object of peculiar vengeance. Sumter has literally fallen, but it has not yielded; its battered walls bid defiance to the whole power of the North.

August 26.—A week ago I was called to Camp Jackson to nurse ——, who has been very sick there. The hospital is very extensive, and in beautiful order. It is under the supervision of Surgeon Hancock, whose whole soul seems engaged in making it an attractive home to the sick and wounded. The beautiful shade-trees and bold spring are delightful to the convalescents during this warm weather. Fast-day was observed there with great solemnity. I heard a Methodist chaplain preach to several hundred soldiers, and I never saw a more attentive congregation.

September 8.—The Government employed the cars yesterday bringing Longstreet's Corps from Fredericksburg, on its way to Chattanooga. We all stood at our gate last night to give the soldiers water; we had nothing else to give them, poor fellows, as there were three long trains, and they had no time to stay. They looked healthy and cheerful, and went off hurrahing for Virginia.

The year of our sojourn at this cottage is nearly over. Our mess must be broken up, as some of our gentlemen are ordered away. We have had a very pleasant time, and it is painful to dissolve our social relations. Not one of the families is provided with a home; we are all looking out for lodgings, and find it very difficult to get them. This change of home, habits, and association is very trying to old persons; the variety seems rather pleasant to the young.

September 16.—This house is to be sold on the 29th, so we must all find resting-places before that time. But where? Room-rent in Richmond is enormously high. We may get one very small cottage here for forty dollars per month, but it has the reputation of being unhealthy. Our connection, Mr. P., is here looking out for a home, and we may get one together. It would be delightful to have him and the dear girls with us. No one thinks of boarding; almost all the boarding-house keepers rent out their rooms, and refugees keep house in them as cheaply as they choose.

Richmond, 24.—We have all been scattered. The Bishop has obtained good rooms; the other members of the household are temporarily fixed. We are here with our son, looking for rooms every day; very few are vacant, and they are too high for our means. We shall probably have to take the little cottage at Ashland, notwithstanding its reputation—either the cottage or a country-house near Richmond, about which we are in correspondence with a gentleman. This plan will be carried out, and work well if the Lord pleases, and with this assurance we should be satisfied; but still we are restless and anxious. Our ladies, who have been brought up in the greatest luxury, are working with their hands to assist their families. The offices given to ladies have been filled long ago, and yet I hear of a number of applicants. Mr. Memminger says that one vacancy will bring a hundred applications. Some young ladies plait straw hats for sale; I saw one sold this morning for twenty dollars—and their fair fingers, which had not been accustomed to work for their living, plait on merrily; they can dispose of them easily; and, so far from being ashamed of it, they take pride in their own handiwork. I went to see Mrs. —— to-day, daughter of one of our gentlemen high in position, and whose husband was a wealthy landholder in Maryland. I found her sitting at her sewing-machine, making an elaborate shirt-bosom. She said she took in sewing, and spoke of it very cheerfully. "How can we rent rooms and live on captain's pay?" She began by sewing for brothers and cousins, then for neighbours, and now for anybody who will give it to her. She laughingly added, that she thought she would hang out her sign, "Plain sewing done here." We certainly are a *great people*, women as well as men. This lady, and all other ladies, have always places at their frugal tables for hungry soldiers. Many ladies take in copying.

25*th.*—There has been a great battle in the West, at Chickamauga, in Tennessee, between Bragg and Rosecranz. We are gloriously victorious! The last telegram from General Bragg tells of 7,000 prisoners, thirty-five pieces of cannon, and 15,000 small-arms, taken by our men. The fight is not over, though they have been fighting three days. Longstreet and his corps of veterans are there to reinforce them. A battle is daily expected on the Rapidan; and, to use Lincoln's expression, they are still "pegging away" at Charleston.

September 26.—Spent this morning seeking information about our plan of living in the country. Nothing satisfactory.

28*th.*—Mrs. M. and myself went to St. John's Church yesterday, and heard an excellent sermon from Bishop Wilmer; service read by Dr. Norwood. Encouraging news continues from the West. I am still anxious about our home. Mr. —— is sick, and the prospect of getting a house diminishing. Perhaps I should take comfort from the fact that a great many persons are homeless as well as ourselves. If Mr. —— were well, I should not feel so hopeless. The girls, too, are visiting the country, expecting us to get an *impossible* home, and I do dislike to disappoint them. Oh, that we could be perfectly satisfied, knowing that we are in the Lord's hands!

CEDAR HILL, *October* 4.—We came to Ashland on the 29th, to attend the sale of the house in which we lived last year. We got a few pieces of furniture, and determined to rent the little cottage. We spent that night at Mrs. T's, and came here next morning, and are now collecting hops, brooms, and the various *et cœteras* necessary for housekeeping. A refugee friend, who will change her location, has lent us her furniture, so that we expect to be very snug. Of course we shall have no curtains nor carpets, which are privations in our old age, but the deficiencies must be made up by large wood fires and bright faces. The war has taught useful lessons, and we can make ourselves comfortable and happy on much less than we ever dreamed of before.

October 24.—Since writing in my diary, our plans have been entirely changed. Our old friend, Mrs. R., offered us rooms in Richmond, on such terms as are within our means, and a remarkable circumstance connected with it is, that they are in the house which my father once occupied, and the pleasant chamber which I now occupy I left this month twenty-nine years ago. It is much more convenient to live in Richmond than in Ashland, so that we have rented the little cottage to another. One room answers the purpose of dining-room and sleeping-room, by putting a large screen around the bed; the girls have a room, and we use the parlour of the family for entertaining our guests. For this we pay $60 per month and half of the gas bill.

But this has been a sad, sad month to me, and I find it very difficult to bring my mind to attend to the ordinary affairs of life. On the 11th of this month, our nephew, Captain William B. Newton, was killed while leading a cavalry charge in Culpeper County. We have the consolation of believing that his redeemed spirit has passed into heaven; but to how many has the earth been left desolate! His young wife and three lovely children; his father, mother, sisters, brothers, uncles and aunts, have seen the pride of their hearts pass away. His country mourns him as a great public loss. The bar, the legislative hall, and the camp proudly acknowledge his brilliant talents. In peace, the country looked to him as one to whom her best interests would hereafter be intrusted; in war, as one of the most gallant officers on the field. An early and ardent Secessionist, he was among the first to turn from the delightful home circle, where he ever sought his happiness, to go to the defence of right. He came into the field as First Lieutenant of the Hanover Troop; shortly after became its Captain, loved and revered by his men; and the commission of Lieutenant-Colonel of his regiment, the Fourth Virginia Cavalry, was on its way to him; but, alas! alas! it reached its destination a few hours too late. God be with my precious —— and her sweet children! I long and yet dread to go to that once bright home, the light of which has faded forever.

I was shocked to hear that on the fatal Sunday on which my darling William fell, three of our E. H. S. boys had come to a glorious, though untimely end, on the same field—

Surgeon John Nelson, Lieutenant Lomax Tayloe, and Private J. Vivian Towles; and at Bristow Station, a few days afterwards, dear little Willie Robinson, son of my old friends, Mr. Conway and Mrs. Mary Susan Robinson. He was but eighteen. I attended his funeral on Wednesday last, and there learned that he was a devoted Christian. These dear boys! Oh, I trust that they sprang from the din of the battle-field to the peace of heaven! Lord, how long must we suffer such things?

25th.—To-day we heard the Rev. Mr. Peterkin, from the text: "Be not weary in well-doing." It was a delightful sermon, persuasive and encouraging. Mr. —— spends Sunday morning always in the hospital. He has Hospital No. 1, in addition to the Officers' Hospital, under his care. They occupy a great deal of his time, in the most interesting way.

27th.—I was surprised this morning by a precious visit from S. S. She went to Petersburg this evening, to join her husband, who is stationed there. She seems to think that she can never return to her Winchester home, so completely is every thing ruined. It is strange how we go on from month to month, living in the present, without any certain prospect for the future. We had some sweet, sad talk of our dear William. She says he was prepared, and God took him. At his funeral, his pastor took out his last letter from him, but became so overwhelmed with tears that he could not read it. It is right, and we must submit; but it is a bitter trial to give up one we loved so dearly.

28th.—Our niece, M. P., came for me to go with her on a shopping expedition. It makes me sad to find our money depreciating so much, except that I know it was worse during the old Revolution. A merino dress cost $150, long cloth $5.50 per yard, fine cotton stockings $6 per pair; handkerchiefs, for which we gave fifty cents before the war, are now $5. There seems no scarcity of dry-goods of the ordinary kinds; bombazines, silks, etc., are scarce and very high; carpets are not to be found—they are too large to run the blockade from Baltimore, from which city many of our goods come.

November 9.—We are now quite comfortably fixed, in what was once my mother's chamber, and most unexpectedly we have a carpet. The other day, while entertaining some friends, in this chamber by night, dining-room by day, and parlour ever and anon, Mrs. Secretary Mallory walked in, who, like ourselves, has had many ups-and-downs during the Confederacy, and therefore her kind heart knows exactly how to sympathize with others. While talking away, she suddenly observed that there was no carpet on the floor, and exclaimed, "Mrs. ——, you have no carpet! My boxes have just come from Montgomery, where I left them two years ago, filled with carpets and bedding. I have five, and I will lend you one. Don't say a word; I couldn't be comfortable, and think of you with this bare floor. Mr. —— is too delicate for it, and you are both too old to begin now on an uncarpeted room." An hour after she left us a servant came with the carpet, which was soon tacked down, and gives a home-like, comfortable air to the room.

11*th*.—Just received a visit from my nephew, W. N., who is on his way to Fauquier to be married. I had not seen him since he lost his leg. He is still on crutches, and it made my heart bleed to see him walk with such difficulty. I believe that neither war, pestilence, nor famine could put an end to the marrying and giving in marriage which is constantly going on. Strange that these sons of Mars can so assiduously devote themselves to Cupid and Hymen; but every respite, every furlough, must be thus employed. I am glad they can accomplish it; and if the "brave deserve the fair," I am sure that the deeds of daring of our Southern soldiers should have their reward. My niece, L. B., of Lexington, would have been married to-morrow night, but her betrothed, Captain S., has been ordered off to meet the enemy. The marriage is, of course, postponed. Poor fellow! I trust that he may come safely home.

I have just written to Colonel Northrup, Commissary-General, to ask an appointment as clerk in his department. So many of the young men have been ordered to the field, that this office has been open to ladies. My cousin, Colonel F. G. Ruffin, of the same office, has interested himself for me. They require us to say that we are really in want of the office—rather a work of supererogation, I should say, as no lady would bind herself to keep accounts for six hours per day without a dire necessity.

13*th*.—My appointment to a clerkship in the Commissary Department has been received, with a salary of $125 per month. The rooms are not ready for us to begin our duties, and Colonel R. has just called to tell me one of the requirements. As our duties are those of accountants, we are to go through a formal examination in arithmetic. If we do not, as the University boys say, "pass," we are considered incompetent, and of course are dropped from the list of appointees. This requirement may be right, but it certainly seems to me both provoking and absurd that I must be examined in arithmetic by a commissary major young enough to be my son. If I could afford it, I would give up the appointment, but, as it is, must submit with the best grace possible, particularly as other ladies of my age have to submit to it.

November 15.—Went this morning to —— Church and heard the Gospel preached, but in a manner so dull, and in a voice so monotonous, that I did not hear with much profit. I mourn that I did not, for I believe that some of the most God-serving, and therefore efficient ministers, are those who are not attractive as preachers, and there must be some defect in the listener who is not profited by the Gospel preached in spirit and in truth, though not set forth in an attractive form. I would that our best preachers could be sent to the field, for the soldiers, having such temptations to spending the Sabbath in idleness, should have the Gospel made impressive and interesting, so that they may be induced to attend the services and to enjoy them.

W. N. and his sweet bride passed through town this week. It was very pleasant to see how she understood his wants; how naturally she would open the doors, gates, etc., and assist him in walking up and down steps. I trust he may soon be able to give up his crutches. L. B. is also married and in town, staying at Judge M's. Captain S. returned *from the wars* a few nights after the one appointed, and was married in quite the old style of bridesmaids and groomsmen, with a bridal supper which I am told reminded one of peace times.

Our army does not seem prospering in the West. Bragg has fallen back. We long to hear better things. A battle seems imminent on the Rappahannock; ninety-three wagons filled with ammunition were yesterday captured by Colonel Rosser—a good capture, at a good time.

December 4.—On Friday last there was a severe fight

on the Rapidan, at Germanna Ford. The enemy were splendidly repulsed; but my dear Raleigh T. Colston, Lieutenant-Colonel of the Second Regiment, was shot through his left leg, which was amputated on the field. I thank God that he is doing well, and feel so thankful that his life was spared! His mother was in Powhatan, on a visit to one of her daughters; but, becoming uneasy at seeing that General Edward Johnson's Division had been engaged, immediately came to Richmond. The cars arrived at night, and she came directly to our rooms. We were surprised to see her, and I, supposing that she had heard of her son's misfortune, was about to say what I could to relieve her mind, when she exclaimed, "I know that my sons are safe, from your countenance." "Yes," said I; "W. is safe, and R. is doing well; he was wounded in his leg." "Severely?" she asked. "His left leg has been amputated below the knee; he is at the University, under the care of Mr. and Mrs. Minor and his sisters, and is doing remarkably well. Colonel Ruffin received a telegram to-day, and I a letter." She passed her hand across her eyes for a minute, and said, "Thank God, his life is spared!" Next morning she left us for the University.

General Bragg has met with a repulse in the South-west, and was pursued; but, being reinforced, has again attacked the enemy and repulsed them. This occurred in the Northwestern part of Georgia. The papers say that the enemy under General Grant has retreated towards Chattanooga. Longstreet, when last heard from, was at Knoxville. Meade, on the Rapidan, after having been in line of battle for several days, has fallen back, finding that General Lee was ready to meet him.

December 6.—I this morning attended the funeral of Mr.

John Seddon, brother of the Secretary of War. It was a most solemn occasion; he was a man of fine talents and high character. The Rev. Dr. Moore, of the Presbyterian Church, preached a most beautiful sermon.

December 12.—To-day I was examined on arithmetic— "Denominate numbers, vulgar and decimal fractions, tare and tret," etc., etc., by Major Brewer, of the Commissary Department. I felt as if I had returned to my childhood. But for the ridiculousness of the thing, I dare say I should have been embarrassed. On Monday I am to enter on the duties of the office. We are to work from nine till three.

We have just received from our relatives in the country some fine Irish and sweet potatoes, cabbages, butter, sausages, chines, and a ham; and from a friend in town two pounds of very good green tea. These things are very acceptable, as potatoes are twelve dollars per bushel, pork and bacon two dollars fifty cents per pound, and good tea at twenty-five dollars per pound. How are the poor to live? Though it is said that the *poor genteel* are the real sufferers. Money is laid aside for paupers by every one who can possibly do it, but persons who do not let their wants be known are the really poor.

Sunday, Dec. 13.—The first anniversary of the battle of Fredericksburg, where we lost so many valuable lives, and where the Federals were thoroughly whipped. Since that time we have lost many lives, which nothing can repay; but we hold our own, have had some victories, and have been upon the whole much blessed by God. At St. James's Church, this morning, and heard a very fine sermon from the Rev. Mr. Peterkin, from the text, "Blessed are the poor in spirit." To-night we expect to hear Bishop Lay.

1864.

January 1, 1864.—A melancholy pause in my diary. After returning from church on the night of the 13th, a telegram was handed me from Professor Minor, of the University of Virginia, saying, "Come at once, Colonel Colston is extremely ill." After the first shock was over, I wrote an explanatory note to Major Brewer, why I could not be at the office next day, packed my trunk, and was in the cars by seven in the morning. That evening I reached the University, and found dear R. desperately ill with pneumonia, which so often follows, as in the case of General Jackson, the amputation of limbs. Surgeons Davis and Cabell were in attendance, and R's uncle, Dr. Brockenbrough, arrived the next day. After ten days of watching and nursing, amid alternate hopes and fears, we saw our friend Dr. Maupin close our darling's eyes, on the morning of the 23d; and on Christmas-day a military escort laid him among many brother soldiers in the Cemetery of the University of Virginia. He died in the faith of Christ, and with the glorious hope of immortality. His poor mother is heart-stricken, but she, together with his sisters, and one dearer still, had the blessed, and what is now the rare privilege, of soothing and nursing him in his last hours. To them, and to us all, his life seemed as a part of our own. His superior judgment and affectionate temper made him the guide of his whole family. To them his loss can never be supplied. His country has lost one of its earliest and best soldiers. Having been educated at the Virginia Military Institute, he raised and drilled a company in his native County of Berkeley, at the time of the John Brown raid. In 1861 he again led that company to Harper's Ferry. From that time he was never absent more than a week or ten days from his command, and even when wounded at Gaines's Mills, he absented himself but three days, and was again at his post during the several last days of those desperate fights. His fatal wound was received in his nineteenth general engagement, in none of which had he his superior in bravery and devotion to the cause. He was proud of belonging to the glorious Stonewall Brigade, and I have been told by those who knew the circumstances, that he was confided in and trusted by General Jackson to a remarkable degree.

Thus we bury, one by one, the dearest, the brightest, the best of our domestic circles. Now, in our excitement, while we are scattered, and many of us homeless, these separations are poignant, nay, overwhelming; but how can we estimate the sadness of heart which will pervade the South when the war is over, and we are again gathered together around our family hearths and altars, and find the circles broken? One and another gone. Sometimes the father and husband, the beloved head of the household, in whom was centred all that made life dear. Again the eldest son and brother of the widowed home, to whom all looked for guidance and direction; or, perhaps, that bright youth, on whom we had not ceased to look as still a child, whose fair, beardless cheek we had but now been in the habit of smoothing with our hands in fondness—one to whom mother and sisters would always give the good-night kiss, as his peculiar due, and repress the sigh that would arise at the thought that college or business days had almost come to take him from us. And then we will remember the mixed feeling of hope and pride when we first saw this household pet don his jacket of gray and shoulder his musket for the field; how we would be bright and cheerful before him, and turn to our chambers to weep oceans of tears when he is fairly gone. And does he, too, sleep his last sleep? Does our precious one fill a hero's grave? O God! help us, for the wail is in the whole land! "Rachel weeping for her children, and will not be comforted, because they are not." In all the broad South there will be scarcely a fold without its missing lamb, a fireside without its vacant chair. And yet we must go on. It is our duty to rid our land of invaders; we must destroy the snake which is endeavouring to entwine us in its coils, though it drain our heart's blood. We know that we are right in the sight of God, and that we must

"With patient mind our course of duty run.
God nothing does, or suffers to be done,
But we would do ourselves, if we could see
The end of all events as well as He."

The Lord reigneth, be the earth never so unquiet.

January 3.—Entered on the duties of my office on the 30th of December. So far I like it well. "The Major" is very kind, and considerate of our comfort; the duties of the office are not very onerous, but rather confining for one who left school thirty-four years ago, and has had no restraint of the kind during the interim. The ladies, thirty-five in number, are of all ages, and representing various parts of Virginia, also Maryland and Louisiana. Many of them are refugees. It is melancholy to see how many wear mourning for brothers or other relatives, the victims of war. One sad young girl sits near me, whose two brothers have fallen on the field, but she is too poor to buy mourning. I found many acquaintances, and when I learned the history of others, it was often that of fallen fortunes and destroyed homes. One young lady, of high-sounding Maryland name, was banished from Baltimore, because of her zeal in going to the assistance of our Gettysburg wounded. The society is pleasant, and we hope to get along very agreeably. I am now obliged to visit the hospital in the afternoon, and I give it two evenings in the week. It is a cross to me not to be able to give it more time; but we have very few patients just now, so that it makes very little difference.

January 15.—Nothing new from the armies—all quiet. At home we are in *statu quo*, except that we have had a very agreeable accession to our family party in the person of Colonel C. F. M. G. He sleeps in his office, and messes with us. He cheers us every day by bringing the latest news, in the most pleasant form which the nature of the case will admit. My occupation at home just now is as new as that in the office—it is shoe-making. I am busy upon the second pair of gaiter boots. They are made of canvas, presented me by a friend. It was taken from one of our James River vessels, and has been often spread to the breeze, under the " Stars and Bars." The vessel was sunk among the obstructions at Drury's Bluff. The gaiters are cut out by a shoemaker, stitched and bound by the ladies, then soled by a shoemaker, for the moderate sum of fifty dollars. Last year he put soles on a pair for ten dollars. They are then blacked with the material used for blacking guns in the navy. They are very handsome gaiters, and bear polishing by blacking and the shoe-brush as well as morocco. They are lasting, and very cheap when compared with those we buy, which are from $125 to $150 per pair. We are certainly becoming very independent of foreign aid. The girls make beautifully fitting gloves, of dark flannel, cloth, linen, and any other material we can command. We make very nice blacking, and a friend has just sent me a bottle of brilliant black ink, made of elderberries.

February 15.—A pause in my diary; but nothing of importance has occurred, either at home or with the country. The armies are mud-bound—I wish they could continue so. I dread the approach of Spring, with its excitements and horrors.

Prices of provisions have risen enormously—bacon $8 per pound, butter $15, etc. Our old friends from the lower part of Essex, Mr. ——'s parishioners for many years, sent over a wagon filled most generously with all manner of necessary things for our larder. We have no right to complain, for Providence is certainly supplying our wants. The clerks' salaries, too, have been raised to $250 per month, which sounds very large; but when we remember that flour is $300 per barrel, it sinks into insignificance.

28th.—Our hearts ache for the poor. A few days ago, as E. was walking out, she met a wretchedly dressed woman, of miserable appearance, who said she was seeking the Young Men's Christian Association, where she hoped to get assistance and work to do. E. carried her to the door, but it was closed, and the poor woman's wants were pressing. She then brought her home, supplied her with food, and told her to return to see me the following afternoon. She came, and with an honest countenance and manner told me her history. Her name is Brown ; her husband had been a workman in Fredericksburg; he joined the army, and was killed at the second battle of Manassas. Many of her acquaintances in Fredericksburg fled last winter during the bombardment ; she became alarmed, and with her three little children fled too. She had tried to get work in Richmond ; sometimes she succeeded, but could not supply her wants. A kind woman had lent her a room and a part of a garden, but it was outside of the corporation ; and although it saved house-rent, it debarred her from the relief of the associations formed for supplying the city poor with meal, wood, etc. She had evidently been in a situation little short of starvation. I asked her if she could get bread enough for her children by her work ? She said she could sometimes, and when she could not, she "got turnip-tops from her piece of a garden, which were now putting up smartly, and she boiled them, with a little salt, and fed them on that." " But do they satisfy your hunger," said I ? " Well, it is something to go upon for awhile, but it does not stick by us like as bread does, and then we gets hungry again, and I am afraid to let the children eat them too often, lest they should get sick ; so I tries to get them to go to sleep; and sometimes the woman in the next room will bring the children her leavings, but she is monstrous poor." When I gave her meat for her children, taken from the bounty of our Essex friends, tears of gratitude ran down her cheeks ; she said they "had not seen meat for so long." Poor thing, I promised her that her case should be known, and that she should not suffer so again. A soldier's widow shall not suffer from hunger in Richmond. It must not be, and will not be when her case is known. Others are now interested for her. This evening Mrs. R. and myself went in pursuit of her; but though we went through all the streets and lanes of "Butcher Flat" and other vicinities, we could get no clue to her. We went into many small and squalid-looking houses, yet we saw no such abject poverty as Mrs. Brown's. All who needed it were supplied with meal by the corporation, and many were supporting themselves with Government work. One woman stood at a table cutting out work ; we asked her the stereotyped question—" Is there a very poor widow named Brown in this direction?" "No, ladies; I knows two Mrs. Browns, but they ain't so poor, and ain't no widows nuther." As neither of them was our Mrs. B., we turned away ; but she suddenly exclaimed, "Ladies, will one of you read my husband's last letter to me ? for you see I can't read writing." As Mrs. R. took it, she remarked that it was four weeks old, and asked if no one had read it to her?" Oh yes, a gentleman has read it to me four or five times ; but you see I loves to hear it, for may-be I shan't hear from him no more." The tears now poured down her cheeks. "He always writes to me every chance, and it has been so long since he wrote that, and they tell me that they have been fighting, and may-be something has happened to him." We assured her that there had been no fighting— not even a skirmish. This quieted her, and Mrs. R. read the badly written but affectionate letter, in which he expresses his anxiety to see her and his children, and his inability to get a furlough. She then turned to the mantel-piece, and with evident pride took from a nail an old felt hat, through the crown of which were two bullet-holes. It was her husband's hat, through which a bullet had passed in the battle of Chancellorsville, and, as she remarked, must have come "very nigh grazing his head." We remarked upon its being a proof of his bravery, which gratified her very much ; she then hung it up carefully, saying that it was just opposite her bed, and she never let it be out of her sight. She said she wanted her husband to fight for his country, and not " to stand back, like some women's husbands, to be drafted; she would have been ashamed of that, but she felt uneasy, because something told her that he would never get back." Poor woman! we felt very much interested in her, and tried to comfort her.

March 10.—There has been much excitement in Richmond about Kilpatrick's and Dahlgren's raids, and the death of the latter. The cannon roared around the city, the alarm-bell rang, the reserves went out; but Richmond was safe, and we felt no alarm. As usual, they did all the injury they could to country-people, by pillaging and burning. They steal every thing they can; but the people have become very adroit in hiding. Bacon, flour, etc., are put in most mysterious places; plate and handsome china are kept under ground; horses are driven into deuse woods, and the cattle and sheep are driven off. It is astonishing, though much is taken, how much is left. I suppose the raiders are too much hurried for close inspection.

20th.—Our Lent services in St. Paul's Lecture-room, at seven o'clock in the morning, are delightful. The room is always crowded to overflowing—the old, the young, the grave, the gay, collect there soon after sunrise; also military officers in numbers. When General Lee is in town, as he now is, he is never absent, and always one of the most devout worshippers. Within a few days I have seen General Whiting there; also Generals Ransom, Pegram, and others. Starred officers of all grades, colonels, majors, etc., together with many others belonging to the rank and file; and civilians of every degree. It is delightful to see them, all bending together before high Heaven, imploring the help which we so much need.

The Transportation Office is just opposite to us, where crowds of furloughed soldiers, returning to their commands, are constantly standing waiting for transportation. As I pass them on my way to the office in the morning, I always stop to have a cheerful word with them. Yesterday morning I said to them: "Gentlemen, whom do you suppose I have seen this morning?" In answer to their inquiring looks, I said: "General Lee." "General Lee," they exclaimed: "I did not know he was in town; God bless him!" and they looked excited, as if they were about to burst forth with "Hurrah for General Lee!" "And where do you suppose I saw him so early?" "Where, Madam—where?" "At prayer-meeting, down upon his knees, praying for you and for the country." In an instant they seemed subdued; tears started to the eyes of many of those hardy, sunburnt veterans. Some were utterly silent, while others exclaimed, with various ejaculations, "God bless him!" "God bless his dear old soul!" etc. As I walked away, some followed me to know where he was to be seen. One had never seen him at all, and wanted to see him "monstrous bad;" others had seen him often, but wanted to see him in town, "just to look at him." I told them where his family residence was, but as they feared that they could not leave the Transportation Office long enough to find "Franklin Street," I dare say the poor fellows did not see General Lee. This morning I had almost the same conversation with another crowd in the same place. It is delightful to see how they reverence him, and almost as much for his goodness as for his greatness.

April 1.—My diary has been somewhat neglected, for after looking over commissary accounts for six hours in the day, and attending to home or hospital duties in the afternoon, I am too much wearied to write much at night. There are reports of movements in the armies which portend bloody work as the season advances. Oh that the Lord may have us in his holy keeping!

We continue quite comfortable at home. Of course provisious are scarce; but, thanks to our country friends and relatives, we have never been obliged to give up meat entirely. My brother-in-law, Mr. N., has lately sent us twelve hams, so that we are much better supplied than most persons. Groceries are extremely high. We were fortunate in buying ten pounds of tea, when it only sold for $22 per pound. Coffee now sells for $12, and brown sugar at $10 per pound. White sugar is not to be thought of by persons of moderate means. Milk is very scarce and high, so that we have only had it once for many months; and we, the Colonel, Mr. ——, and myself, are very glad to get a cup of tea, night and morning, sweetened with brown sugar, and without milk or cream. Before the war we would have scorned it, but now we enjoy it exceedingly, and feel ourselves very much blessed to have it. The girls have given up tea and coffee; I attempted to do it, and for several days drank only water, but such is the effect of habit upon old people, it made me perfectly miserable; I lost my elasticity of spirit; the accounts in the office went on heavily, everybody asked me if I had heard any bad news, and the family begged me not to look so unhappy. I struggled and strived against the feeling, but the girls pronounced me utterly subjugated, and insisted on my returning to my old beverage. I found myself much more easily persuaded than it is my wont to be, and was happy to resume my brown-sugar tea without cream.

On going down-stairs this evening, I found my friend Mrs. Upshur awaiting me in the parlour. She is the widow of the Hon. Abel P. Upshur, Secretary of War in Mr. Tyler's administration, whose untimely end we remember so well. She is a refugee from Washington, and called to ask me to assist her in finding a room to accommodate herself, her sister, and her little grandson. Her present room, in the third story of a very nice house, suited her very well, but the price was raised every month, until it had become beyond her means. She is rich, but it is almost impossible for her to get funds from Washington. To obtain a room is a most difficult task, but I cheerfully promised her to do what I could; but that I must first go up the street to get some flour, for as it was $300 per barrel, we could not get one, but must purchase it at $1.25 per pound, until we could get some wheat, which we were then expecting from the country, and have it ground. She at once insisted on lending me flour until ours was ground; this being agreed to, we continued on our walk in pursuit of the room. We naturally talked of the past. She related to me a circumstance which occurred when I was a young girl, and was a striking illustration of the change which time and the war had brought on us both. She said that during the political Convention of 1829-30, she came to Richmond with her husband, who was a member of it. The first entertainment to which she was invited was given at my father's house. When she entered the room my mother was standing about the centre of it, receiving her guests, and seeing that Mrs. Upshur was young and a perfect stranger, she took her by the hand and seated her by Mrs. Madison, at the same time introducing her to that celebrated woman. She said it was one of the most pleasant evenings of her life, and she looked back upon it with peculiar satisfaction, for she was then introduced to Mr. Madison, Mr. Monroe, Mr. Benjamin Watkins Leigh, and many others of the celebrated men of the day, who were attending the Convention. Could we then have looked through the vista of time, and have seen ourselves in this same city, the one looking for a cheap room in somebody's third story, the other looking for *cheap bread*, would we have believed it? The anecdote saddened us both for a time, but we soon recovered, and went on our way in cheerful, hopeful conversation. But we did not find the room.

April 25.—Our family in *statu quo*. The country in great excitement. We have lately had a splendid little victory at Plymouth, North Carolina. We have also had successes in Florida, at Shreveport, and other places in the South and South-west. The God of battles is helping us, or how could we thus succeed? This city is quite excited by Mr. Memminger having ordered off the Note-signing Department, consisting entirely of ladies, to Columbia, South Carolina. It has caused much distress, for many of them, whose living depends on the salary, can't possibly go. Mothers cannot leave their children, nor wives their husbands. No one seems to understand the motive which prompted the order. It seems to be very arbitrary. It is thought by some persons that all the departments will be ordered off. I trust not; for I, among many others, would be obliged to resign, and I cannot imagine how we would live without the salary. I see no reason to believe that any such move is intended, and I will not be unhappy about it. "Sufficient unto the day is the evil thereof."

The enemy threatens Richmond, and is coming against it with an immense army. They boast that they can and will have it this summer; but, with the help of God, we hope to drive them back again. Our Government is making every effort to defeat them. I don't think that any one doubts our ability to do it; but the awful loss of life necessary upon the fights is what we dread.

April 27.—Another day and night have passed, and nothing of importance has occurred to the country. We are expecting movements in every direction. O God! direct our leaders!

Our daughter M. is with us, quite sick; her husband has just arrived from North Carolina, where he is attached to General Whiting's command.

29*th.*—The country seems to continue quiet, but the campaign on the Rapidan is expected to open every day. Oh, how I dread it! The morning is bright and beautiful; it seems hardly possible that such strife is abroad in the land.

May 2.—Just taken leave of J. J., who has gone to Halifax, where the Bishop resides. It seems so strange that she does not want to go to the country. If I could only get to some quiet nook, some lodge in a vast wilderness, where rumours of unsuccessful or successful war could never reach me more, I think I should be happy. The Bishop says it is too expensive here for his income, and so it is for everybody's income, but were we to leave it we should have none; our whole dependence is now upon the Government, except the interest on a small amount invested in Confederate bonds.

Our army, it is said, is fighting at or near Newbern, North Carolina. I trust they are following up the Plymouth victory.

Tuesday Morning, May 3.—Yesterday passed as usual. We attended Mr. Peterkin's prayer-meeting before breakfast, which we generally do, and which was very interesting. Then came by market for our daily supplies; and at nine I commenced my labour in the office, while Mr. —— went to his hospital, which occupies a great deal of his time.

Washington, North Carolina, has been evacuated by the Federals, who have retired to Newbern. All quiet on the Rapidan. Six steamers have run the blockade within a few days, laden with ammunition, etc. Surely God is with us. It is a delightful thing to contemplate that so many of our officers of high position, who are leading and giving an example to our soldiers, should be God-fearing men; from the President and General Lee down, I believe a majority of them are professing Christians. On Sunday I saw General R. Ransom (who has lately been put in command here) and General Kemper, who has just recovered from the wound received at Gettysburg, both at the communion-table.

On Saturday our President had a most heart-rending accident in his family. His little son was playing on the back-portico, fell over, and was picked up apparently lifeless. Both parents were absent, nor did they get home in time to see their child alive. The neighbours collected around him, physicians were immediately called in, but the little fellow could not be aroused; he breathed for about three-quarters of an hour. His devoted parents returned to find their boy, whom they had left two hours before full of " life in every limb," now cold in death. They have the deep sympathy of the community.

May 5.—Our army on the Rapidan is in line of battle. Grant is moving his mighty columns. Where the battle will take place Heaven only knows. I pray that God may be with us, and that the enemy may be driven far from our borders.

We are now attending the prayer-meetings held by the Young Men's Christian Association, which are very interesting; three of them will be held this week for our dear army, and for the battle now pending.

May 6, 1864.—The Federals are this morning ascending James River, with a fleet of thirty-nine vessels—four monitors among them. The battle between Lee and Grant imminent. God help us! We feel strengthened by the prayers of so many good people. All the city seems quiet and trusting. We feel that the Lord will keep the city. We were at our own prayer-meeting at St. James's this morning at half-past six. Yesterday evening we heard most fervent prayers from the Young Men's Christian Association. To-day Dr. Reid's Church will be open all day for prayer. I am sorry that I shall not be able to go before the afternoon.

Grant's force is said to be between one hundred and fifty and one hundred and eighty thousand men. The "battle is not always to the strong," as we have often experienced during the past three years.

We spent last evening at the Ballard House, with Dr. S. and my dear S. She is hastening to her ill child; he must return to his post; private griefs cannot now be indulged.

Sunday, May 8.—By the blessing of God, I now record that, as far as heard from, our arms have been signally victorious. On Thursday and Friday the enemy were driven off, and the telegram of yesterday from General Lee spoke of our cause as going on prosperously, and with comparatively little loss to us. Grant had been driven back, and 10,000 prisoners taken, but how far he has gone is not yet known. General Lee's telegram last night was very encouraging; he speaks of having captured two major-generals and killed three brigadiers. We have not yet heard of our casualties, except in one or two instances. We have been dreadfully shocked by the death of Colonel William Randolph, of Clarke County. He fell on the 6th of May. The country has lost no more devoted patriot, the army no more gallant officer, and society no more brilliant member. It was but last Sunday that his sister-in-law, Miss M. S., said to me with natural pride and pleasure : " William Randolph has been promoted; he is now colonel of the Second." I expressed the pleasure which I then felt; but as she passed out of the room, and my thoughts again turned to the subject, a superstitious horror came over me, and I said to those around me, " This is a fatal honour conferred upon W. R.," and I could not get rid of the impression. The Second Regiment has invariably lost its field officers. It is one of the most gallant regiments of the Stonewall Brigade, and has frequently had what is called the post of honour. Colonel Allen, Colonel Botts, Lieutenant-Colonel Lackland, Lieutenant-Colonel Colston, Major Jones, and now Colonel Randolph, have fallen ! and Colonel Nadenbonsh, of the same regiment, has been so mutilated by wounds, as to be obliged to retire from the service.

The fleet upon James River has landed about 30,000 or 40,000 troops. One of their gunboats ran upon a torpedo, which blew it to atoms. We repulsed them near Port Walthall. Yesterday they came with a very strong force upon the Petersburg Railroad. They were too strong for us, and we had to fall back; the enemy consequently took the road, and, of course, injured it very much; but they have fallen back; why, we do not know, unless they have heard of Grant's failure. The alarm-bell is constantly ringing, making us nervous and anxious. The militia have been called out, and have left the city, but where they have gone I know not. It is strange how little apprehension seems to be felt in the city. Our trust is first in God, and, under Him, in our brave men. At this moment Yankee prisoners are passing by. I do not know where they were captured. Those taken at the battle of "The Wilderness" were sent South.

I went to the Monumental Church this morning. Mr. —— read the service, and Mr. Johnston, of Alexandria, preached.

Wednesday, May 11.—The last three days have been most exciting. The enemy on the south side of the river have made heavy demonstrations; their force is perhaps 40,000; ours not half that number. The militia, the City Battalion, and the clerks have gone from Richmond. They have had a heavy fight at Port Walthall, and another near Chester, in which we had, upon the whole, the advantage of them. In the mean time a large body of raiders are going over the country. They have cut the Central Railroad, and burnt three trains of cars, laden with provisions for General Lee's army, and are doing all manner of mischief to public and private property. Not a word can we hear from General Lee, except through private telegrams sent from Guiney's Station. The wires (telegraph) above that place have been cut. Our accounts from Guiney's are very encouraging. It is astonishing how quiet everybody is—all owing, I must believe, to an abiding faith in the goodness of God. Prayer-meetings are held in almost all the churches, and we take great comfort in them. It seems to me evident that the Lord is fighting our battles for us.

The last was a most disturbed night. We knew that the attachés of the War Department had received orders to spend the night there, and our son had promised us that if any thing exciting occurred he would come up and let us know. We were first aroused by hearing a number of soldiers pass up Broad Street. I sprang up, and saw at least a brigade passing by. As we were composing ourselves to sleep, I heard several pebbles come against the window. On looking out, I saw J. standing below. In a moment the door was opened and he was in our room, with the information, brought by a courier, that 7,000 raiders were within sixteen miles of us, making their way to the city. He also said that 3,000 infantry had marched to meet them. Every lady in the house dressed immediately, and some of us went down to the porch. There we saw ladies in every porch, and walking on the pavements, as if it were evening. We saw but one person who seemed really alarmed; every one else seemed to expect something to occur to stop the raiders. Our city had too often been saved as if by a miracle. About two o'clock a telegram came from General Stuart that he was in pursuit of the enemy. J. came up to bring us the information, and we felt that all was right. In a very short time families had retired to their chambers, and quietness reigned in this hitherto perturbed street. For ourselves, we were soon asleep. To-day General Stuart telegraphs that the enemy were overtaken at Ashland by Lomax's Brigade, and handsomely repulsed. We have just heard that they have taken the road to Dover's Mills, and our men are in hot pursuit.

Thursday, May 12.—The cannon is now roaring in our ears. It cannot be more than three miles off. The Lord reigneth; in that is our trust. There was a severe cavalry fight yesterday morning, in which our brilliant cavalry leader, General J. E. B. Stuart, was severely wounded. He was brought to the city last night. One of his aids, our relative, Lieutenant T. S. Garnett, has told us with what difficulty they got him here; in an ambulance, going out of the way, hither and thither, to avoid the enemy; of course, every jolt inflicting intense agony. He is now at the house of his brother-in-law, Dr. Brewer, surrounded by the most efficient surgeons and devoted friends. The prayers of the community are with him.

My time, when out of the office, is much absorbed by the hospital. Many wounded are brought in from both sides of the river. This morning, as I entered St. James's Church, I saw the smoke from the cannon distinctly. I stood for a moment on the steps and listened to the continued roaring, and felt that the contest was fearfully near to us. The prayers, hymns, psalms, and address were most comforting. God be praised for his goodness, that we are still surrounded by Christian people, and have the faith and trust of Christians. The town is as calm as if it were not the great object of desire to hundreds of thousands of implacable enemies, who desire nothing so much as its destruction.

General Lee's telegram last night gave us an account of another repulse given General Grant, with great slaughter. "We suffered little in comparison;" such was his telegram, signed "R. E. Lee." His signature is always cheering to our people. For some time we had not seen it, in consequence of cut telegraphic wires. Both armies are now fortifying. The Yankees have such indomitable perseverance, that they will never give up.

May 13.—General Stuart died of his wounds last night, twenty-four hours after he was shot. He was a member of the Episcopal Church, and expressed to the Rev. Dr. Peterkin his resignation to the will of God. After much conversation with his friends and Dr. P., and joining them in a hymn which he requested should be sung, he calmly resigned his redeemed spirit to the God who gave it. Thus passed away our great cavalry general, just one year after the immortal Jackson. This seems darkly mysterious to us, but God's will be done. The funeral took place this evening, from St. James's Church. My duty to the living prevented my attending it, for which I am very sorry ; but I was in the hospital from three o'clock until eight, soothing the sufferers in the only way I could, by fanning them, bathing their wounds, and giving them a word of comfort. Mr. —— and others of our household were at the funeral. They represent the scene as being very imposing.

14*th*.—The cavalry fight on the Chickahominy was very severe. The Yankees escaped on Thursday night ; they should not have been allowed to get off. Our sad deficiency in numbers is always in our way.

The death of another of our beloved E. H. S. boys has shocked us greatly—I mean that of Colonel Robert Randolph, of Fauquier, for a long time the chivalric captain of the famous "Black Horse Company." After fighting desperately for hours, he was ordered to change his position; he immediately raised himself in his saddle, exclaiming, " Boys, we will give them one round more before we go !"

fired, and was at that moment struck in the forehead by a Minié ball, and laid low, a few hours after the fall of his General. Thus our young men, of the first blood of the country—first in character and education, and, what is more important to us now, first in gallantry and patriotism—fall one by one. What a noble army of martyrs has already passed away! I tremble for the future; but we must not think of the future. "Sufficient unto the day is the evil thereof."

General Lee's last telegram tells of a furious fight on Thursday, near Spottsylvania Court-House. The enemy was repulsed, and driven back; and yet General Grant prepares for a fresh attack. It is said that 15,000 wounded Yankees are in Fredericksburg. We have heard cannon all day in the direction of Drury's Bluff; yet we are calm!

Tuesday Morning, May 17.—For some days the cannon has been resounding in our ears, from the south side of James River. Colonel Garnett has come in to tell us that for the first two days there was only heavy skirmishing, but that on yesterday there was a terrific fight all along the lines. Yesterday evening a brigadier, his staff, and 840 men, were lodged in the Libby Prison. Nothing definite has been heard since that time. The impression is, that we have been generally successful. Very brilliant reports are afloat on the streets, but whether they are reliable is the question. My nephew, Major B., has just called to tell me that his brother W. is reported "missing." His battery suffered dreadfully, and he has not been seen. God grant that he may be only a prisoner! We suppose that it would have been known to the fragment of his battery which is left, if he had fallen.

18th.—W. B. certainly captured. I thank God for it, as the least of casualties.

Generals Lee and Grant still fighting.

On the south side, Beauregard has driven Butler to Bermuda Hundreds, where he is under shelter of his gunboats. Oh! when will this fearful state of things end?

23d.—Our young relative, Lieutenant G., a member of General Stuart's staff, who was always near his person, has just been giving us a most gratifying account of General Stuart's habits. He says, that although he considered him one of the most sprightly men he has ever seen, devoted to society, particularly to that of the ladies, always social and cheerful, yet he has never seen him do any thing, even under the strongest excitement, unbecoming his Christian profession or his high position as a soldier; he never saw him drink, or heard an oath escape his lips; his sentiments were always high-minded, pure, and honourable, and his actions entirely coincided with them. In short, he considered him, whether on the field or in the private circle, the model of a Christian gentleman and soldier. When speaking of his gallantry as an officer, Lieutenant G's admiration knows no bounds. He speaks of the devotion of the soldiers to him as enthusiastic in the extreme. The evening before his fatal wound, he sent his troops on in pursuit of Sheridan, under the command of General Fitz Lee, as he was unavoidably detained for some three or four hours. General Lee overtook the enemy, and a sharp skirmish ensued, in which Sheridan's rear suffered very much. In the mean time, General Stuart determined to overtake General Lee, and, with his staff, rode very rapidly sixteen miles, and reached him about nightfall. They were halting for a few moments, as General Stuart rode up quietly, no one suspecting he was there, until a plain-looking soldier crossed the road, stopped, peered through the darkness into his face, and shouted out, "Old Jeb has come!" In an instant the air was rent with huzzas. General Stuart waved his cap in recognition; but called out in rather a sad voice, "My friends, we won't halloo until we get out of the woods!" intimating that there was serious work before them. At that hour the next night he was pursuing his weary and suffering way to Richmond. A friend, who knows how much I regretted not being able to serve General Stuart in any way, or even to be at his funeral, has been so kind as to write me a minute account of his sickness, death, and burial. "Perhaps (she says) it is not generally known how entirely General Stuart sacrificed his life to save Richmond. An officer of high rank, who knew the circumstances, told me that in all the war there was not one man more truly a martyr to our cause. In the many raids upon Richmond there was none in which we seemed in such imminent peril as the one in which General Stuart has just fallen. How we listened, and watched, and prayed, as the cannon sounded nearer and nearer, and even the volleys of musketry could be heard out on the roads by which the enemy were approaching! We knew that General Stuart had a band of about 2,000 cavalry against overwhelming odds on the Yankee side, and that he knew that upon this 2,000 men alone it depended to bar the enemy's approach on that side. He met the Yankees, 5,000 strong, beat them back, and fell in the encounter! It was with difficulty that he could be rescued from those who were bearing him away, but one of his own troopers saved him, and with his staff and surgeon (Dr. John Fontaine) bore him to the city. We heard that he was dying, and, in spite of the anxiety and confusion reigning at such a time, many of us rushed to Dr. Brewer's house to hear tidings of the beloved commander, whose gallantry, whose youthful gayety and chivalrous character, made him the prince among our cavalry officers. His life was ebbing out from internal hemorrhage; but his senses were as clear and his mind as calm as noontide. He asked repeatedly for his wife, who, though but fifteen miles away, could not be reached, so completely was the city hemmed in by the enemy. By his side stood our President, who, upon hearing of his situation, had hastened to thank him in the name of his country. 'I have but done my duty,' was the soldier's reply. And near him was the minister of God, good Mr. Peterkin, of whose church (Episcopal) General S. was a member. He asked for his favourite hymn, and joined his feeble voice with the touching words: 'I would not live alway.' From time to time, he turned his head to ask, 'Is she come?' But she, for whom his loving heart so yearned, came not till that heart was stilled forever. At the funeral—at the head of his coffin—sat the soldier who had rescued him, all battle-stained and soiled; and near by, the members of his staff, who all adored him. Upon the coffin lay a sword, formed of delicate white flowers, a cross of white roses, and above these the heavenly crown, symbolized by one of green bay-leaves. We followed him to the church, where, after appropriate ceremonies, attended by many persons, his body was taken to Hollywood Cemetery. No martial pomp, no soldier's funeral, but—

> "'Slowly and sadly we laid him down,
>   From the field of his fame fresh and gory;
> We carved not a line, we raised not a stone,
>   But we left him alone with his glory.'

Everybody was struck with the resemblance to the funeral so beautifully described in the lines just quoted. As we passed, in slow procession—

"'We knew by the distant and random gun,
That the foe was sullenly firing.'

These guns were his funeral knell, sounding at intervals the solemn peal, with which, in the haste and uncertainty of the time, it was impossible for us to honour him."

One of the morning papers has some lines on the same subject, more poetic, though not so graphic, as the account given by my friend:

"J. E. B. STUART.

"We could not pause, while yet the noontide air
Shook with the cannonade's incessant pealing,
The funeral pageant, fitly to prepare,
A nation's grief revealing.

"The smoke above the glimmering woodland wide,
That skirts our southward border with its beauty,
Marked where our heroes stood, and fought and died,
For love, and faith, and duty

"And still what time the doubtful strife went on,
We might not find expression for our sorrow;
We could but lay our dear, dumb warrior down,
And gird us for the morrow.

"One weary year ago, when came a lull
With victory, in the conflicts' stormy closes,
When the glad Spring, all flushed and beautiful,
First mocked us with her roses—

"With dirge and bell, and minute-gun, we paid
Some few poor rites, an inexpressive token

Of a great people's pain, to Jackson's shade,
  In agony unspoken.

"No wailing trumpet, and no tolling bell,
  No cannon, save the battle's boom receding,
When Stuart to the grave we bore, might tell
  With hearts all crushed and bleeding.

"The crisis suited not with pomp, and she,
  Whose anguish bears the seal of consecration,
Had wished his Christian obsequies should be
  Thus void of ostentation.

"Only the maidens came, sweet flowers to twine
  Above his form, so still, and cold, and painless,
Whose deeds upon our brightest records shine,
  Whose life and sword were stainless.

"We well remembered how he loved to dash
  Into the fight, festooned from summer bowers·
How like a fountain's spray, his sabre's flash
  Leaped from a mass of flowers.

"And so we carried to his place of rest,
  All that of our Paladin was mortal;
The cross, and not the sabre, on his breast,
  That opes the heavenly portal.

"No more of tribute might to us remain;
  But there will come a time when freedom's martyrs
A richer guerdon of renown shall gain
  Than gleams in stars and garters.

"I claim no prophet's vision, but I see,
  Through coming years now near at hand, now distant,
My rescued country, glorious and free,
  And strong and self-existent.

"I hear from out that sunlit land which lies
    Beyond these clouds which darkly gather o'er us,
The happy sounds of industry arise,
    In swelling, peaceful chorus.

"And mingling with these sounds, the glad acclaim
    Of millions, undisturbed by war's afflictions,
Crowning each martyr's never-dying name
    With grateful benedictions.

"In some fair, future garden of delights,
    Where flowers shall bloom, and song-birds sweetly warble.
Art shall erect the statues of our knights,
    In living bronze and marble.

"And none of all that bright, heroic throng
    Shall wear to far-off time a semblance grander,
Shall still be decked with fresher wreaths of song,
    Than the beloved commander.

"The Spanish legends tell us of the Cid,
    That after death he rode erect and stately
Along his lines, e'en as in life he did,
    In presence yet more stately.

"And thus our Stuart at this moment seems
    To ride out of our dark and troubled story,
Into the region of romance and dreams,
    A realm of light and glory.

"And sometimes when the silver bugles blow,
    That radiant form in battle reappearing,
Shall lead his horsemen headlong on the foe,
    In victory careering."

May 26.—We are now anticipating a fight at Hanover Junction. General Lee fell back to that point on

Sunday last, for some good purpose, no doubt. Our army is in line of battle on the Cedar Hill plantation. The ladies of the family have come to Richmond to avoid the awful collision about to take place. That house, I sadly fear, is to be another sacrifice. Our successes have been wonderful, and evidently, I think, directed by God. We have, however, just met with a sad reverse in Charles City County. General Fitz Lee, commanding two brigades, fought a much larger body of men, who were strongly fortified, and was of course repulsed. Alas, alas for our gallant army! bravery cannot always contend safely against overwhelming numbers. We are very uneasy about our dear ones who were in that fight. Strange stories are told of the wounded having been bayoneted. It is difficult to believe that men of human hearts could do such things; and while I feel unhappy about the rumour, I cannot credit it.

May 27.—News from Fitz Lee's fight; it was not disastrous as at first reported; many were wounded, many captured, and but four killed. But four desolated homes by this stroke! but four widows, or broken-hearted mothers, in addition to the bereaved of the land! God be with them to comfort them! Nothing farther of the bayoneted wounded: I trust that it was all a fabrication.

We returned to the office yesterday, which had been closed for a week. It is pitiable to see how the rations are being reduced by degrees. The Government is exerting itself for the relief of the soldiers. God have mercy upon and help us!

June 4.—There has been skirmishing for some days. One day a fight at Ashland, another at Cold Harbour; but yesterday the heaviest cannonading I ever heard continued all day, until after dark. The fighting was between Bethesda

Church and Cold Harbour. We were well fortified, and General Lee reports great success to our arms. " It is the Lord's doings, and it is marvellous in our eyes." We went to church this evening and returned thanks.

June 5.—Our daughter-in-law, Mrs. Dr. ——, came from Charlottesville this evening. The regular communication being cut off, she went up to Lynchburg, taking that route to Richmond; but the Government having impressed the cars, she was obliged to take a freight-train, and was fortunate in finding a friend coming down in the same way, who acted as her escort. At Burkesville (shall I record it of a Virginia house of any degree?) she was treated with such inhospitality, that she was compelled to pass the night in a car filled with bags of corn, which the gentlemen fixed so carefully as to give her *almost* a comfortable resting-place. When she returned from her unsuccessful application for quarters, one of the soldiers said to her, (she was the only lady in the company,) " Lady, where are you from?" "The Valley of Virginia," was her reply. He instantly sprang up: " Boys, we must burn that house!" he exclaimed; " they won't take in this lady from the ' Valley,' where we have been treated so kindly." Of course he had no idea of burning the house, though he seemed highly indignant. She came to us looking well after a three days' journey, having borne her difficulties with great cheerfulness.

11*th*.—Just heard from W. and S. H. Both places in ruins, except the dwelling-houses. Large portions of the Federal army were on them for eight days. S. H. was used as a hospital for the wounded brought from the battle-fields; this protected the house. At W. several generals had their head-quarters in the grounds near the house, which, of course, protected it. General Warren had his tent in the "shrubbery" for two days, General Burnside for a day or two, and those of lesser rank were there from time to time. General Grant was encamped at S. H. for a time. Dr. B. was at home, with several Confederate wounded from the battle of "Haw's Shop" in the house. Being absent a mile or two from home when they arrived, they so quickly threw out pickets, spread their tents over the surrounding fields and hills, that he could not return to his house, where his wife and only child were alone, until he had obtained a pass from a Yankee officer. As he approached the house, thousands and tens of thousands of horses and cattle were roaming over the fine wheat fields on his and the adjoining estate, (that of his niece, Mrs. N.,) which were now ripe for the sickle. The clover fields and fields of young corn were sharing the same fate. He found his front porch filled with officers. They asked him of his sentiments with regard to the war. He told them frankly that he was an original Secessionist, and ardently hoped to see the North and South separate and distinct nations now and forever. One of them replied that he "honoured his candour," and from that moment he was treated with great courtesy. After some difficulty he was allowed to keep his wounded Confederates, and in one or two instances the Federal surgeons assisted him in dressing their wounds. At S. H. the parlour was used for an amputating room, and Yankee blood streamed through that beautiful apartment and the adjoining passage. Poor M. had her stricken heart sorely lacerated in every way, particularly when her little son came running in and nestled up to her in alarm. A soldier had asked him, "Are you the son of Captain Newton, who was killed in Culpeper?" "Yes," replied the child. "Well, I belong to the

Eighth Illinois, and was one of the soldiers that fired at him when he fell," was the barbarous reply.

On these highly cultivated plantations not a fence is left, except mutilated garden enclosures. The fields were as free from vegetation after a few days as the Arabian desert; the very roots seemed eradicated from the earth. A fortification stretched across W., in which were embedded the fence rails of that and the adjoining farms. Ten thousand cavalry were drawn up in line of battle for two days on the two plantations, expecting the approach of the Confederates; bands of music were constantly playing martial airs in all parts of the premises; and whiskey flowed freely. The poor servants could not resist these intoxicating influences, particularly as Abolition preachers were constantly collecting immense crowds, preaching to them the cruelty of the servitude which had been so long imposed upon them, and that Abraham Lincoln was the Moses sent by God to deliver them from the "land of Egypt and the house of bondage," and to lead them to the promised land. After the eight days were accomplished, the army moved off, leaving not a quadruped, except two pigs, which had ensconced themselves under the ruins of a servant's house, and perhaps a dog to one plantation; to the other, by some miraculous oversight, two cows and a few pigs were left. Not a wheeled vehicle of any kind was to be found; all the grain, flour, meat, and other supplies were swept off, except the few things hid in those wonderful places which could not be fathomed even by the "Grand Army." Scarcely a representative of the sons and daughters of Africa remained in that whole section of country; they had all gone to Canaan, by way of York River, Chesapeake Bay, and the Potomac—not dry-shod, for the waters were not rolled back at the presence of these modern Israelites, but in vessels crowded to suffocation in this excessively warm weather. They have gone to homeless poverty, an unfriendly climate, and hard work; many of them to die without sympathy, for the invalid, the decrepit, and the infant of days have left their houses, beds, and many comforts, the homes of their birth, the masters and mistresses who regarded them not so much as property as humble friends and members of their families. Poor, deluded creatures! I am grieved not so much on account of the loss of their services, though that it excessively inconvenient and annoying, but for their grievous disappointment. Those who have trades, or who are brought up as lady's maids or house servants, may do well, but woe to the masses who have gone with the blissful hope of idleness and free supplies! We have lost several who were great comforts to us, and others who were sources of care, responsibility, and great expense. These particulars from W. and S. H. I have from our nephew, J. P., who is now a scout for General W. H. F. Lee. He called by to rest a few hours at his uncle's house, and says he would scarcely have known the barren wilderness. The Northern officers seemed disposed to be courteous to the ladies, in the little intercourse which they had with them. General Ferrara, who commanded the negro troops, was humane, in having a coffin made for a young Confederate officer who died in Dr B's house, and was kind in other respects. The surgeons, too, assisted in attending to the Confederate wounded. An officer one morning sent for Mrs. N. to ask her where he should place a box of French china for safety; he said that some soldiers had discovered it buried in her garden, dug it up and opened it, but he had come up at this crisis and had placed a guard over it, and desired to know where she wished it put. A place of safety of course was not on the premises, but she had it taken to her chamber. She thanked him for his kindness. He seemed moved, and said, "Mrs. N., I will do what I can for you, for I cannot be too thankful that my wife is not in an invaded country." She then asked him how he could, with his feelings, come to the South. He replied that he was in the regular army, and was obliged to come. Many little acts of kindness were done at both houses, which were received in the spirit in which they were extended. *Per contra:* On one occasion Miss D., a young relative of Mrs. N's, was in one of the tents set aside for the Confederate wounded, writing a letter from a dying soldier to his friends at home. She was interrupted by a young Yankee surgeon, to whom she was a perfect stranger, putting his head in and remarking pertly, "Ah, Miss D., are you writing? Have you friends in Richmond? I shall be there in a few days, and will with pleasure take your communications." She looked up calmly into his face, and replied, "Thank you; *I* have no friends in the Libby!" It was heard by his comrades on the outside of the tent, and shouts and peals of laughter resounded at the expense of the discomfited surgeon. The ladies frequently afterwards heard him bored with the question, "Doctor, when do you go to the Libby?"

12th.—I am grieved to say that we have had a reverse in the "Valley," and that General Jones, of the cavalry, has been killed, and his command repulsed. They have fallen back to Waynesborough, leaving Staunton in the hands of the enemy. General Johnston is doing well in Georgia. Oh, that he may use up Sherman entirely! We are getting on well at home; everybody looks as calm as if there were no belligerent armies near.

24th.—I have been much occupied nursing the sick, not only in the hospital, but among our own friends; and a sad, sad week has the last been to us. We have had very little time to think of public affairs, but now that the last sad offices have been performed for one very, very dear to us, with sore hearts we must go back to busy life again. It is wonderful to me that we retain our senses. While the cannon is booming in our ears from the neighbourhood of Petersburg, we know that Hunter is raiding among our friends in the most relentless way; that the Military Institute has been burnt, and that we have nothing to hope for the West, unless General Early and General Breckinridge can destroy him utterly.

July 18.—Since the last note in my diary we have been pursuing our usual course. The tenor of our way is singularly rough and uneven, marked by the sound of cannon, the marching of troops, and all the paraphernalia of grim-visaged war; but we still visit our friends and relatives, and have our pleasant social and family meetings, as though we were at peace with all the world. The theme of every tongue is our army in Maryland. What is it doing? What will be the result of the venture? The last accounts are from the Washington papers. Early, they say, is before Washington, throwing in shells, having cut the railroads and burnt the bridges. We are of course all anxiety, and rumour is busier than ever. The army, it is said, has driven innumerable horses, beeves, etc., into Virginia. I trust so; it is surmised that to supply the commissariat is the chief object of the trip. Grant still before Petersburg, sending transports, etc., with troops to defend Washington.

24th.—Amid all the turbulent scenes which surround us, our only grandchild has first seen the light, and the dear little fellow looks as quiet as though all were peace. We thank God for this precious gift, this little object of all-absorbing interest, which so pleasantly diverts our troubled minds. His father has left his far-off military post to welcome him, and before he returns we must by baptism receive him into the Church on earth, praying that he may be a "member of Christ, a child of God, and an inheritor of the kingdom of heaven." This rite thus early administered, bringing him into the Episcopal Church, seems to belong to him by inheritance, as he is the grandson of a Presbyter on one side, and of a Bishop on the other.

The city looks warlike, though the inhabitants are quiet. Troops are constantly passing to and fro; army wagons, ambulances, etc., rattle by, morning, noon, and night. Grant remains passive on the Appomattox, occasionally throwing a shell into Petersburg, which may probably explode among women and children—but what matters it? They are rebels—what difference does it make about their lives or limbs?

July 27.—General Early has returned from Maryland, bringing horses, cattle, etc. While near Washington, the army burned Mr. Montgomery Blair's house, which I cannot persuade myself to regret, and spared the residence of his father, by order, it is said, of General Breckinridge. I know that General B. was right, but I think it required great forbearance, particularly in the soldiers, who have felt in their own persons and families the horrors of this cruel war of invasion. It seems to our human view that unless the war is severely felt by those in high authority, it will never cease. Hunter has just passed through the upper part of the Valley of Virginia, his pathway marked by fire and sword; and Sheridan has followed Early into Virginia, with no very gentle intent, I fear. I am glad that Maryland was spared as a general thing, particularly as our friends might have suffered with our foes, for it would have been difficult to discriminate; but I cannot avoid thinking that if other places, besides Governor Bradford's house and the town of Chambersburg, had been burnt, it would shorten the war. Yet God has said, "Vengeance is mine, I will repay;" and I hope that Christian principles will ever be observed by our commanders. There seems to be no touch of pity in the hearts of many of the Federal generals. Women and children are made homeless at midnight, and not allowed to save any thing, even their clothes. When houses are not burned, they are robbed of every thing which a rapacious soldiery may desire. The last barrel of flour, the last ham, is taken from store-rooms; and this is done, not in Virginia only; nor are Hunter, Sheridan, Kilpatrick, or Stoneman the only men who do it; but every State in the Confederacy has felt the heel of the despot. North and South Carolina have suffered on their eastern borders most severely; the same of Georgia and Florida. Alabama has had much to bear. The Mississippi country in Louisiana, Arkansas, and the State of Mississippi, has been ravaged and desolated; Tennessee has perhaps had more to bear than any of them. But poor old Virginia has been furrowed and scarred until her original likeness is gone. From the Potomac to the Roanoke, from the seaboard to the Kentucky boundary, including the down-trodden Eastern Shore, she could scarcely be recognized by her sons. Marked by a hundred battle-fields, and checkered by fortifications, almost every spot is classic ground. From the beginning she has acted her part nobly, and has already covered herself with glory; but when the war is over, where shall we find her old churches, where her noble homesteads, scenes of domestic comfort and generous hospitality? Either laid low by the firebrand, or desecrated and desolated. In the march of the army, or in the rapid evolutions of raiding parties, woe betide the houses which are found deserted! In many cases the men of the family having gone to the war, the women and children dare not stay; then the lawless are allowed to plunder. They seem to take the greatest delight in breaking up the most elegant or the most humble furniture, as the case may be; cut the portraits from the frames, split pianos in pieces, ruin libraries, in any way that suits their fancy; break doors from their hinges, and locks from the doors; cut the windows from the frames, and leave no pane of glass unbroken; carry off house-linen and carpets; the contents of the store-rooms and pantries, sugar, flour, vinegar, molasses, pickles, preserves, which cannot be eaten or carried off, are poured together in one general mass; the horses are of course taken from the stables; cattle and stock of all kinds driven off or shot in the woods and fields. Generally, indeed I believe always when the whole army is moving, inhabited houses are protected. To raiders such as Hunter and Co. is reserved the credit of committing such outrages in the presence of ladies—of taking their watches from their belts, their rings from their fingers, and their ear-rings from their ears; of searching their bureaux and wardrobes, and filling pockets and haversacks in their presence. Is it not then wonderful that soldiers whose families have suffered such things could be restrained when in a hostile conutry? It seems to me to show a marvellous degree of forbearance in the officers themselves, and of discipline in the troops.

August 11.—Sheridan's and Early's troops are fighting

in the Valley. We suffered a disaster near Martinsburg, and our troops fell back to Strasburg; had a fight on the old battle-ground at Kernstown, and we drove the enemy through Winchester to Martinsburg, which our troops took possession of. Poor Winchester, how checkered its history throughout the war! Abounding with patriotism as it is, what a blessing it must be to have a breath of free air, even though it be for a short time! Their welcome of our soldiers is always so joyous, so bounding, so generous! How they must enjoy the blessed privilege of speaking their own sentiments without having their servants listening and acting as spies in their houses, and of being able to hear from or write to their friends! Oh! I would that there was a prospect of their being disenthralled forever.

12*th.*—I am sorry to record a defeat near Moorfield, in Hardy County. These disasters are very distressing to us all, except to the croakers, who find in them so much food for their gloom, that I am afraid they are rather pleased than otherwise. They always, on such occasions, elongate their mournful countenances, prophesy evil, and chew the cud of discontent with a better show of reason than they can generally produce. The signal failure of Grant's mine to blow up our army, and its recoil upon his own devoted troops, amply repay us for our failure in Hardy. God's hand was in it, and to Him be the praise.

One of my friends in the office is a victim of Millroy's reign in Winchester. She wrote to a friend of hers at the North, expressing her feelings rather imprudently. The letter was intercepted, and she was immediately arrested, and brought in an ambulance through the enemy's lines to our picket-post, where she was deposited by the roadside. She says that she was terribly distressed at leaving her mother and sisters, but when she got into Confederate lines the air seemed wonderfully fresh, pure and free, and she soon found friends. She came to Richmond and entered our office. About the same time a mother and daughters who lived perhaps in the handsomest house in the town, were arrested, for some alleged imprudence of one of the daughters. An ambulance was driven to the door, and the mother was taken from her sick-bed and put into it, together with the daughters. Time was not allowed them to prepare a lunch for the journey. Before Mrs. —— was taken from her house Mrs. Millroy had entered it, the General having taken it for his head-quarters; and before the ambulance had been driven off, one of their own officers was heard to say to Mrs. M., seeing her so entirely at home in the house, "For goodness' sake, madam, wait until the poor woman gets off." Is it wonderful, then, that the Winchester ladies welcome our troops with gladness? that they rush out and join the band, singing "The bonnie blue flag" and "Dixie," as the troops enter the streets, until their enthusiasm and melody melt all hearts? Was it strange that even the great and glorious, though grave and thoughtful, Stonewall Jackson should, when pursuing Banks through its streets, have been excited until he waved his cap with tears of enthusiasm, as they broke forth in harmonious songs of welcome? Or that the ladies, not being satisfied by saluting them with their voices, waving their handkerchiefs, and shouting for joy, should follow them with more substantial offerings, filling their haversacks with all that their depleted pantries could afford? Or is it wonderful that our soldiers should love Winchester so dearly and fight for it so valiantly? No, it is beautiful to contemplate the long-suffering, the firmness under oppression, the patience, the generosity, the patriotism of Winchester. Other towns, I dare say, have borne their tyranny as well, and when their history is known they will call forth our admiration as much; but we *know* of no such instance. The "Valley" throughout shows the same devotion to our cause, and the sufferings of the country people are even greater than those in town.

Some amusing incidents sometimes occur, showing the eagerness of the ladies to serve our troops after a long separation. A lady living near Berryville, but a little remote from the main road, says, that when our troops are passing through the country, she sometimes feels sick with anxiety to do something for them. She, one morning, stood in her porch, and could see them turn in crowds to neighbouring houses which happened to be on the road, but no one turned out of the way far enough to come to her house. At last one man came along, and finding that he was passing her gate, she ran out with the greatest alacrity to invite him to come in to get his breakfast. He turned to her with an amused expression and replied: " I am much obliged to you, madam; I wish I could breakfast with you, but as I have already eaten *four* breakfasts to please the ladies, I must beg you to excuse me."

14*th*.—Norfolk, poor Norfolk! nothing can exceed its long-suffering, its night of gloom and darkness. Unlike Winchester, it has no bright spots—no oasis in its blank desert of wretchedness. Like Alexandria, it has no relief, but must submit, and drag on its chain of servility, till the final cry of victory bursts its bonds, and makes it free. I have no time to write of all I hear and know of the indignities offered to our countrymen and countrywomen in Alexandria, Norfolk, Portsmouth, and other places which remain incarcerated in the sloughs of Federal tyrauny. God help them, and give us strength speedily to break the chain that binds them.

August 15.—An account from my relatives, of the raid of the 19th of June into the village of Tappahannock, has lately reached me. The village had been frequently visited and pillaged before, and both sides of the beautiful Rappahannock, above and below, had been sadly devastated; but the last visit seems to carry with it more of the spirit of revenge than any before. My aunt writes:

"About daybreak on that peaceful Sabbath morn six gun-boats were seen returning down the river. A rumour that Hampton was after them, had driven them from their work of devastation in the country above us to their boats for safety. By six o'clock six hundred negroes and four hundred cavalry and marines were let loose upon the defenceless town. The first visit I received was from six cavalrymen; the pantry-door was unceremoniously broken open, and a search made for wine and plate ; but all such things had been removed to a place of safety, and when I called loudly for an officer to be sent for, the ruffians quietly went to their horses and departed. Next came a surgeon from Point Lookout, to search the house, and deliver the key to Dr. R's store, which he had sent for as soon as he landed—making a great virtue of his not breaking open the door, and of his honesty in only taking a few pills. This dignitary walked through the rooms, talking and murdering the 'king's English' most ludicrously. However, he behaved quite well through the day, and was, under Heaven, the means of protecting us from aggressions by his frequent visits. In a short time every unoccupied house in the village was forcibly entered, and every thing taken from them or destroyed. Dr. R's house was completely sacked. L.

had made all necessary preparations for returning home, but all was swept by the Vandals. Dr. R.'s surgical instruments, books, medicines, his own and his sister's clothes, as well as those of their dead parents, were taken, the officers sharing the plunder with the soldiers. The furniture, such as was not broken up, was carried off in dray-loads to the boats, and these two young people were as destitute of domestic comforts as though a consuming fire had passed over their pleasant residence. My lot was filled with the creatures going in and out at pleasure, unless the cry, 'The Johnnies are coming,' sent them running like scared beasts to their rendezvous, and gave us a few moments of quiet. The poor negroes belonging to the town seemed to lose all power over themselves, and to be bereft of reason. Some seemed completely brutalized by the suggestions that were constantly whispered in their ears; others so frightened by the threats made, that reason deserted them; others so stupefied that they lost all power to direct themselves, and gave up to the control of others. It is impossible to describe the madness that possessed them. For myself, I had but one care left—to keep them from polluting my house any farther by keeping them out; and this I was enabled to do after shutting and locking the door in the face of one of them. The most painful event of the day was when a little coloured girl, a great pet with us, was dragged from the house. The aunt of the child was determined to take her with her, but she resisted all her aunt's efforts, and came to the house for protection. An officer came for her, and after talking with her, and telling her that he would not 'trouble her, but she was not old enough to know what was good for her,' he went off. About night a white man and the most fiendish-looking negro I ever saw came for her in the name of the aunt, and vowed they would have her at all risks.

"The officers had all gone to the boats, and it was in vain to resist them, and with feelings of anguish we saw the poor child dragged from us. I cannot think of this event without pain. But night now set in, and our apprehensions increased as the light disappeared; we knew not what was before us, or what we should be called on to encounter during the hours of darkness. We only knew that we were surrounded by lawless banditti, from whom we had no reason to expect mercy, much less kindness; but above all, there was an eye that never slumbered, and an arm mighty to defend those who trusted to it, so we made the house as secure as we could, and kept ready a parcel of *sharp case-knives* (don't laugh at our weapons) for our defence, if needed, and went up-stairs, determined to keep close vigils all night. Our two faithful servants, Jacob and Anthony, kept watch in the kitchen. Among the many faithless, those two stood as examples of the comfort that good servants can give in time of distress. About nine o'clock we heard the sound of horses' feet, and Jacob's voice under the window. Upon demanding to know what was the matter, I was answered by the voice of a gun-boat captain, in broken German, that they were going to fire over my house at the 'Rebs' on the hill, and that we had better leave the house, and seek protection in the streets. I quietly told our counsellor that I preferred remaining in my own house, and should go to the basement, where we should be safe. So we hastily snatched up blankets and comforts, and repaired to the basement, where pallets were spread, and G's little baby laid down to sleep, sweetly unconscious of our fears and troubles. We sent to apprise the Misses G. of the danger, and urge them to come to us. They came, accompanied by an ensign, who had warded off danger from them several times during the day. He was a grave, middle-aged man, and was very kind. At the request of the ladies, he came into the room with us and remained until twelve o'clock. He was then obliged to return to the gun-boat, but gave us an efficient guard until daybreak. He pronounced Captain Schultz's communication false, as they had no idea of firing. We knew at once that the object had been to rob the house, as all unoccupied houses were robbed with impunity. This gentleman's name was Nelson. I can never forget his kindness. During the night our relative, Mrs. B——m, came to us in great agitation; she had attempted to stay at home, though entirely alone, to protect her property. She had been driven from her house at midnight, and chased across several lots to the adjoining one, where she had fallen from exhaustion. Jacob, hearing cries for help, went to her, and brought her to us. Our party now consisted of twelve females of all ages. As soon as the guard left us at daybreak, they came in streams to the hen-yard, and woe to the luckless chicken who thought itself safe from robbers! At one o'clock on Monday the fleet of now eight steamers took its departure. Two of the steamers were filled with the deluded negroes who were leaving their homes. We felt that the incubus which had pressed so heavily upon us for thirty hours had been removed, and we once more breathed freely, but the village was left desolate and destitute."

18*th*.—For several days our whole time has been occupied nursing the dear little grandchild, whose life was despaired of for two days. We are most thankful for his recovery

The army is now on the north side of James River, and this evening, at this moment, we hear heavy cannonading, and musketry is distinctly heard from the hills around the city. Oh, Heavenly Father! guide our generals and troops, and cause this sanguinary conflict to end by a desirable, an honourable peace!

20*th*.—A friend from the Valley has described a successful attack made by Mosby on a Federal wagon-train near Berryville. It was on its way to the army near Strasburg, and Mosby was on the other side of the Shenandoah. He crossed in the night with one cannon and about seventy-five men, and at daylight surprised the drivers and guard as they were beginning to hitch their mules, by a salute from the cannon and seventy-five pistols. There was a general stampede in an instant of all who were unhurt. As quick as thought, 600 mules were turned towards the river, and driven to the command in Loudoun. In the mean time, the wagons were set on fire, and most of them and their contents were consumed before the luckless drivers could return to their charge.

It is said that our new steamer, the "Tallahassee," has been within sixty miles of the city of New York, very much to the terror of the citizens. It also destroyed six large vessels. I bid it God-speed with all my heart; I want the North to feel the war to its core, and then it will end, and not before.

22*d*.—Just been on a shopping expedition for my sister and niece, and spent $1,500 in about an hour. I gave $110 for ladies' morocco boots; $22 per yard for linen; $5 apiece for spools of cotton; $5 for a paper of pins, etc. It would be utterly absurd, except that it is melancholy, to see our currency depreciating so rapidly.

31*st*.—The last day of this exciting, troubled summer of

1864. How many young spirits have fled—how many bleeding, breaking hearts have been left upon earth, from the sanguinary work of this summer! Grant still remains near Petersburg; still by that means is he besieging Richmond. He has been baffled at all points, and yet his indomitable perseverance knows no bounds. Sherman still besieges Atlanta. God help us!

We are again troubled in mind and body about engaging rooms; we find we must give up these by the 1st of October, and have begun the usual refugee occupation of room-hunting.

Letters from our friends in the Valley, describing the horrors now going on there. A relative witnessed the burning of three very large residences on the 20th of August. General Custar was stationed with his brigade of Michigan Cavalry near Berryville. He had thrown out pickets on all the roads, some of which were fired on by Mosby's men. This so exasperated the Federals, that an order was at once issued that whenever a picket-post was fired on the nearest house should be burned. On the morning of the 20th this dreadful order was put into execution, and three large houses were burnt to the ground, together with barns, wheat-stacks, and outhouses. The house of Mr. —— was near a picket-post, and about midnight on the 19th a messenger arrived with a note announcing the sudden death of Mrs. ——'s sister, on a plantation not many miles distant. A lamp was lighted to read the note, and, unfortunately, a little while afterwards the picket-post was fired on and one man wounded. The lighting of the lamp was regarded as a signal to Colonel Mosby. During the same night the pickets near two other large houses were fired on. This being reported at head-quarters, the order was at once issued to burn all three houses. Two companies of the Fifth Michigan Cavalry, commanded by Captain Drake, executed the fearful order. They drew up in front of Mr. ——'s house and asked for him. "Are you Mr. ——?" demanded the Captain. "I have orders to burn your house." In vain Mr. —— remonstrated. He begged for one hour, that he might see General Custar and explain the circumstances of the night before; he also pleaded the illness of his son-in-law, then in the house. No reply was vouchsafed to the old gentleman, but with a look of hardened ferocity, he turned to the soldiers, with the order: "Men, to your work, and do it thoroughly!" In an instant the torch was applied to that home of domestic elegance and comfort. One soldier seized the sick son-in-law, who is a surgeon in our service, threatening to carry him to head-quarters, and was with difficulty prevented by the kind interposition of Dr. Sinclair, the surgeon of the regiment. They allowed the family to save as much furniture as they could, but the servants were all gone, and there was no one near to help them. The soldiers at once went to Mr. ——'s secretary, containing $40,000 in bonds, destroyed it, and scattered the mutilated papers to the winds. Matches were applied to window and bed curtains; burning coals were sprinkled in the linen-closet, containing every variety of house and table linen. Mrs. ——, the daughter, opened a drawer, and taking her jewelry, embracing an elegant diamond ring and other valuables, was escaping with them to the yard, when she was seized by two ruffians on the stair-steps, held by the arms by one, while the other forcibly took the jewels; they then, as she is a very small woman, lifted her over the banister and let her drop into the passage below; fortunately it was not very far and she was not at all injured. Nothing daunted, she rushed up-stairs, to rescue a box containing her bridal presents of silver, which was concealed in the wall above a closet. She climbed up to the highest shelf of the closet, seized the box, and, with unnatural strength, threw it through the window into the yard below. While still on the shelf, securing other things from their hiding-place, all unconscious of danger, a soldier set fire to some dresses hanging on the pegs below the shelf on which she stood. The first intimation she had of it was feeling the heat; she then leaped over the flames to the floor; her stockings were scorched, but she was not injured. She next saw a man with the sign of the Cross on his coat; she asked him if he was a chaplain? He replied that he was. She said, "Then in mercy come, and help me to save some of my mother's things." They went into her mother's chamber, and she hurriedly opened the bureau drawer, and began taking out the clothes, the chaplain assisting, but what was her horror to see him putting whatever he fancied into his pocket—among other things a paper of pins. She says she could not help saying, as she turned to him, "A minister of Christ stealing pins!!" In a moment the chaplain was gone, but the pins were returned to the bureau. Mrs. —— is the only daughter of Mr. ——, and was the only lady on the spot. Her first care, when she found the house burning, was to secure her baby, which was sleeping in its cradle up-stairs. A guard was at the foot of the steps, and refused to let her pass; she told him that she was going to rescue her child from the flames. "Let the little d——d rebel burn!" was the brutal reply. But his bayonet could not stop her; she ran by, and soon returned, bearing her child to a place of safety. When the house had become a heap of ruins, the mother returned from the bedside of her dead sister, whither she had gone at daylight that morning, on horseback, (for her harness had been destroyed by the enemy, making her carriage useless.) She was, of course, overwhelmed with grief and with horror at the scene before her. As soon as she dismounted, a soldier leaped on the horse, and rode off with it. Their work of destruction in one place being now over, they left it for another scene of vengeance.

The same ceremony of Captain Drake's announcing his orders to the mistress of the mansion (the master was a prisoner) being over, the torch was applied. The men had dismounted; the work of pillage was going on merrily; the house was burning in every part, to insure total destruction. The hurried tramp of horses' feet could not be heard amidst the crackling of flames and falling of rafters, but the sudden shout and cry of "No quarter! no quarter!" from many voices, resounded in the ears of the unsuspecting marauders as a death-knell. A company of Mosby's men rushed up the hill and charged them furiously; they were aroused by the sound of danger, and fled hither and thither. Terrified and helpless, they were utterly unprepared for resistance. The cry of "No quarter! no quarter!" still continued. They hid behind the burning ruins; they crouched in the corners of fences; they begged for life; but their day of grace was past. The defenceless women, children, and old men of the neighbourhood had borne their tortures too long; something must be done, and all that this one company of braves could do, was done. Thirty were killed on the spot, and others, wounded and bleeding, sought refuge, and asked pity of those whom they were endeavouring to ruin. —— writes: "Two came to us, the most pitiable objects you ever beheld, and we did what we could for them; for, after all, the men are not to blame half so much as the officers. Whether these things have been ordered by Sheridan or Custar, we do not know. These two wounded men, and all who took refuge among Secessionists, were removed that night, contrary to our wishes, for we knew that their tortures in the ambulances would be unbearable; but they were unwilling to trust them, and unable to believe that persons who were suffering so severely from them could return good for evil.

"One man gruffly remarked: 'If we leave any of them with you all, Mosby will come and kill them over again.' We have since heard that those two men died that night. The pickets were then drawn in nearer to head quarters. All was quiet for the rest of the day, and as Colonel Mosby had but one company in that section of the country, it had of course retired. That night, two regiments (for they could not trust themselves in smaller numbers) were seen passing along the road; their course was marked by the torches which they carried. They rode to the third devoted house, and burned it to the ground. No one knows whose house will be the next object of revenge. Some fancied wrong may make us all homeless. We keep clothes, house-linen, and every thing compressible, tied up in bundles, so that they can be easily removed."

Such are some of the horrors that are being enacted in Virginia at this time. These instances, among many, many others, I note in my diary, that my children's children may know what we suffer during this unnatural war. Sheridan does not mean that Hunter or Butler shall bear the palm of cruelty—honours will at least be divided. I fear, from appearances, that he will exceed them, before his reign of terror is over. —— says she feels as if she were nightly encircled by fire—camp-fires, picket-fires, with here and there stacks of wheat burning, and a large fire now and then in the distance, denote the destruction of something— it may be a dwelling, or it may be a barn.

September 1.— —— has this day entered on her duties as clerk in the "Surgeon-General's Department," which she obtained with very little trouble on her part. We had always objected to her applying for an office, because we were afraid of the effect of sedentary employment on her health; but now it seems necessary to us, as the prices of provisions and house-rent have become so very high. Providence has dealt most mercifully with us from the beginning of the war: at first it seemed to be the pleasure of our friends as well as ourselves that we should be with them; then, when it became evident that the war would continue, Mr. —— obtained an office, which gave us a limited, but independent, support. Then, when prices became high, and we could not live on the salary, the chaplaincy came, with a little better income. As provisions continued to increase in price, and our prospect seemed very poor for the winter, my office was obtained without the least effort on my part, though I had often sought one in the Treasury without success; and now, when difficulties seem to be increasing with the great scarcity of provisions, the way is again made comparatively easy. So it seems that the Lord intends us to work for our daily bread, and to be independent, but not to abound.

10*th*.—We must give up our rooms by the last of this month, and the question now arises about our future abode. We are searching hither and thither. We had thought for a week past that our arrangements were most delightfully made, and that we had procured, together with Dr. M. and Colonel G., six rooms in a house on Franklin Street. The arrangement had been made, and the proprietor gone from town. The M's and ourselves were to take four rooms in the third story; the back parlour on the first floor was to be used by all parties; and Colonel G. would take the large front basement room as his chamber, and at his request, as our dining-room, as we could not be allowed to use the upper chambers as eating-rooms. Our large screen was to be transferred to the Colonel's bedstead and washing apparatus, and the rest of the room furnished in dining-room style. These rooms are all furnished and carpeted. Nothing could have suited us better, and we have been for some days anticipating our comfortable winter-quarters. The M's have left town with the blissful assurance of a nice home; to add to it all, the family of the proprietor is all that we could desire as friends and companions. Last night I met with a friend, who asked me where we had obtained rooms. I described them with great alacrity and pleasure. She looked surprised, and said, "Are you not mistaken? those rooms are already occupied." "Impossible," said I; "we have engaged them." She shook her head, saying, "There was some mistake; they have been occupied for some days by a family, who say that they have rented them." None but persons situated exactly in the same way can imagine our disappointment. The Colonel looked aghast; Mr. —— pronounced it a mistake; the girls were indignant, and I went a little farther, and pronounced it bad treatment. This morning I went up before breakfast to hear the truth of the story—the family is still absent, but the servants confirmed the statement by saying that a family had been in the rooms that we looked at for a week, and that a gentleman, a third party, had been up the day before to claim the rooms, and said that the party occupying them had no right to them, and must be turned out. The servant added, that this third gentleman had sent up a dray with flour which was now in the house, and had put his coal in the coal-cellar. All this seems passing strange. Thus have we but three weeks before us in which to provide ourselves with an almost impossible shelter. The "Colonel" has written to Mr. —— for an explanation, and the M's have been apprised of their dashed hopes. I often think how little the possessors of the luxurious homes of Richmond know of the difficulties with which refugees are surrounded, and how little we ever appreciated the secure home-feeling which we had all enjoyed before the war began. We have this evening been out again in pursuit of quarters. The advertisements of "Rooms to let" were sprinkled over the morning papers, so that one could scarcely believe that there would be any difficulty in our being supplied. A small house that would accommodate our whole party, five or six rooms in a large house, or two rooms for ourselves, if it were impossible to do better, would answer our purpose—any thing for a comfortable home. The first advertisement alluded to basement rooms—damp, and redolent of rheumatism. The next was more attractive—good rooms, well furnished, and up *but two* flights of stairs; but the price was enormous, far beyond the means of any of the party, and so evidently an extortion designed to take all that could be extracted from the necessity of others, that we turned from our hard-featured proprietor with disgust. The rooms of the third advertisement had been already rented, and the fourth seemed more like answering our purpose than any we had seen. There were only two rooms, and though small, and rather dark, yet persons whose shelter was likely to be the "blue vault of heaven" could not be very particular. The price, too, was exorbitant, but with a little more self-denial it might be paid. The next inquiry was about kitchen, servant's room and coal-house ; but we got no further than the answer about the kitchen. The lady said there was no kitchen that we could possibly use; her stove was small, and she required it all; we must either be supplied from a restaurant, or do our own cooking in one of the rooms. As neither plan was to be thought of, we ended the parley. A *part of a kitchen* is indispensable, though perhaps the most annoying thing to which refugees are subjected. The mistress is generally polite enough, but save me from the self-sufficient cook. "I would like to oblige you, madam, but you can't have loaf-bread to-morrow morning, because my mistress has ordered loaf-bread and rolls, and our stove is small;" or, "No, madam, you can't '*bile*' a ham, nor nothing else to-day, because it is our washing-day;" or, "No, ma'am, you can't have biscuits for tea, because the stove is cold, and I've got no time to heat it." So that we must either submit, or go to the mistress for redress, and probably find none, and thus run the risk of offending both mistress and maid, both of whom have us very much in their power. As I walked home from this unsuccessful effort, it was nearly dark; the gas was being lighted in hall, parlour, and chamber. I looked in as I passed, and saw cheerful countenances collecting around centre-tables, or sitting here and there on handsome porticoes or marble steps, to enjoy the cool evening breeze—countenances of those whose families I had known from infancy, and who were still numbered among my friends and acquaintances. I felt sad, and asked myself, if those persons could realize the wants of others, would they not cheerfully rent some of their extra rooms? Rooms once opened on grand occasions, and now, as such occasions are few and far between, not opened at all for weeks and months together.

Would they not cheerfully remove some of their showy and fragile furniture for a time, and allow those who had once been accustomed to as large rooms of their own, to occupy and take care of them? The *rent* would perhaps be no object with them, but their kindness might be twice blessed—the refugees would be made comfortable and happy, and the money might be applied to the wants of the soldiers or the city poor. And yet a third blessing might be added—the luxury of doing good. Ah, they would then find that the "quality of mercy is not strained," but that it would indeed, like the "gentle dew from heaven," fall into their very souls, and diffuse a happiness of which they know not. These thoughts filled my mind until I reached the present home of a refugee friend from Washington. It was very late, but I thought I would run in, and see if she could throw any light upon our difficulties. I was sorry to find that she was in a similar situation, her husband having that day been notified that their rooms would be required on the first of October. We compared notes of our room-hunting experiences, and soon found ourselves laughing heartily over occurrences and conversations which were both provoking and ridiculous. I then wended my way home, amid brilliantly lighted houses and badly lighted streets. Squads of soldiers were sauntering along, impregnating the air with tobacco-smoke; men were standing at every corner, lamenting the fall of Atlanta or the untimely end of General Morgan. I too often caught a word, conveying blame of the President for having removed General Johnston. This blame always irritates me, because the public became so impatient at General Johnston's want of action, that they were clamorous for his removal. For weeks the President was abused without measure because he was not removed, and now the same people are using the same terms towards him because the course which they absolutely required at his hands has disappointed them. The same people who a month ago curled the lip in scorn at General Johnston's sloth and want of energy, and praised General Hood's course from the beginning of the war, now shrug their unmilitary shoulders, whose straps have never graced a battle-field, and pronounce the change "unfortunate and uncalled for." General Hood, they say, was an "admirable Brigadier," but his "promotion was most unfortunate ;" while General Johnston's "Fabian policy" is now pronounced the very thing for the "situation "— the course which would have saved Atlanta, and have made all right. This may all be true, but it is very distressing to hear it harped upon now; quite as much so as it was six weeks ago to hear the President called obstinate, because he was ruining the country by not removing General J. But I will no longer make myself uneasy about what I hear, for I have implicit confidence in our leaders, both in the Cabinet and on the field. Were I a credulous woman, and ready to believe all that I hear in the office, in the hospital, in my visits and on the streets, I should think that Richmond is now filled with the most accomplished military geniuses on which the sun shines. Each man expresses himself, as an old friend would say, with the most "dogmatic infallibility" of the conduct of the President, General Lee, General Johnston, General Hampton, General

Beauregard, General Wise, together with all the other lights of every degree. It is true that there are as many varieties of opinion as there are men expressing them, or I should profoundly regret that so much military light should be obscured among the shades of the Richmond Departments; but I do wish that some of them would refrain from condemning the acts of our leaders, and from uttering such awful prophecies, provided the President or General Lee does not do so and so. Although I do not believe their forebodings, yet the reiteration of such opinions, in the most assured tones, makes me nervous and uneasy. I would that all such men could be sent to the field; I think at least a regiment could be spared from Richmond, for then the women of the city at least would be more peaceful.

12*th.*—After holding a consultation with a particular friend of Dr. M., together with Mr. —— and the "Colonel," we have determined to await the decision of Mr. —— about the rooms on Franklin Street, and not to attempt to get others, hoping that as there are so many competitors for them, we may be considered the rightful claimants. There can be no doubt that they were promised to us.

The morning papers report "all quiet" at Petersburg, except that shells are daily thrown into the city, and that many of the women and children are living in tents in the country, so as to be out of the reach of shells.

The death of the bold and dashing General Morgan is deeply regretted. He has done us great service throughout the war, but particularly since his wonderful escape from his incarceration in the Ohio Penitentiary. It seems so short a time since he was here, all classes delighting to do him reverence. It is hard for us to have to give up such men.

General Hood telegraphs that the inhabitants of Atlanta

have been ordered to leave their homes, to go they know not whither. Lord, how long must we suffer such things? I pray that the enemy's hands may be stayed, and that they may be driven from our fair borders to their own land. I ask not vengeance upon them, but that they may be driven to their own homes, and that we may be henceforward and forever a separate people.

16th.—A visit to-day from my · brother Dr. B., who bears the utter desolation of his home quietly, though so sudden a change of circumstances is of course very depressing. He tells me that he has lately had a visit from a very interesting young South Carolinian, who came to look for the body of his brother. The two brothers were being educated in Germany when the war broke out; and as soon as they were of military age, with the consent of their parents, they hastened home to take part in their country's struggle. In one of the cavalry fights in Hanover, in May last, one brother was killed, and the other, "not being able to find the body at the time, was now seeking it." His mother was on the ocean returning to her home, and he could not meet her with the information that her son's body could not be found. He had heard that some of the fallen had been buried at S. H. or W. He mentioned that their intimate friend, young Middleton, had fallen in the same fight. Mr. Middleton had been buried at S. H., and his grave had been marked by Mrs. N.; but young Pringle (the name of the brothers) had been carried to neither place. Mr. Pringle had seen in a New York paper an account given by a Yankee officer of several wounded Confederates who had been captured, and having died on their way to the "White House," they were buried by the roadside, and he had some reason to believe that his brother was among them. It was then remembered that there were three graves on the opposite side of the Pamunky River, and one was marked with the name "*Tingle.*" It was an excessively warm Sunday morning ; but as the young soldier's furlough only extended to the following day, there was no time to be lost. Dr. B. and the brother set out upon their melancholy mission, having obtained a cart, one or two men, and given an order at a neighbouring carpenter's shop for a coffin. After crossing the river they found the three graves, at the place designated, in the county of King William. The one marked " Tingle " contained the body of a Federal and one of a Confederate soldier, but not the brother. The next one opened was not the right one; but the third contained the much-loved remains, which were easily recognized by the anxious brother. Tenderly and gently, all wrapped in his blanket, he was transferred from his shallow grave to his soldier's coffin, and then conveyed to S. H., to be placed by his friend Middleton. It was now night, the moon shone brightly, and all was ready. The families from both houses gathered around the grave. " Slowly and sadly they laid him down." No minister of the Gospel was near to perform the services. Dr. B. stood at the head with a Prayer-Book for the purpose, but his defective sight obliged him to yield the book to Mrs. N., who, with a clear, calm voice read by the light of a single lantern the beautiful ritual of the Episcopal Church. The grave was filled in solemn silence, the brother standing at the foot. When all was over, the young ladies and children of the families advanced with wreaths and bouquets, and in an instant the soldier's grave was a mound of fresh flowers. The brother could no longer restrain his feelings ; he was completely overwhelmed, and was obliged to retire to his room, where he could indulge them freely. Next morning he returned to his command, after a leave-taking in which the feelings expressed by all parties evinced more of the friendship of years than the acquaintance of hours. It seems strange indeed that this scene, so similar to that of the burial of the lamented Captain Latané, should have occurred at the same place. But who could relate, who could number the sad scenes of this war? Many such have probably occurred in various parts of the country.

18*th*.—Nothing yet from Mr. —— about our rooms. All the furnished rooms that I have seen, except those, would cost us from $100 to $110 per month for each room, which, of course, we cannot pay; but we will try and not be anxious overmuch, for the Lord has never let us want comforts since we left our own dear home, and if we use the means which He has given us properly and in His fear, He will not desert us now.

I went with Mr. —— as usual this morning to the " Officers' Hospital," where he read a part of the service and delivered an address to such patients among the soldiers as were well enough to attend. I acted as his chorister, and when the services were over, and he went around to the bedsides of the patients, I crossed the street, as I have done several times before, to the cemetery—the old " Shockoe Hill Cemetery." It is, to me, the most interesting spot in the city. It is a melancholy thought, that, after an absence of thirty years, I am almost a stranger in my native place. In this cemetery I go from spot to spot, and find the names that were the household words of my childhood and youth ; the names of my father's and mother's friends ; of the friends of my sisters, and of my own school-days. The first that struck me was that of the venerable and venerated Bishop Moore, on the monument erected by his church; then, that of his daughter, the admirable Miss Christian; then the monument to Colonel Ambler, erected by his children. Mrs. Ambler lies by him. Mr. and Mrs. Chapman Johnson, Judge and Mrs. Cabell, Mr. and Mrs. John Wickham, surrounded by their children, who were the companions of my youth; also, their lovely grand-daughter, Mrs. W. H. F. Lee, who passed away last winter, at an early age, while her husband was prisoner of war. Near them is the grave of the Hon. Benjamin Watkins Leigh; of Judge and Mrs. Stanard, and of their gifted son; of dear Mrs. Henningham Lyons and her son James, from whose untimely end she never recovered; of our sweet friend, Mrs. Lucy Green. Then there is the handsome monument of Mrs. Abraham Warwick and the grave of her son, dear Clarence, who died so nobly at Gaines's Mill in 1862. His grave seems to be always covered with fresh flowers, a beautiful offering to one whose young life was so freely given to his country. Again I stood beside the tombs of two friends, whom I dearly loved, Mrs. Virginia Heth and Mrs. Mary Ann Barney, the lovely daughters of Mr. and Mrs. Robert Gwathney, whose graves are also there. Then the tomb of our old friend, Mr. James Rawlings, and those of Mr. and Mrs. Herbert A. Claiborne and their daughter, Mary Burnet. Just by them is the newly-made grave of our sweet niece, Mary Anna, the wife of Mr. H. Augustine Claiborne, freshly turfed and decked with the flowers she loved so dearly. A little farther on lies my young cousin, Virginia, wife of Major J. H. Claiborne, and her two little daughters. But why should I go on? Time would fail me to enumerate all the loved and lost. Their graves look so peaceful in that lovely spot. Most of them died before war came to distress them. The names of two persons I cannot omit, before whose tombs I pause with a feeling of veneration for their many virtues. One was that of Mrs. Sully, my music-teacher, a lady who was known and respected by the whole community for her admirable character, accompanied by the most quiet and gentle manner. The other was that of Mr. Joseph Danforth, the humble but excellent friend of my precious father. The cemetery at Hollywood is of later date, though many very dear to me repose amid its beautiful shades.

But enough of the past and of sadness. I must now turn to busy life again, and note a little victory, of which General Lee telegraphed yesterday, by which we gained some four hundred prisoners, many horses and wagons, and 2,500 beeves. These last are most acceptable to our commissariat!

The Southern Army are having an armistice of ten days, for the inhabitants of Atlanta to get off from their homes. Exiled by Sherman, my heart bleeds for them. May the good Lord have mercy upon them, and have them in His holy keeping!

21st.—Bad news this morning. General Early has had a defeat in the Valley, near Winchester, and has fallen back to Strasburg. Our loss reported heavy. Major-General Rodes killed, and Brigadier-General Godwin and General Fitz Lee wounded. No other casualties heard of; and I dread to hear more.

28th.—Mr. P. came home, and at once decided that we were entitled to the rooms. By this arrangement we are greatly relieved. The family who occupied them have moved off, and Mr. —— having convinced the third party of his mistake, has taken off his hands the coal and flour which he had stored away, and now all is straight. The "Colonel" and ourselves moved our goods and chattels to these rooms yesterday. The M's will be here in a day or two. We have a long walk to our offices, but it is very near my hospital. Mr. ——'s hospital is very far from every point, as it is on the outskirts of the city; but he thinks the walk is conducive to his health, so that we are, upon the whole, very comfortable.

October 10.—I am cast down by hearing that J. P. has been captured; he was caught while scouting in the enemy's lines, on James River. Poor child! I feel very, very anxious about him.

Our army in the Valley has regained its foothold, the enemy having retreated. E. C. had his horse killed under him in a fight near Waynesborough, but he escaped unhurt.

The Federal Army below Richmond advanced a few days ago, and took "Fort Harrison." We live now amid perpetual firing of cannon. The loss of Fort Harrison is, I am afraid, a very serious loss to us. The enemy made a second advance, which has been handsomely repulsed. They seem to be putting forth their utmost efforts against us. I pray that our armies may be able to resist them and drive them to their own land.

12*th*.—The armies around Richmond remain quiet. Butler is digging the canal at "Dutch Gap," and Grant is fortifying "Fort Harrison" most vigorously. General Rosser has had a little reverse in the Valley, losing some guns. He had a cavalry fight, overcame the enemy, and drove them for miles; but encountering a body of infantry which was too much for him, he had to retreat, leaving his guns to the enemy.

The hospitals are full of the wounded; my afternoons

are very much engaged, nursing them. I was very sorry yesterday to find R. S. painfully wounded.

13th.—The day has passed as usual—six hours in the Commissary Department, and the remainder occupied in various ways. Rumours of fighting below Richmond; we hear the cannon, but it is said to be merely a skirmish.

20th.—Nothing new in the field. Armies quiet; perhaps preparing for dreadful work. I got a note last night from J. P., written with a pencil. He and other prisoners are working ten hours a day on "Dutch Gap Canal." They work under the fire of our own batteries. Poor fellow! my heart yearns over him.

26th.—The armies around Richmond continue quiet. General Early's second misfortune was very depressing to us all. We are now recovering from it. I trust that God will turn it all to our good. A striking and admirable address from him to his soldiers was in the morning papers. Oh, I trust they will retrieve their fortunes hereafter.

28th.—Very much interested lately in the hospitals; not only in our own, " the Robertson hospital," but in Mr. ——'s, " the officers' hospital."

He has just told me of a case which has interested me deeply. An officer from the far South was brought in mortally wounded. He had lost both legs in a fight below Petersburg. The poor fellow suffered excessively; could not be still a moment; and was evidently near his end. His brother, who was with him, exhibited the bitterest grief, watching and waiting on him with silent tenderness and flowing tears. Mr. —— was glad to find that he was not unprepared to die. He had been a professor of religion for some years, and told him that he was suffering too much to think on that or any other subject, but he constantly tried to look to God for mercy. Mr. —— then recognized him, for the first time, as a patient who had been in the hospital last spring, and whose admirable character had then much impressed him. He was a gallant and brave officer, yet so kind and gentle to those under his control that his men were deeply attached to him, and the soldier who nursed him showed his love by his anxious care of his beloved captain. After saying to him a few words about Christ and his free salvation, offering up a fervent prayer in which he seemed to join, and watching the sad scene for a short time, Mr. —— left him for the night. The surgeons apprehended that he would die before morning, and so it turned out; at the chaplain's early call there was nothing in his room but the chilling signal of the empty "hospital bunk." He was buried that day, and we trust will be found among the redeemed in the day of the Lord. This, it was thought, would be the last of this good man; but in the dead of night came hurriedly a single carriage to the gate of the hospital. A lone woman, tall, straight, and dressed in deep mourning, got quickly out, and moved rapidly up the steps into the large hall, where, meeting the guard, she asked anxiously, "Where's Captain T.?" Taken by surprise, the man answered hesitatingly, "Captain T. is dead, madam, and was buried to-day." This terrible announcement was as a thunderbolt at the very feet of the poor lady, who fell to the floor as one dead. Starting up, oh, how she made that immense building ring with her bitter lamentations! Worn down with apprehension and weary with travelling over a thousand miles by day and night, without stopping for a moment's rest, and wild with grief, she could hear no voice of sympathy—she regarded not the presence of one or many; she told the story of her married life, as if she were alone—

how her husband was the best man that ever lived; how everybody loved him; how kind he was to all; how devoted to herself; how he loved his children, took care of, and did every thing for them; how, from her earliest years almost, she had loved him as herself; how tender he was of her, watching over her in sickness, never seeming to weary of it, never to be unwilling to make any sacrifice for her comfort and happiness; how that, when the telegraph brought the dreadful news that he was dangerously wounded, she never waited an instant nor stopped a moment by the way, day nor night, and now "I drove as fast as the horses could come from the depot to this place, and he is dead and buried!—I never shall see his face again!" "What *shall* I do?"—"But where is he buried?" They told her where. "I must go there; he must be taken up; I must see him!" "But, madam, you can't see him; he has been buried some hours." "But I must see him; I can't live without seeing him; I must hire some one to go and take him up; can't you get some one to take him up? I'll pay him well; just get some men to take him up. I *must* take him home; he must go home with me. The last thing I said to his children was, that they must be good children, and I would bring their father home, and they are waiting for him now! He must go; I can't go without him; I can't meet his children without him!" and so, with her woman's heart, she could not be turned aside—nothing could alter her purpose. The next day she had his body taken up and embalmed. She watched by it until every thing was ready, and then carried him back to his own house and his children, only to seek a grave for the dead father close by those he loved, among kindred and friends in the fair sunny land he died to defend.

Many painfully interesting scenes occur, which I would like

so much to write in my diary, but time fails me at night, and my hours of daylight are very closely occupied.

November 13.—The "military situation" seems very much the same. Some cheering intimations from Georgia. Hood has made movements on Sherman's flank, and Forrest upon his rear, which it is thought promise most valuable results, but nothing final has been yet accomplished, and we may be too sanguine.

General Price is still successful in Missouri.

In the Valley of Virginia an immense amount of private property has been destroyed. Sheridan, glorying in his shame, boasts of, and probably magnifies, what has been done in that way. He telegraphs to Grant that he has burned 2,000 barns. The Lord shorten his dreadful work, and have mercy upon the sufferers!

Nothing new about Richmond. A few days ago the enemy made several attempts to advance upon the Darbytown road, and were handsomely repulsed. The firing of cannon is so common a sound that it is rather remarkable when we do not hear it.

Mr. —— has been telling us of some other interesting cases in his hospital; among them, that of Captain Brown, of North Carolina, has awakened our sympathies. He came into the hospital bright and cheerful, with every appearance of speedy recovery. He talked a great deal of his wife and six children at home, one of whom he had never seen. Knowing that his wife would be sick, he had obtained a furlough, and made arrangements to go home, but the recent battles coming on, he would not leave his post. Through many a hard-fought action God had kept him unharmed; he had never been touched by a solitary weapon, until he began to feel that there was not the slightest danger to him, even amid the harvest of death. He wrote that he should be at home as soon as this fight was over ; but it was not to be so, and he soon came into the hospital severely wounded. As he lay upon his bed of suffering, the image of his dear wife in her sickness and sorrow, and then with her new-born infant, seemed constantly before him. "I intended to be there," he would say dreamily ; "I made all my arrangements to be there ; I know she wants me ; she wrote to me to come to her ; oh, I wish I was there, but now I can't go, but I hope I did right ; I hope it is all right." A letter from her, speaking of herself and infant as doing well, relieved his anxiety, and he tried to bear the disappointment with patience, still hoping soon to be at home. God, however, had ordered it otherwise. The word had gone forth, "He shall not return to his house, neither shall his place know him any more." Gangrene appeared, and it was melancholy to see his strength giving way, his hopes fading, and death coming steadily on. He was a professor of religion, and Mr. —— says he was always ready to hear the word of God, and, though anxious to live, yet he put himself into the Lord's hand, with humble faith and hope, such as may give his friends assurance that death was gain to him.

The war news seems encouraging. Many persons are very despondent, but I do not feel so—perhaps I do not understand the military signs. Our men below Richmond have certainly had many successes of late. Sheridan, instead of capturing Lynchburg, as he promised, is retreating down the Valley. In the South, the army of Tennessee is in Sherman's rear, and Forrest still carries every thing before him. General Price seems to be doing well in Missouri ; Arkansas and Texas seem to be all right. Kentucky, too, (poor Kentucky!) seems more hopeful. Then why should we despond? Maryland, alas for Maryland! the tyrant's heel appears too heavy for her, and we grievously fear that the prospect of her union with the South is rapidly passing away. If we must give her up, it will not be without sorrow and mortification. We shall mournfully bewail her dishonour and shame. If her noble sons who have come to the South must return, they will take with them our gratitude and admiration for their gallant bearing in many a hard-fought battle. Readily will we receive those who choose to remain among us; and in holy ground take care of her honoured dead, who so freely gave their lives for Southern rights. The Potomac may seem to some the natural boundary between North and South; but it is hard to make up one's mind yet to the entire surrender of our sister State; and if we could, gladly would we hope for Maryland, even as we hope for the Southern Confederacy herself.

21st.—We attended hospital services yesterday as usual. There are few patients, and none are very ill. On Friday night a most unexpected death took place, under very painful circumstances. A young adjutant lost his life by jumping out of a window at the head of his bed, about ten feet from the ground. His attendants were a sister, brother, and two servants. His suffering with a wound in his foot had been so intense that he would not allow any one to touch it except the ward-master, who handled it with the greatest tenderness. Yet while his attendants were asleep (for they thought it unnecessary to be up with him all night) he managed to get up, raise the window, and throw himself out, without disturbing one of them. His mind was no doubt unsettled, as it had been before. He lived about an hour after being found. His poor sister was wild with grief and horror, and his other attendants dreadfully shocked.

23d.—Military movements are kept very much in the dark. Nothing going on about Richmond, except cannonading, particularly at Dutch Gap.

Sherman is moving across Georgia in direction of Milledgeville, looking towards Savannah, or perhaps Charleston, or to some intermediate point on the coast, where he may, if necessary, meet with reinforcements and supplies from Federal shipping already there, or on their way down the Atlantic coast for that very purpose. Efforts are being made by the Governors of South Carolina and Georgia to arrest him. Beauregard, too, has made a short, stirring address, assuring them that he was hastening down to their aid, and that with proper exertions which might be made on their part, the destruction of the enemy would be certain. Nothing equal to the demands of these trying times has yet been done by any of the authorities. Oh that they would strain every nerve to put a stop to this bold and desolating invader! It would require united effort, made without delay. No hesitation, no doubting and holding back must there be; every human being capable of bearing arms must fly to the rescue; all the stores of every kind should be destroyed or removed; bridges burned, roads torn up or obstructed; every difficulty should be thrown in the way. He should be harassed day and night, that he might be delayed, and entrapped, and ruined. Oh that these things could be done! It may be a woman's thought, but I believe that had Georgia one tithe of the experience of the ruined, homeless Virginians, she would exert every fibre of her frame to destroy the enemy; she would have no delusive hope of escape. I trust that the doctrines of

Brown, Stephens, and such like, are not now bearing their bitter fruits! that the people of patriotic Georgia have not been rendered unfit for the sacrifices and dangers of this fearful day, when every man is required to stand in the deadly breach, and every earthly interest, even life itself, must be surrendered rather than yield to the barbarous foe, by their treasonable doctrines of reconstruction, reunion, etc. Oh, I trust not; and I hope that our now uncertain mails may bring information that all Georgia and South Carolina are aroused to their awful condition.

December 4, Sunday.—We attended this evening the funeral of Colonel Angus W. McDonald, the relative of Mr. ——. His is a sad story. He was educated at West Point, but in early life resigned his position in the regular army and joined a company of fur traders, went with them to the Rocky Mountains, where he led an adventurous life, well suited to his excitable temper. For years his life was full of adventure, with the broad heavens for his roof and the cold earth for his couch. With a bold spirit and great muscular power, he soon acquired extensive influence with the Indian tribes among which he moved, and was chosen as the chief of one of them, where he was known as the "Big Warrior." As such he led his braves to many a hard-fought battle, and taught surrounding tribes to fear him and them, by such courage and prowess as always so deeply impress the savage mind. Many incidents of his life among the Indians are full of interest. On one occasion, having received an injury from a neighbouring tribe, he sent to them that he was coming to settle with them for it, and that they must meet him for the purpose, at a certain time and place. Accordingly, all their warriors were assembled and seated in due form, at the proper distance from and around a central post, ready and waiting for the conference. At the appointed time, the "Big Warrior," in full dress, made his appearance, and striding through to the centre of the dark, silent circle, he struck his tomahawk deep into the "post," and looking quietly but sternly around from one gloomy warrior to another, he in few words told them why he was there, and what he required of them. "You have insulted me," said he ; "you robbed some of my men, and you killed two of them ; you must restore the goods and give up the murderers, or you must *fight* it out, and I am here for that purpose." His imposing appearance, his boldness, the justice of his cause, and his steady purpose of retaliating to the full, so awed them, that his terms were promptly assented to, and he quickly returned to his people with the most ample satisfaction for the injuries they had received. He grew weary of this life after some years, and determined to return to his early home and associations. Acting upon this impulse, we next find him in Romney, Hampshire County, among his kindred, where he quietly resumed the duties of civilized life, was married, and practised law for years. Still restless and different from other men, he was constantly speculating in one thing and another—politics, property, etc. At one time he was in the Virginia Legislature, and controlled the vote of his county in a way new to our republican experience. For this purpose he got possession of a large mountain region, filling it with a population whom he ruled very much as a Scottish chief would have done in his ancestral Highlands, and using their votes to decide any public controversy in which he chose to engage. This, of course, did not last long ; it was too much opposed to the public views and feelings, and under the consequent changes around him, he found it expedient to return to private life. From this retirement, however, his native State soon recalled him, as one of the three commissioners to settle the boundary line between Maryland and Virginia. In his capacity as such, the Virginia Legislature sent him to England to examine the public records bearing upon this subject. He discharged the duties of his mission with ability and success, as his voluminous report will show. The present war found him residing with his large family near Winchester, his native place. The Confederate Government having given him the commission of a colonel, it was hoped that he would be of great use in the bloody contest; but a discipline better suited in its severity to Indian warriors than to our high-minded volunteers, together with advanced years and declining health, disappointed the expectations of himself and his friends. He found, indeed, that bodily infirmity alone rendered him unfit for active service, and this, with other difficulties, made it proper to break up his command. Thus it happened that when that brute, Hunter, marched through Lexington, spreading desolation in his path, Colonel McDonald, then a resident of the town, believing that the enemy, who had manifested great harshness towards him, injuring his property near Winchester, etc., would arrest him, determined to keep out of their way, and with others took refuge in a neighbouring forest. Here, unfortunately, the enemy found him, with his son Harry, a youth of some sixteen years, and took them prisoners. It is somewhat singular that the presence of this devoted son caused the father's arrest. He had always determined that he would never surrender, never be taken alive. But when he looked at this boy, who had fought so nobly by his side, and who would surely be sacrificed if he refused to surrender, he could fight no longer ; it seemed to him, as he afterwards said, as the voice from Heaven which stayed the armed hand of Abraham, and he could not fire another shot. Father and son were thus captured. Harry escaped in a day or two ; but the father was tied and dragged along at a rapid pace towards the Maryland line. When he could no longer walk a step, they allowed him to get into a wagon with nothing to rest upon but some old iron, rough tools, etc. Thus they hastened him to Cumberland, Maryland, where they handcuffed him and put him into solitary confinement ; thence he was hurried to Wheeling, where he was again, with his manacles on, shut up in a dungeon, seven feet by ten, with nothing to relieve the sufferings incident to such a fate, nothing to expect or hope for, but the bitterest cruelty. From this dreadful captivity he was released two or three weeks ago, and reached the house of his daughter, in this city, with health, bad for years, now worse than ever, and constitution entirely broken by hard and cruel bondage. Cheered by freedom, and the society of his children who were here, he flattered himself that he would be enabled to return to his home of refuge in Lexington. This hope proved delusive. It soon appeared that his whole nervous system was shattered, and his end rapidly approaching ; his wife was sent for, but did not arrive until the day after he died. Not dreaming of what awaited her, she came full of hope and joy at the anticipated meeting. But who may describe the grief which overwhelmed her on her arrival? His checkered life was closed in his sixty-sixth year. The funeral took place this evening at St. Paul's Church. He was buried with military honors, at Hollywood Cemetery. While manacled in the horrid dungeon, his only petition was to be allowed to keep a Bible, from which he professed to have derived great peace and comfort. His family think that he returned from prison a changed man. His spirit, which was naturally stern, had become gentle and loving, and strangely grateful to every being who showed him the least kindness. The Bible was still his daily companion; from it he seemed to derive great comfort and an abiding faith in Christ his Saviour.

17th.—The military movements are important, but to what they tend we know not. More troops have been added from Sheridan to Grant, and Early to Lee, and Sherman has crossed Georgia with little opposition or loss. Our last news is, that he has taken Fort McAllister, some miles below Savannah. What fate awaits that city we tremble to think of. A raid on Bristol and up the railroad, towards Saltville, has alarmed us for the salt-works; but General Breckinridge having turned up in the right place, suddenly appeared in their front and drove them off, to the great relief of the public mind.

24th.—Savannah has been evacuated, without loss to us, except of some stores, which could not be removed. The city was surrendered by its mayor, Arnold by name, and he seems to be worthy of the traitorous name. Our troops marched towards Charleston. Savannah was of little use to us for a year past, it has been so closely blockaded, and its surrender relieves troops which were there for its defence, which may be more useful elsewhere; but the moral effect of its fall is dreadful. The enemy are encouraged, and our people depressed. I never saw them more so.

On the 22d General Rosser beat a division of the enemy near Harrisonburg, and on the 23d General Lomax repulsed and severely punished another, near Gordonsville.

To-morrow is Christmas-day. Our girls and B. have gone to Cedar Hill to spend a week. Our office has suspended its labours, and I am anticipating very quiet holidays. A Christmas present has just been handed me from my sweet young friend S. W.—a box filled with all manner of working materials, which are now so scarce and expensive, with a beautiful mat for my toilet at the bottom of it. Christmas will come on the Sabbath. The "Colonel" is gone, but J. and C. will take their usual Sunday dinner, and I have gotten up a little dessert, because Christmas would not be Christmas without something better than usual; but it is a sad season to me. On last Christmas-day our dear R. T. C. was buried; and yesterday I saw my sweet young cousin E. M. die, and to-morrow expect to attend her funeral. Full of brightness and animation, full of Christian hope and charity, she was the life of her father's house, the solace and comfort of her already afflicted mother, one of the many mothers whose first-born has fallen a sacrifice to the war. This interesting girl, with scarcely a warning, has passed into heaven, leaving a blank in the hearts of her family never to be filled.

26th.—The sad Christmas has passed away. J. and C. were with us, and very cheerful. We exerted ourselves to be so too. The Church services in the morning were sweet and comforting. St. Paul's was dressed most elaborately and beautifully with evergreens; all looked as usual; but there is much sadness on account of the failure of the South to keep Sherman back. When we got home our family circle was small, but pleasant. The Christmas turkey and ham were not. We had aspired to a turkey, but finding the prices range from $50 to $100 in the market on Saturday, we contented ourselves with roast-beef and the various little dishes which Confederate times have made us believe are tolerable substitutes for the viands of better days. At night I treated our little party to tea and ginger cakes—two very rare indulgences; and but for the sorghum, grown in our own fields, the cakes would be an impossible indulgence. Nothing but the well-ascertained fact that Christmas comes but once a year would make such extravagance at all excusable. We propose to have a family gathering when the girls come home, on the day before or after New Year's day, (as that day will come on Sunday,) to enjoy together, and with one or two refugee friends, the contents of a box sent the girls by a young officer who captured it from the enemy, consisting of white sugar, raisins, preserves, pickles, spices, etc. They threaten to give us a plum-cake, and I hope they will carry it out, particularly if we have any of our army friends with us. Poor fellows, how they enjoy our plain dinners when they come, and how we love to see them enjoy them! Two meals a day has become the universal system among refugees, and many citizens, from necessity. The want of our accustomed tea or coffee is very much felt by the elders. The rule with us is only to have tea when sickness makes it necessary, and the headaches gotten up about dark have become the joke of the family. A country lady, from one of the few spots in all Virginia where the enemy has never been, and consequently where they retain their comforts, asked me gravely why we did not substitute milk for tea. She could scarcely believe me when I told her that we had not had milk more than twice in eighteen months, and then it was sent by a country friend. It is now $4 a quart.

28th.—A bright spot in our military horizon. The enemy's fleet of more than thirty gun-boats made a furious attack on Fort Fisher, near Wilmington, N. C., on the 24th, (last Saturday;) they kept up an average fire of thirty shots per minute until night. On the 25th the attack was renewed, and on the 27th, after being three times repulsed, the enemy abandoned his position above Fort Fisher, and re-embarked. The damage done to us was very slight—only two guns disabled, and but few other casualties. Thus failed utterly this great expedition of land and sea forces, from which the Federal authorities and the whole North confidently expected such grand results. And so may it ever be; the Lord help us, and deliver us in every such hour of need.

Yesterday we had a pleasant little dinner-party at Dr. G's—so rare a thing now, that I must note it in my diary. Many nice things on the table were sent by country friends. What would we do without our country friends? Their hearts seem warm and generous to those who are not so well off as themselves. They set a good example, which I trust will not be lost on us. Our relatives and friends, though they have been preyed upon by the enemy almost to exhaustion, never seem to forget us. Sausage from one, a piece of beef from another, a bushel of dried fruit, a turkey, etc., come ever and anon to our assistance. One can scarcely restrain tears of affection when it is remembered that these things are evidences of self-denial, and not given from their abundance, as at the beginning of the war. The soldiers are not forgotten by these country friends—those who remember the refugees are never forgetful of the soldiers. Take our people as a whole, they are full of generosity and patriotism. The speculators and money-makers of these trying times are a peculiar class, of which I neither like to speak, think, nor write; they are objects of my implacable disgust. They do not belong to our noble Southern patriots. They are with us, but not of us! I should think that a man who had made a fortune during the war would, when the war is over, wish to hide it, and not own his ill-gotten gains. I trust there are not many such. The year 1864 has almost passed away. Oh, what a fearful account it has rendered to Heaven! What calamities and sorrows crowd into its history, in this afflicted country of ours! God help us, and guide us onward and upward, for the Saviour's sake!

1865.

January 1st, 1865.—At St. James's Church this morning. Our children came over from Union Hill yesterday, to take their dinner from the contents of the captured box, and were detained by snow and rain. We were too much pleased to have them with us not to *make it convenient* to accommodate them, which we did with the assistance of our kind friend Mrs. P. To-morrow F. and myself will return to our offices, after a good rest, for which we are very thankful.

2d.—This bitter cold morning, when we entered the office, we found that our good "Major" had provided us a New Year's treat of hot coffee. Of course we all enjoyed it highly, and were very grateful to him; and when I returned home, the first thing that met my eye was a box sent from the express office. We opened it, and found it a Christmas box, filled with nice and substantial things from a friend now staying in Buckingham County, for whom I once had an opportunity of doing some trifling kindness. The Lord is certainly taking care of us through His people. The refugees in some of the villages are much worse off than we are. We hear amusing stories of a friend in an inland place, where nothing can possibly be bought, *hiring a skillet from a servant for one dollar* per month, and other cooking utensils, which are absolutely necessary, at the same rate; another in the same village, whose health seems to require that she should drink something *hot* at night, has been obliged to resort to *hot water*, as she has neither tea, coffee, sugar, nor milk. These ladies belong to wealthy Virginia families. Many persons have no meat on their tables for months at a time; and they are the real patriots, who submit patiently, and without murmuring, to any privation, provided the country is doing well. The flesh-pots of Egypt have no charms for them; they look forward hopefully to the time when their country shall be disenthralled, never caring for the trials of the past or the present, provided they can hope for the future.

8th. — Some persons in this beleaguered city seem crazed on the subject of gayety. In the midst of the wounded and dying, the low state of the commissariat, the anxiety of the whole country, the troubles of every kind by which we are surrounded, I am mortified to say that there are gay parties given in the city. There are those denominated "starvation parties," where young persons meet for innocent enjoyment, and retire at a reasonable hour; but there are others where the most elegant suppers are served— cakes, jellies, ices in profusion, and meats of the finest kinds in abundance, such as might furnish a meal for a regiment of General Lee's army. I wish these things were not so, and that every extra pound of meat could be sent to the army. When returning from the hospital, after witnessing the dying scene of a brother, whose young sister hung over him in agony, with my heart full of the sorrows of hospital-life, I passed a house where there were music and dancing. The revulsion of feeling was sickening. I thought of the gayety of Paris during the French Revolution, of the "cholera ball" in Paris, the ball at Brussels the night before the battle of Waterloo, and felt shocked that our own Virginians, at such a time, should remind me of scenes which we were wont to think only belonged to the lightness of foreign society. It seems to me that the army, when it hears of the gayety of Richmond, must think it heartless, particularly while it is suffering such hardships in her defence. The weddings, of which there are many, seem to be conducted with great quietness. We were all very much interested in a marriage which took place in this house a short time ago. Our sweet young friend, Miss A. P., was married to a Confederate States' surgeon from South Carolina. We assembled in the parlour, which was brilliantly lighted, before the dawn of day. The bride appeared in travelling costume; as soon as the solemn ceremony was done the folding-doors were thrown open, revealing a beautifully spread breakfast-table in the adjoining room. Breakfast being over, the bride and groom were hurried off to the cars, which were to bear them South. But, as usual in these war-times, the honeymoon was not to be uninterrupted. The furlough of the groom was of short continuance—the bright young bride will remain in the country with a sister, while he returns to his duty on the field. As soon as the wedding was over and the bridal party had gone, the excitement of the week had passed with us, leaving a blank in the house; but the times are too unquiet for a long calm—the gap was closed, and we returned to busy life. There seems to be a perfect mania on the subject of matrimony. Some of the churches may be seen open and lighted almost every night for bridals, and wherever I turn I hear of marriages in prospect.

>"In peace Love tunes the shepherd's reed;
>In war he mounts the warrior's steed,"

sings the "Last Minstrel" of the Scottish days of romance; and I do not think that our modern warriors are a whit behind them either in love or war. My only wonder is, that they find the time for the love-making amid the storms of warfare. Just at this time, however, I suppose our valiant knights and ladies fair are taking advantage of the short respite, caused by the alternate snows and sunshine of our variable climate having made the roads impassable to Grant's artillery and baggage-wagons. A soldier in our hospital called to me as I passed his bed the other day, "I say, Mrs. ——, when do you think my wound will be well enough for me to go to the country?" "Before very long, I hope." "But what does the doctor say, for I am mighty anxious to go?" I looked at his disabled limb, and talked to him hopefully of his being able to enjoy country air in a short time. "Well, try to get me up, for, you see, it ain't the country air I am after, but I wants to get married, and the lady don't know that I am wounded, and maybe she'll think I don't want to come." "Ah," said I, "but you must show her your scars, and if she is a girl worth having she will love you all the better for having bled for your country; and you must tell her that

> "'It is always the heart that is bravest in war,
> That is fondest and truest in love.'"

He looked perfectly delighted with the idea; and as I passed him again he called out, "Lady, please stop a minute and tell me the verse over again, for, you see, when I do get there, if she is affronted, I wants to give her the prettiest excuse I can, and I think that verse is beautiful."

11th.—Every thing seems unchanging in the outer world during the few past days. We were most delightfully surprised last night. While sitting quietly in the Colonel's room, (in the basement,) the window was suddenly thrown up, and in sprang our son J., just returned from Northern captivity. Finding that we had changed our quarters since he was here, he walked up the street in search of us, and while stopping to ascertain the right house, he espied us through the half-open window-shutter, and was too impatient for the preliminaries of ringing a bell and waiting for a servant to open the door. He was in exuberant spirits, but much disappointed that his wife was not with us. So, after a short sojourn and a cup of tea, he went off to join her on "Union Hill." They both dined with us to-day. His confinement has not been so bad as we feared, from the treatment which many other prisoners had received, but it was disagreeable enough. He was among the surgeons in Winchester in charge of the sick and wounded; and when we retreated before Sheridan after the battle of the 19th of August, it fell to his lot, among eighteen or twenty other surgeons, to be left there to take care of our captured wounded. When those duties were at an end, instead of sending them under flag of truce to our own army, they were taken first to the old Capitol, where they remained ten days, thence to Fort Delaware, for one night, and thence to Fort Hamilton, near Fortress Monroe, where they were detained four weeks. They there met with much kindness from Southern ladies, and also from a Federal officer, Captain Blake.

16th.— Fort Fisher has fallen; Wilmington will of course follow. This was our last port into which blockade-runners were successful in entering, and which furnished us with an immense amount of stores. What will be the effect of this disaster we know not; we can only hope and pray.

21st.—We hear nothing cheering except in the proceedings of Congress and the Virginia Legislature, particularly the latter. Both bodies look to stern resistance to Federal authority. The city and country are full of rumours and evil surmising; and while we do not believe one word of the croaking, it makes us feel restless and unhappy.

29th, Sunday.— As usual, we attended Mr. Peterkin's church, and enjoyed his sermon. Every thing looks so dark without that our only comfort is in looking to God for His blessing. The Union Prayer-Meetings are great comforts to us. They are attended by crowds; ministers of all denominations officiate at them. Prayers for the country, hymns of praise, and exhortations, fill up the time. Some of the addresses are very stirring, urging the laity to work and to give, and to every branch of the Christian Church to do its duty to the country. Our brave old Bishop Meade, on his dying bed, admonished one of his presbyters to speak boldly to the people in behalf of the country; and I am glad to hear the ministers do it. They speak cheerfully, too, on the subject; they are sanguine of our success, depending upon the Lord and on the bravery of our troops —on the "sword of the Lord and of Gideon."

February 8.—I feel more and more anxious about Richmond. I can't believe that it will be given up; yet so many persons are doubtful that it makes me very unhappy. I can't keep a regular diary now, because I do not like to write all that I feel and hear. I am constantly expecting the blessing of God in a way that we know not. I believe that all of our difficulties are to be overruled for good. A croaker accuses me of expecting a miracle to be wrought in our favour, which I do not; but we have been so often led on in a manner so wonderful, that we have no right to doubt the mercy of God towards us. Our troops, too, are standing up under such hardships and trials, which require the most sublime moral as well as personal courage to endure, that I cannot avoid expecting a blessing upon them!

Sherman moves on in his desolating path. Oh for men to oppose and crush him!

In the midst of our trials, *Hymen* still comes in to assert his claims, and to amuse and interest us. We have lately seen our beautiful young friend, M. G., led to his altar; and two of our young office associates are bidding us farewell for the same *sacrifice*. One of them, Miss T. W., has sat by my side for more than a year, with her bright face and sweet manners. She will be a real loss to me, but I cannot find it in my heart to regret that she will bless with her sweetness one of our brave Confederate officers.

28th.—Our new Commissary-General is giving us brighter hopes for Richmond by his energy. Not a stone is left unturned to collect all the provisions from the country. Ministers of the Gospel and others have gone out to the various county towns and court-houses, to urge the people to send in every extra bushel of corn or pound of meat for the army. The people only want enlightening on the subject; it is no want of patriotism which makes them keep any portion of their provisions. Circulars are sent out to the various civil and military officers in all disenthralled counties in the State,—which, alas! when compared with the whole, are very few,—to ask for their superfluities. All will answer promptly, I know, and generously.

Since I last wrote in my diary, our Essex friends have again most liberally replenished our larder just as they did this time last year—if possible, more generously. The Lord reward them!

March 10.—Still we go on as heretofore, hoping and praying that Richmond may be safe. Before Mr. Hunter (Hon. R. M. T.) left Richmond, I watched his countenance whenever I heard the subject mentioned before him, and though he said nothing, I thought he looked sad. I know that he understands the situation of affairs perfectly, and I may have fancied the sad look, but I think not; and whenever it arises before my mind's eye, it makes me unhappy. I imagine, too, from a conversation which I had with Mr. Secretary Mallory, that he fears much for Richmond. Though it was an unexpressed opinion, yet I fear that I understood it rightly. I know that we ought to feel that whatever General Lee and the President deem right for the cause must be right, and that we should be satisfied that all will be well; but it would almost break my heart to see this dear old city, with its hallowed associations, given over to the Federals. Fearful orders have been given in the offices to keep the papers packed, except such as we are working on. The packed boxes remain in the front room, as if uncertainty still existed about moving them. As we walk in every morning, all eyes are turned to the boxes to see if any have been removed, and we breathe more freely when we find them still there.

To-day I have spent in the hospital, and was very much interested in our old Irishman. He has been there for more than two years; first as a patient sent from Drury's Bluff, with ague and fever. Though apparently long past the military age, he had enlisted as a soldier in a Georgia regiment, but it was soon discovered that he was physically unable to stand camp-life; he was therefore detailed to work in the gardens, which supplied the soldiers at the Bluff with vegetables. He got well, and returned to his post, but was soon sent back again, too sick for service. The climate did not suit him, and when he again recovered Miss T. employed him as gardener and marketman to her hospital. We all became interested in him, because of his quiet, subdued manner, faithfulness to his duty, and respectful bearing. Some months ago his health began to decline, and day after day he has been watched and cared for by the surgeon and ladies with deep interest; but he steadily declines in strength, and is now confined to his cot, and it is but too evident that his end is approaching. We had all remarked that he never alluded to his early history, and was singularly reserved with regard to his religious faith; yet, as long as he was able to go out, he might be seen every Sunday seated alone in a corner of the gallery of St. James's Church. This evening, as I was walking around the room in which he lies, and had just administered to him some nourishment, he said to me : "When you get through with the men won't you come back and let me talk to ye?" When I returned and took my seat by him, he looked earnestly in my face, and said : "Mrs. ——, you have an Irish name—have you friends there?" "No, my husband's grandfather was from Ireland, but we have no relatives there now." "Yes," was his reply, "it is a good name in Ireland, and you have been kind to me, and I want to talk to you a bit before I die. You know that I am a Protestant, and I have been constantly to Mr Peterkin's church since I came here, because I like the church, and I like him; and I hope that now I am prepared to die. But I was not brought up an Episcopalian in the old country—our house was divided, like.

My father was a Catholic, and my mother was a Presbyterian; neither went to the church of the other, but they were a loving couple for all that. He said to her, when we were but wee things: 'Mary,' said he, ' the children must go to your church sometimes, and to mine sometimes; you may teach them the Bible; but when they are old enough, they must judge for themselves.' And so it was; we were obliged every Sunday to go to one church or the other, but we determined for ourselves. I most always went with mother, because she was so good and gentle, and I loved her so much. We grew up a cheerful, happy family. My father was a gardener, three-quarters of a mile from Loudonderry; he had a good little farm, and sold his fruit and vegetables in Derry, and had made a great deal of money; and we had a good house, and were so comfortable. We all went to school, and kept on so until I, the eldest child, was grown. In the neighbourhood was a man that my father hated. Oh, how he hated that man! But I loved that man's daughter; with my whole heart I loved that girl."

Here his voice became excited, his eyes were suffused with tears, and his emaciated, pock-marked face almost glowed with animation. The room had become still; the sick and wounded and visitors to the room were all listening with deep attention to the old man's story. "I knew," he continued, "that my father would see me dead before he would agree to my marrying into that family, and he was a stern man, and I was afraid to let him know; and I tried to get over my love; but I saw her whenever I went to church, and at last I told her that I loved her, and she said she would marry me, and then, Mrs. ——," he said with energy, "no mortal man could have made me give her up. After awhile my father said to me, 'Johnny,' said he, ' you are of age, and must work for yourself now ; I will give you ten acres of my farm; begin early in spring, break it up, and make a garden; in a few years you will be an independent man.' Said I, ' Father, may I put a house on it ?' ' No, my son; when I die you will have this house ; can't you live now with your mother and me ?' ' But, father,' said I, ' suppose I get married, where can I live then ?' ' If I like the match,' said he, ' you may live here.' I said no more then, but I saw Mary Dare,' (he added, in a subdued voice, ' her name was Mary Dare,) and I told her I would try my father again, and if he would not agree to what I said, I would go to America, and make a home for her. She was distressed, and I was in misery. Towards the spring my father said to me every now and then, ' Johnny, why don't you break up your ground ? I have seeds for ye ; it is time to begin.' But I could not begin ; and I could not tell him why, I had such a dread of him. At last he said, 'Johnny, you are behindhand ; why don't you go to work ?' I knew from his look that I must speak now, and my mother looked so tender-like into my face, that I said, 'Father, I can't live here, unless I can bring my wife here, or build a house for her. I am going to marry Mary Dare, and if you object to it, I will go to America.' My father looked sternly at me, and said, ' I will not have you in my house or on my land, if you marry that girl ; think about it ; if you will give her up, you may live here and be well off ; if not, you can go to America at once, and I will bear your expenses. Let me know to-morrow morning.' My mother looked heart-broken, but she did not speak. She never opposed my father. This was Sunday. Next morning he asked me if I had made up my mind. I said, ' Yes, sir ; to go to

America.' 'Then, Johnny, on Wednesday morning I will go to Derry and get you ready.' On Wednesday he called me to get his pony, and to walk to town, and meet him at a tailor's. He was there before me, and selected cloth to make me two good suits of clothes. We then went to a draper's and got linen (for we wear linen in Ireland, not cotton) to make me twelve shirts, and other clothes besides. Then we went to the packet office, where we were told that a packet would sail on that day week for Liverpool, to meet an emigrant ship just ready to sail for New York. He paid my passage without saying a word to me, though his manner was kind to me all the time. As we turned to go home he said, 'I have four pounds to give you for pocket-money, and I shall deposit fifty pounds in New York for you, which you can draw if you are in want ; but I advise you not to draw it unless you are in want, for it is all I shall give you.' When we got home my mother collected her friends and neighbours to make my clothes. She and my sisters looked sorry enough, but not a word did they say about it. I knew that my father had told them not to do it, and my heart was too full to speak to anybody except to Mary Dare—she knew that as soon as I could come for her that I would come. When I took leave of my mother she almost died, like. I told her, 'Mother,' said I, 'I am coming back when I am independent, and can do as I please. Write to me, mother dear ; I will write to you and my sisters when I get to New York, and tell you where I am ;' and I did write to Mary and to my mother. I could not write to my father ; I could not forgive him, when I thought how he had grieved Mary and me ; and I could not be deceitful. As soon as I got to New York, I engaged with a gentleman at Williamsburg, on Long Island, to work his garden. For two years I worked, and laid up my wages; and not a single letter came for me. I grieved and sorrowed, and thought about Mary—I thought maybe her letters were stopped by somebody. I knew she would not forget me. Sometimes I thought I would go home to Ireland, and see what was the matter. At last, one day, my employer came into the garden with a newspaper in his hand. 'Mr. Crumley,' says he, 'here is something for you;' and sure enough there was a line to John Crumley, asking me to meet an old friend that had just come from Derry. I could not work another stroke, but went to the city, and there he was. I asked him first about my mother. 'All well; I have a letter from her to you.' 'And haven't you another letter? Didn't Mary Dare write to me?' 'Mary Dare!' he said; 'don't you know that Mary Dare died soon after you left the old country?'" The old man stopped a moment to recover himself. Then, striking the side of his cot with his hard, sunburnt hand, he added, "Yes, she was dead, and I was then left the lone man that you see me now, Mrs. ——. My mother had not written before, because she hated to distress me, but she wrote to beg that I would come home; my father's health was failing, and he wanted me, his first-born, to come and take the homestead. But Ireland and home were nothing to me now. I wrote to her that my next brother must take the homestead, and take care of my father and her, God bless her! I should never see Ireland again, but I loved her and my sisters all the same. The next letter was long after that. My mother wrote, 'Your father is dead; come back, Johnny, and take your own home.' I could not go; and then I went to Georgia, and never heard from home again. I tried to fight for the South, because the Southern people were good to me, and I thought if I got killed there was nobody to care for me."

His story was done. He looked at me, and said, "You have all been so good to me, particularly Miss T. God bless you all for it! I am now almost at my journey's end." When I looked up I found the men subdued and sorrowful. The story, and the weak, sad tones with which it was told, had touched them all, and brought tears from some.

11th.—Sheridan's raid through the country is perfectly awful, and he has joined Grant, without being caught. Oh, how we listened to hear that he had been arrested in his direful career! It was, I suppose, the most cruel and desolating raid upon record—more lawless, if possible, than Hunter's. He had an overwhelming force, spreading ruin through the Upper Valley, the Piedmont country, the tide-water country, until he reached Grant. His soldiers were allowed to commit any cruelty on non-combatants that suited their rapacious tempers—stealing every thing they could find; ear-rings, breastpins, and finger-rings were taken from the first ladies of the land; nothing escaped them which was worth carrying off from the already desolated country. And can we feel patient at the idea of such soldiers coming to Richmond, the target at which their whole nation, from their President to the meanest soldier upon their army-rolls, has been aiming for four years? Oh, I would that I could see Richmond burnt to the ground by its own people, with not one brick left upon another, before its defenceless inhabitants should be subjected to such degradation!

Fighting is still going on; so near the city, that the sound of cannon is ever in our ears. Farmers are sending in produce which they cannot spare, but which they give with a spirit of self-denial rarely equalled. Ladies are offering their jewelry, their plate, any thing which can be converted into money, for the country. I have heard some of them declare, that, if necessary, they will cut off their long suits of hair, and send them to Paris to be sold for bread for the soldiers; and there is not a woman, worthy of the name of Southerner, who would not do it, if we could get it out of the country, and bread or meat in return. Some gentlemen are giving up their watches, when every thing else has been given. A colonel of our army was seen the other night, after a stirring appeal had been made for food for the soldiers, to approach the speaker's stand with his watch in his hand, saying: "I have no money, nor provisions; my property was ruined by Hunter's raid last summer; my watch is very dear to me from association, but it must be sold for bread." Remembering, as he put it down, that it had been long worn by his wife, now dead, though not a man who liked or approved *of scenes*, he obeyed the affectionate impulse of his heart, took it up quickly, kissed it, and replaced it on the table.

12*th*.—A deep gloom has just been thrown over the city by the untimely death of one of its own heroic sons. General John Pegram fell while nobly leading his brigade against the enemy in the neighbourhood of Petersburg. But two weeks before he had been married in St. Paul's Church, in the presence of a crowd of relatives and friends, to the celebrated Miss H. C., of Baltimore. All was bright and beautiful. Happiness beamed from every eye. Again has St. Paul's, his own beloved church, been opened to receive the soldier and his bride—the one coffined for a hero's grave, the other, pale and trembling, though still by his side, in widow's garb.

31st.—A long pause in my diary. Every thing seems so dark and uncertain that I have no heart for keeping records. The croakers croak about Richmond being evacuated, but I can't and won't believe it.

There is hard fighting about Petersburg, and General A. P. Hill has been killed. Dreadful to think of losing such a man at such a time; but yet it comes nearer home when we hear of the young soldiers whom we have loved, and whose youth we have watched with anxiety and hope as those on whom our country must depend in days to come, being cut down when their country most needs them. We have just heard of the death of Barksdale Warwick, another of our E. H. S. boys—another son of the parents who yielded up their noble first-born son on the field of battle three years ago. He fell a day or two ago; I did not hear precisely when or where; I only know that he has passed away, as myriads of our young countrymen have done before him, and in the way in which our men would prefer to die.

A week ago we made a furious attack upon the enemy's fortifications near Petersburg, and several were taken before daylight, but we could not hold them against overwhelming numbers, and batteries vastly too strong for any thing we could command; and so it is still—the enemy is far too strong in numbers and military resources. The Lord save us, or we perish! Many persons think that Richmond is in the greatest possible danger, and may be evacuated at any time. Perhaps we are apathetic or too hopeful, but none of us are desponding at all, and I find myself planning for the future, and feeling excessively annoyed when I find persons less sanguine than myself.

April 3.— Agitated and nervous, I turn to my diary to-night as the means of soothing my feelings. We have passed through a fatal thirty-six hours. Yesterday morning (it seems a week ago) we went, as usual, to St. James's Church, hoping for a day of peace and quietness, as well as of religious improvement and enjoyment. How short-sighted we are, and how little do we know of what is coming, either of judgment or mercy! The sermon being over, as it was the first Sunday in the month, the sacrament of the Lord's Supper was administered. The day was bright, beautiful, and peaceful, and a general quietness and repose seemed to rest upon the congregation, undisturbed by rumours and apprehensions. While the sacred elements were being administered, the sexton came in with a note to General Cooper, which was handed him as he walked from the chancel, and he immediately left the church. It made me anxious; but such things are not uncommon, and caused no excitement in the congregation. The services being over, we left the church, and as the congregations from the various churches were being mingled on Grace Street, our children, who had been at St. Paul's, joined us, on their way to the usual family gathering in our room on Sunday. After the salutations of the morning, J. remarked, in an agitated voice, to his father, that he had just returned from the War Department, and that there was sad news—General Lee's lines had been broken, and the city would probably be evacuated within twenty-four hours. Not until then did I observe that every countenance was wild with excitement. The inquiry, "What is the matter?" ran from lip to lip. Nobody seemed to hear or to answer. An old friend ran across the street, pale with excitement, repeating what J. had just told us, that unless we heard better news from General Lee the city would be evacuated. We could do nothing; no one suggested any thing to be done. We reached home with a strange, unrealizing feeling. In an hour J. (who is now Professor of Mathematics in the Naval School) received orders to accompany Captain Parker to the South with the Corps of Midshipmen. Then we began to understand that the Government was moving, and that the evacuation was indeed going on. The office-holders were now making arrangements to get off. Every car was ordered to be ready to take them south. Baggage-wagons, carts, drays, and ambulances were driving about the streets; every one was going off that could go, and now there were all the indications of alarm and excitement of every kind which could attend such an awful scene. The people were rushing up and down the streets, vehicles of all kinds were flying along, bearing goods of all sorts and people of all ages and classes who could go beyond the corporation lines. We tried to keep ourselves quiet. We could not go south, nor could we leave the city at all in this hurried way. J. and his wife had gone. The "Colonel," with B., intended going in the northern train this morning—he to his home in Hanover County, and she to her father's house in Clarke County, as soon as she could get there. Last night, when we went out to hire a servant to go to Camp Jackson for our sister, we for the first time realized that our money was worthless here, and that we are in fact penniless. About midnight she walked in, escorted by two of the convalescent soldiers. Poor fellows! all the soldiers will go who can, but the sick and wounded must be captured. We collected in one room, and tried to comfort one another; we made large pockets and filled them with as many of our valuables as we could suspend from our waists. The gentlemen walked down to the War Office in the night to see what was going on. Alas! every sight and sound was grievous and heavy.

A telegram just received from General Lee hastened the evacuation. The public offices were all forsaken. They said that by three o'clock in the morning the work must be completed, and the city ready for the enemy to take possession. Oh, who shall tell the horror of the past night! Hope seemed to fade; none but despairing words were heard, except from a few brave hearts. Union men began to show themselves; treason walked abroad. A gloomy pall seemed to hang over us; but I do not think that any of us felt keenly, or have yet realized our overwhelming calamity. The suddenness and extent of it is too great for us to feel its poignancy at once. About two o'clock in the morning we were startled by a loud sound like thunder; the house shook and the windows rattled; it seemed like an earthquake in our midst. We knew not what it was, nor did we care. It was soon understood to be the blowing up of a magazine below the city. In a few hours another exploded on the outskirts of the city, much louder than the first, and shivering innumerable plate-glass windows all over Shockoe Hill. It was then daylight, and we were standing out upon the pavement. The Colonel and B. had just gone. Shall we ever meet again? Many ladies were now upon the streets. The lower part of the city was burning. About seven o'clock I set off to go to the central depot to see if the cars would go out. As I went from Franklin to Broad Street, and on Broad, the pavements were covered with broken glass; women, both white and coloured, were walking in multitudes from the Commissary offices and burning stores with bags of flour, meal, coffee, sugar, rolls of cotton cloth, etc.; coloured men were rolling wheelbarrows filled in the same way. I went on and on towards the depot, and as I proceeded shouts and screams became louder. The rabble

15*

rushed by me in one stream. At last I exclaimed, "Who are those shouting? What is the matter?" I seemed to be answered by a hundred voices, "The Yankees have come." I turned to come home, but what was my horror, when I reached Ninth Street, to see a regiment of Yankee cavalry come dashing up, yelling, shouting, hallooing, screaming! All Bedlam let loose could not have vied with them in diabolical roarings. I stood riveted to the spot; I could not move nor speak. Then I saw the iron gates of our time-honoured and beautiful Capitol Square, on the walks and greensward of which no hoof had been allowed to tread, thrown open and the cavalry dash in. I could see no more; I must go on with a mighty effort, or faint where I stood. I came home amid what I thought was the firing of cannon. I thought that they were thundering forth a salute that they had reached the goal of their ardent desires; but I afterwards found that the Armory was on fire, and that the flames having reached the shells deposited there for our army, they were exploding. These explosions were kept up until a late hour this evening; I am rejoiced they are gone; they, at least, can never be turned against us. I found the family collected around the breakfast-table, and was glad to see Captain M's family with them. The captain has gone, and the ladies have left their home on "Union Hill" to stay here among friends, Colonel P. having kindly given them rooms. An hour or two after breakfast we all retired to our rooms exhausted. No one had slept; no one had sought repose or thought of their own comfort. The Federal soldiers were roaming about the streets; either whiskey or the excess of joy had given some of them the appearance of being beside themselves. We had hoped that very little whiskey would be found in the city, as, by order of the Mayor, casks were emptied yesterday evening in the streets, and it flowed like water through the gutters; but the rabble had managed to find it secreted in the burning shops, and bore it away in pitchers and buckets. It soon became evident that protection would be necessary for the residences, and at the request of Colonel P. I went to the Provost Marshal's office to ask for it. Mrs. P. was unfortunately in the country, and only ladies were allowed to apply for guards. Of course this was a very unpleasant duty, but I must undertake it. Mrs. D. agreed to accompany me, and we proceeded to the City Hall—the City Hall, which from my childhood I had regarded with respect and reverence, as the place where my father had for years held his courts, and in which our lawyers, whose names stand among the highest in the Temple of Fame, for fifty years expounded the Constitution and the laws, which must now be trodden under foot. We reached it. After passing through crowds of negro soldiers there, we found on the steps some of the elderly gentlemen of the city seeking admittance, which was denied them. I stopped to speak to Mr. ——, in whose commission house I was two days ago, and saw him surrounded by all the stores which usually make up the establishment of such a merchant; it was now a mass of blackened ruins. He had come to ask protection for his residence, but was not allowed to enter. We passed the sentinel, and an officer escorted us to the room in which we were to ask our country's foe to allow us to remain undisturbed in our own houses. Mrs. D. leant on me tremblingly; she shrank from the humiliating duty. For my own part, though my heart beat loudly and my blood boiled, I never felt more high-spirited or lofty than at that moment. A large table was surrounded by officials, writing or talking to the ladies, who came on the same mission that brought us. I approached the officer who sat at the head of the table, and asked him politely if he was the Provost Marshal. "I am the Commandant, madam," was the respectful reply. "Then to whom am I to apply for protection for our residence?" "You need none, madam; our troops are perfectly disciplined, and dare not enter your premises." "I am sorry to be obliged to undeceive you, sir, but when I left home seven of your soldiers were in the yard of the residence opposite to us, and one has already been into our kitchen." He looked surprised, and said, "Then, madam, you are entitled to a guard. Captain, write a protection for the residence on the corner of First and Franklin Streets, and give these ladies a guard." This was quickly done, and as I turned to go out, I saw standing near me our old friend, Mrs. ——. Oh! how my heart sank when I looked into her calm, sad face, and remembered that she and her venerable and highly esteemed husband must ask leave to remain in peace in their home of many years. The next person who attracted my attention was that sweet young girl, S. W. Having no mother, she of course must go and ask that her father's beautiful mansion may be allowed to stand uninjured. Tears rolled down her cheeks as she pressed my hand in passing. Other friends were there; we did not speak, we could not; we sadly looked at each other and passed on. Mrs. D. and myself came out, accompanied by our guard. The fire was progressing rapidly, and the crashing sound of falling timbers was distinctly heard. Dr. Read's church was blazing. Yankees, citizens, and negroes were attempting to arrest the flames. The War Department was falling in; burning papers were being wafted about the streets. The Commissary Department, with our desks and papers, was consumed already. Warwick & Barksdale's mill was sending its flames to the sky. Cary and Main Streets seemed doomed throughout; Bank Street was beginning to burn, and now it had reached Franklin. At any other moment it would have distracted me, but I had ceased to feel any thing. We brought our guard to Colonel P., who posted him; about three o'clock he came to tell me that the guard was drunk, and threatening to shoot the servants in the yard. Again I went to the City Hall to procure another. I approached the Commandant and told him why I came. He immediately ordered another guard, and a corporal to be sent for the arrest of the drunken man. The flames had decreased, but the business part of the city was in ruins. The second guard was soon posted, and the first carried off by the collar. Almost every house is guarded; and the streets are now (ten o'clock) perfectly quiet. The moon is shining brightly on our captivity. God guide and watch over us!

April 5.—I feel as if we were groping in the dark; no one knows what to do. The Yankees, so far, have behaved humanely. As usual, they begin with professions of kindness to those whom they have ruined without justifiable cause, without reasonable motive, without right to be here, or anywhere else within the Southern boundary. General Ord is said to be polite and gentlemanly, and seems to do every thing in his power to lessen the horrors of this dire calamity. Other officers are kind in their departments, and the negro regiments look quite subdued. No one can tell how long this will last. Norfolk had its day of grace, and even New Orleans was not down-trodden at once. There are already apprehensions of evil. Is the Church to pray for the Northern President? How is it possible, except as we pray for all other sinners? But I pause for further developments.

6th.—Mr. Lincoln has visited our devoted city to-day. His reception was any thing but complimentary. Our people were in nothing rude or disrespectful; they only kept themselves away from a scene so painful. There are very few Unionists of the least respectability here; these met them (he was attended by Stanton and others) with cringing loyalty, I hear, but the rest of the small collection were of the low, lower, lowest of creation. They drove through several streets, but the greeting was so feeble from the motley crew of vulgar men and women, that the Federal officers themselves, I suppose, were ashamed of it, for they very soon escaped from the disgraceful association. It is said that they took a collation at General Ord's—our President's house!! Ah! it is a bitter pill. I would that dear old house, with all its associations, so sacred to the Southerners, so sweet to us as a family, had shared in the general conflagration. Then its history would have been unsullied, though sad. Oh, how gladly would I have seen it burn! I have been nowhere since Monday, except to see my dear old friend Mrs. R., and to the hospital. There I am not much subjected to the harrowing sights and sounds by which we are surrounded. The wounded must be nursed; poor fellows, they are so sorrowful! Our poor old Irishman died on Sunday. The son of a very old acquaintance was brought to our hospital a few days ago, most severely wounded—Colonel Charles Richardson, of the artillery. We feared at first that he must die, but now there is a little more hope. It is so sad that after four years of bravery and devotion to the cause, he should be brought to his native city, for the defence of which he would have gladly given his life, dangerously if not mortally wounded, when its sad fate is just decided. I love to sit by his bedside and try to cheer him; his friends seem to vie with each other in kind attentions to him.

We hear rumours of battles, and of victories gained by our troops, but we have no certain information beyond the city lines.

10*th.*—Another gloomy Sabbath-day and harrowing night. We went to St. Paul's in the morning, and heard a very fine sermon from Dr. Minnegerode—at least so said my companions. My attention, which is generally riveted by his sermons, wandered continually. I could not listen; I felt so strangely, as if in a vivid, horrible dream. Neither President was prayed for; in compliance with some arrangement with the Federal authorities, the prayer was used as for all in authority! How fervently did we all pray for our own President! Thank God, our silent prayers are free from Federal authority. "The oppressor keeps the body bound, but knows not what a range the spirit takes." Last night, (it seems strange that we have lived to speak or write of it,) between nine and ten o'clock, as some of the ladies of the house were collected in our room, we were startled by the rapid firing of cannon. At first we thought that there must be an attack upon the city; bright thoughts of the return of our army darted through my brain; but the firing was too regular. We began to think it must be a salute for some great event. We threw up the windows, and saw the flashes and smoke of cannon towards Camp Jackson. Some one present counted one hundred guns. What could it be? We called to passers-by : " What do those guns mean ?" Sad voices answered several times :

"I do not know." At last a voice pertly, wickedly replied: "General Lee has surrendered, thank God!" Of course we did not believe him, though the very sound was a knell. Again we called out: "What is the matter?" A voice answered, as if from a broken heart: "They say General Lee has surrendered." We cannot believe it, but my heart became dull and heavy, and every nerve and muscle of my frame seems heavy too. I cannot even now shake it off. We passed the night, I cannot tell how—I know not how we live at all. At daybreak the dreadful salute commenced again. Another hundred guns at twelve to-day. Another hundred—can it be so? No, we do not believe it, but how can we bear such a doubt? Where are all our dear ones, our beloved soldiers, and our noble chief to-night, while the rain falls pitilessly? Are they lying on the cold, hard ground, sleeping for sorrow? or are they moving southward triumphantly, to join General Johnston, still able and willing—ah, far more than willing—to avenge their country's wrongs? God help us!—we must take refuge in unbelief.

Tuesday Night.—No light on our sorrow—still gloomy, dark, and uncertain.

I went to-day to the hospital, as was my duty. My dear friend S. T. cheers me, by being utterly incredulous about the reported surrender. As usual, she is cheerfully devoting her powers of mind and body to her hospital. For four years she has never thought of her own comfort, when by sacrificing it she could alleviate a soldier's sorrow. Miss E. D., who has shared with her every duty, every self-sacrificing effort in behalf of our sick and wounded soldiers, is now enduring the keenest pangs of sorrow from the untimely death of her venerable father. On the day of the evacuation, while walking too near a burning house, he was struck by a piece of falling timber, and the blow soon closed his long life. Alas! the devoted daughter, who had done so much for other wounded, could do nothing for the restoration of one so dear to her.

Wednesday Night.—We have heard nothing new to-day confirming the report of the surrender, which is perhaps the reason my spirit feels a little more light. We must *hope*, though our prospects should be as dark as the sky of this stormy night. Our wounded are doing well—those who remain in our hospital and the convalescents have been ordered to "Camp Jackson." Indeed, all the patients were included in the same order; but Miss T. having represented that several of them were not in a condition to be removed, they have been allowed to remain where they are.

Colonel R. is improving, for which we are most thankful.

Thursday Night.—Fearful rumours are reaching us from sources which it is hard to doubt, that it is all too true, and that General Lee surrendered on Sunday last, the 9th of April. The news came to the enemy by telegram during the day, and to us at night by the hoarse and pitiless voice of the cannon. We know, of course, that circumstances forced it upon our great commander and his gallant army. How all this happened—how Grant's hundreds of thousands overcame our little band, history, not I, must tell my children's children. It is enough for me to tell them that all that bravery and self-denial could do has been done. We do not yet give up all hope. General Johnston is in the field, but there are thousands of the enemy to his tens. The citizens are quiet. The calmness of despair is written on every countenance.

Private sorrows are now coming upon us. We *know* of but few casualties.

Good-Friday.—As usual, I went to the hospital, and found Miss T. in much trouble. A peremptory order has been given by the Surgeon-General to remove *all* patients. In the opinion of our surgeon, to five of them it would be certain death. The ambulances were at the door. Miss T. and myself decided to go at once to the Medical Director and ask him to recall the order. We were conducted to his office, and, for the first time since the entrance of the Federal army, were impolitely treated. On two occasions we had been obliged to make application to officials, and had been received with great respect and consideration, and we believe it has been uniformly the case ; and we were, therefore, very much surprised when a request which seemed to us so reasonable was at first refused most decidedly. We could not give up our application, as it seemed to be a matter of life and death ; so we told him what our surgeon had said, and that we hoped he would reconsider his order. He replied, that he should send a surgeon with the ambulances, and if in *his* judgment they could be removed, it should be done without hesitation, as he was determined to break up the small hospitals *which you have all about town*, (ours is the only small hospital in town,) and that he had ordered neither rations nor medicines to be issued to them. Miss T. told him that nothing of the sort was necessary ; she had never asked nor received rations from the Federal Government; that she had now but five men under her care, and they were desperately wounded, and she would greatly prefer that the hospital should be considered in the light of a private establishment, which we could take care of without asking help. A change came over his countenance, but not his manner ; he brusquely told us that he would "see about it." In an hour afterwards the surgeon and the ambulance came, but after what seemed to me rather a pompous display of surgical examination and learned medical terms, addressed to the lady-nurses, he determined to leave our dear mangled soldiers to our care. One of them is in a dying condition ; he cannot survive many hours.

We had no service in our churches to-day. An order came out in this morning's papers that the prayers for the President of the United States must be used. How could we do it ? Mr. —— went to the hospital by the request of Colonel Richardson, and had prayers in his room. Ambulances are constantly passing with horses in the finest possible condition—even finer than ours were in the beginning of the war. It seems to me passing strange that, with all their advantages, we kept them at bay so long, and conquered them so often. Had one port been left open to us— only one, by which we might have received food and clothing—Richmond would not now be in their hands ; our men were starved into submission.

Sunday Night.—The Episcopal churches being closed, we went to the Rev. Dr. Hoge's church. The rector was absent ; he went off, to be in Confederate lines ; but the Rev. Dr. Read, whose church is in ruins, occupied the pulpit.

Strange rumours are afloat to-night. It is said, and believed, that Lincoln is dead, and Seward much injured. As I passed the house of a friend this evening, she raised the window and told me the report. Of course I treated it as a Sunday rumour ; but the story is strengthened by the way which the Yankees treat it. They, of course, know all about it, and to-morrow's papers will reveal the particulars. I trust that, if true, it may not be by the hand of an assassin, though it would seem to fulfil the warnings of Scripture. His efforts to carry out his abolition theories have caused the shedding of oceans of Southern blood, and by man it now seems has his blood been shed. But what effect will it have on the South? We may have much to fear. Future events will show. This event has made us wild with excitement and speculation.

General Lee has returned. He came unattended, save by his staff—came without notice, and without parade; but he could not come unobserved; as soon as his approach was whispered, a crowd gathered in his path, not boisterously, but respectfully, and increasing rapidly as he advanced to his home on Franklin Street, between 8th and 9th, where, with a courtly bow to the multitude, he at once retired to the bosom of his beloved family. When I called in to see his high-minded and patriotic wife, a day or two after the evacuation, she was busily engaged in her invalid's chair, and very cheerful and hopeful. "The end is not yet," she said, as if to cheer those around her; "Richmond is not the Confederacy." To this we all most willingly assented, and felt very much gratified and buoyed by her brightness. I have not had the heart to visit her since the surrender, but hear that she still is sanguine, saying that "General Lee is not the Confederacy," and that there is "life in the old land yet." He is not the Confederacy; but our hearts sink within us when we remember that he and his noble army are now idle, and that we can no longer look upon them as the bulwark of our land. He has returned from defeat and disaster with the universal and profound admiration of the world, having done all that skill and valour could accomplish. The scenes at the surrender were noble and touching. General Grant's bearing was profoundly respectful; General Lee's as courtly and lofty as the purest chivalry could require. The terms, so honourable to all parties, being complied with to the letter, our arms were laid down with breaking hearts, and tears such as stoutest warriors may shed. "Woe worth the day!"

Tuesday Night.—I try to dwell as little as possible on public events. I only feel that we have no country, no government, no future. I cannot, like some others, look with hope on Johnston's army. He will do what he can; but ah, what can he do? Our anxiety now is that our President and other public men may get off in safety. O God! have mercy upon them and help them! For ourselves, like the rest of the refugees, we are striving to get from the city. The stereotyped question when we meet is, "When and where are you going?" Our country relatives have been very kind. My brother offers us an asylum in his devastated home at W. While there we must look around for some other place, in which to build up a home for our declining years. Property we have none—all gone. Thank God, we have our faculties; the girls and myself, at least, have health. Mr. —— bears up under our difficulties with the same hopeful spirit which he has ever manifested. "The Lord will provide," is still his answer to any doubt on our part. The Northern officials offer free tickets to persons returning to their homes — alas! to their homes! How few of us have homes! Some are confiscated; others destroyed. The families of the army and navy officers are here. The husbands and sons are absent, and they remain with nothing to anticipate and nothing to enjoy. To-day I met a friend, the wife of a high official, whose hospitality

I have often enjoyed in one of the most elegant residences in Virginia, which has been confiscated and used as a hospital for "contrabands." Our conversation naturally turned on our prospects. Hearing where we were going, she replied, "I have no brother, but when I hear from my husband and son, I shall accept the whole-souled invitation of a relative in the country, who has invited me to make his house my home; but," she added, as her beautiful eyes filled with tears, "when are our visits to end? We can't live with our ruined relatives, and when our visits are over, what then? And how long must our visits of charity last?" The question was too sad; neither of us could command our voices, and we parted in silence and tears.

20th.—The cars on the Central Railroad will run to-morrow, for the first time, under Federal rule, and the day after we will use our passports and free tickets to leave the city—dearer than ever, in its captivity and ruin. It is almost impossible to get current money. A whole-hearted friend from Alexandria met me the other day, and with the straightforward simplicity due to friendship in these trying times, asked me at once, "Has your husband any money?" I told him I thought not. He replied, "Tell him I have between twenty-five and thirty dollars—that's all—and he shall have half of it; tell him I say so." Ten dollars were accepted, for the circumstances of want which pressed so hard, and for the kindly spirit in which it was offered. Two other friends came forward to share with us their little all. God help the warm hearts of our conquered but precious country! I know they will be blessed, and that light will yet shine through the blackness of darkness which now surrounds them.

W., 24th.—On Saturday evening my brother's wagon

met us at the depot and brought us to this place, beautiful in its ruins. We have not been here since the besom of destruction swept over it, and to us, who have been in the habit of enjoying its hospitality when all was bright and cheerful, the change is very depressing. We miss the respectful and respectable servants, born in the family and brought up with an affection for the household which seemed a part of their nature, and which so largely contributed to the happiness both of master and servant. Even the nurse of our precious little J., the sole child of the house, whose heart seemed bound up in her happiness, has gone. It is touching to hear the sweet child's account of the shock she experienced when she found that her "mammy," deceived and misled by the minions who followed Grant's army, had left her; and to see how her affection still clings to her, showing itself in the ardent hope that her "mammy" has found a comfortable home. The army had respected the interior of the house, because of the protection of the officers. Only one ornament was missing, and that was the likeness of this dear child. Since the fall of Richmond, a servant of the estate, who had been living in Washington, told me that it was in the possession of a maid-servant of the house, who showed it to him, saying that she "looked at it every day." We all try to be cheerful and to find a bright side; and we occupy the time as cheerfully as we can. The governess having returned to her home in Norfolk, I shall employ myself in teaching my bright little niece here and the dear children at S. H., and feel blessed to have so pleasant a duty.

25th.—J. P. arrived to-day direct from Mosby's command, which is disbanded, but has not surrendered. He is full of enthusiasm and visions of coming success, and is bent on joining Johnston. Dear boy, his hopeful spirit has infected me, and aroused a hope which I am afraid to indulge.

28th.—We have no mail communication, and can hear nothing from General Johnston. We go on as usual, but are almost despairing. Dear M., in her sadness, has put some Confederate money and postage stamps into a Confederate envelope, sealed it up, and endorsed it, " In memory of our beloved Confederacy." I feel like doing the same, and treasuring up the buttons, and the stars, and the dear gray coats, faded and worn as they are, with the soiled and tattered banner, which has no dishonouring blot, the untarnished sword, and other arms, though defeated, still crowned with glory. But not yet—I cannot feel that all is over yet.

May 4.—General Johnston surrendered on the 26th of April. " My native land, good-night!"

NOTE TO PAGE 60.

THE capture attributed to the 27th Virginia is probably a mistake. The honor claimed for that regiment has since been ascribed to Fisher's 6th North Carolina regiment. In the excitement of the occasion, the writer of the letter may have been misinformed. The author is glad to make the correction. All honor is certainly due to the noble " Old North State," which, it has always been said, sent a larger number of troops to the field, in proportion to its population, than any other State in the Confederacy, and which buried so many thousands of its gallant sons, in defence of our "lost cause."

NOTE BY THE PUBLISHERS.—Both the statements are probably true, to some extent. We have unquestionable evidence that Fisher's regiment captured *one section* of Sherman's battery just before Col. Fisher received his mortal wound. But the same evidence shows that there was another section (both under Captain Ricketts) which was captured by other troops; our friend does not know what troops, but no doubt the 27th Virginia.

www.ingramcontent.com/pod-product-compliance
Lightning Source LLC
Chambersburg PA
CBHW020321240426
43673CB00039B/876